THE CAPTAIN'S STRATEGY
Your direct route to strategic know-how

By Dr. Amos Raviv

Producer & International Distributor
eBookPro Publishing
www.ebook-pro.com

The Captain's Strategy
Dr. Amos Raviv

Copyright © 2020 Amos Raviv

All rights reserved; No parts of this book may be reproduced or transmitted in any form or by any means, electronic or mechanical, including photocopying, recording, taping, or by any information retrieval system, without the permission, in writing, of the author.

Edited by Ephrat Abisror

Contact: amosea@gmail.com
ISBN 9798670199377

THE CAPTAIN'S STRATEGY

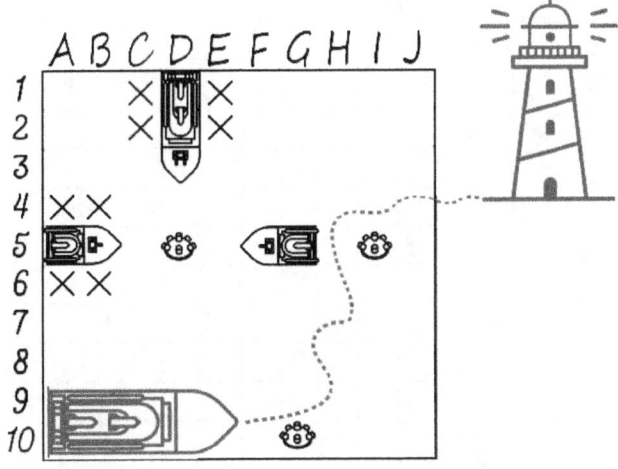

Your direct route to strategic know-how

Dr. Amos Raviv

Contents

Introduction 7

Chapter 1: *Welcome aboard, Captain!... Okay, now what??* 10
Introducing the Strategic Model 10
Strategy Defined 10
The Term 'Strategy' – Famous Definitions 12
Introducing: the CAPTAIN Strategy Acronym: 15
Strategic Management – Managing our Journey 17
Strategic Models 19

Chapter 2: *MODELS* 25
The BCG Model in Captain's eye View 25
The Connection Between Cows, Dogs, Stars, and Your Product Portfolio ...25
Porter's Five Forces Model in Captain's eye View 35
Porter's Diamond in Captain's eye View 47
PEST Model in in Captain's eye View 54
Canez's Make-or-buy in Captain's eye View 62
ServQual Model in Captain's eye View 71
The MSD – Money-Spending-Determination Model in Captain's eye View,
Based on Sasser's Customer Value Model 83

Chapter 3: *Guidelines for Understanding all Strategic Models in Captain's eye View* 96
Introducing: CAPTAIN STRATEGY 96

Chapter 4: *The AMOSEA Strategic Business Model for Marinas* 109
The AMOSEA Strategic Business Model for Marinas 109
Introduction 112
Studies on the Tourism Industry 113
Marketing Services 115
Strategic Management and Strategic Models 125
Occupancy at the Marina as a Dependent Variable 133
Research Hypotheses 144
Findings 152

Bibliography 193

INTRODUCTION

Imagine that your business is a ship, and you are its captain, leading it to market shores. You cannot control the vast seas, the winds or the currents, the low or high tides, nightfall or daybreak, nor can you affect the weather conditions in any way.

However, you can set guidelines for your ship and crew, giving them instructions as to how to plan ahead, how to behave in certain conditions, which measures to undertake, what factors to consider, take down and analyze, and what actions to perform upon which conclusions are reached – while at sea, in real time.

These instructions are designed to help maneuver your ship toward your "Americas," under your specific set of values, beliefs, and culture orientation.

Captains of ships whose "Americas" are defined as pirating, will have a different set of guidelines than captains of ships engaged in various forms of fishing, and theirs will differ from those of others who transport merchandise for sale.

It must be emphasized here that the purpose of this set of guidelines exceeds beyond survival goals such as overcoming currents, weather, enemies, competition, obstacles, accidents, turbulence, rebellions, wear, leadership issues, etc. The purposes are much more far-reaching and involve winning, succeeding, profiting, and exceeding.

For example, let's consider the one parameter of navigation, simply the factor of finding one's direction at sea, and let's place it under our strategy microscope. The strategies one can use when navigating one's ship at sea are ample. They range from dead reckoning (DR), which refers to the process of estimating your present position by projecting course and speed from a known past position, through piloting, which involves navigating a vessel in restricted waters and fixing its position as precisely as possible at frequent intervals, to celestial navigation systems based on observation of the position of the sun, moon, planets, and navigational stars, or inertial navigation, which is a system that computes its position based on motion sensors.

And we still haven't said a word about electronic navigation, which includes methods such as the radio direction finder (RDF), or the Decca, OMEGA, and LORAN-C which are hyperbolic navigation systems, and of course, the GPS, radar navigation, and global navigation satellite systems or GNSS, and so forth.

By combining our navigation strategy with the rest of the parameters, which must be taken into consideration, we create a strategizing mix which will, as we believe, get us where we want to go, as fast as we want to get there. Forming the right strategizing mix and using it efficiently, in light of all other surface and undersurface, inner and outer conditions, will impact the immediacy of our success in reaching the market shores of our goals, as well as our relevance once we reach them.

Simplified, this means, for example, that if your ship and other ships carry the same merchandise, and you manage to beat your competitors to a certain market shores thanks to an excellent navigation strategy, then your competitors will become less relevant once they reach the same shores. However, if you did manage to beat your competitors, yet you had arrived at the wrong shore due to a navigational crash at sea, your relevance will be questionable to begin with, and all the work and effort invested up to your arrival will have been... sunk at sea, so to speak...

Whether we are talking about market shores, or market shares, navigation strategies for reaching and achieving business goals in competitive environments – are crucial, critical, and could not be underestimated in importance. In business, like at sea, we use a wide range of proven and tested strategic models for guidance, by which we create strategies that lead our business activities, in relevance to our markets, industry, culture, goals, image, values, etc.

We use these strategic models as foundations for analyzing our business and the market environment in which it operates, and on the basis of this work we draw conclusions, develop insights, and make skillful business decisions by which we navigate our businesses toward success, market dominance, competitive edge, and profits, or whatever our goals may be.

As can be anticipated, each one of the strategic models we are about to introduce to you in this book evaluates different parameters, and analyzes different relationships between the multiple impacting factors, trends, currents, and developments which are sizzling simultaneously above and under the surface. These will be influencing our success – elevating or killing our efforts – in the same manner by which every navigation strategy mentioned above relies on different parameters.

Implemented parallelly, a smart mix of relevant and effective strategic models can provide us with the bigger strategic picture, leading to better business insights and actions, and to the formation of a superior business strategy.

I have been a strategy lecturer, researcher, and thinker for many years, and a relentless collector of strategic models. Up to this point I do not know of any book which covers comprehensively all major strategic models used and studied today, in an organized, concise, and workable format.

It is my intention in this book to provide you with a strategic working tool, which will constitute **your direct route to strategic know-how in the turbulent seas of the 21st century marketplace**, and be the most comprehensive, rich, and complete book on strategy you can hold.

This book is intended to help you dive in to the complex world of strategy and strategy models in a straightforward yet not oversimplified way, whether you start from the beginning, from the end, or open the book in the middle and charge from there.

My vision is that this book will be the most marked, eared, creased, and coffee-specked book on your desk (note that I have written 'on your desk' and not 'on your shelf'), to return to, to ruffle and shuffle time and again whenever you need a mind-invigorating reference for creative strategic insight and innovativeness.

Whether you are a manager, a CEO, or business leader, whether you are a consultant, an analyzer, or still a student, this book will serve as a premium tool with which you can enrich your professional abilities and scope of knowledge, thoughts, inventiveness, and creativity in all matters of strategy.

If you are a business professional, you can use this book to incorporate new points of view and perspectives into your strategic thinking and management rather than using the same old and fully used up ways. A broad rather than a limited approach to strategy will take the fulfillment of your business's potential miles forward, as well as help you reclaim strategic control, which has been tending to leak lately from our hands to know-it-all advisors and consultants.

With this book in hand you will be able to work with third parties in a synergic manner, from a knowing and skillful position, while maintaining your leadership as a contributor and direction setter for your business.

On the other hand, if you are one of those third parties, i.e., if you are an advisor or a consultant, you can use this book to renew or refresh your arsenal of strategic tools and provide your clients with fresh thinking and strategic brainstorming paths.

If you are a student searching for the one single book to hold, that can free your shelves from the heavy weight of densely written volumes, while providing you with the widest perspective on strategy, as well as the richest treasury of strategic information, well, you've found it.

This book is built on the principle of scope rather than depth. It includes "instant descriptions" of all major strategic models known and used today – in abridged user-friendly formats – therefore, it is a prize for all learners.

Every model is demonstrated with a diagram, followed by a detailed yet simple and easily comprehensible explanation, and one or more examples from the marketplace or business world, illustrating the usefulness and powerfulness of each model as manifested in true stories from the front lines.

For your convenience, this is the first book written on strategy in which all strategic models are organized in three major logical categories, which I have identified in my research and studies. Each category provides a distinct angle focusing on one major aspect of the process of strategy formation, logically explained, for easy recollection and orientation.

I named them Descriptive Models, Market Oriented Models, and Focused Models. All categories are explained in detail at the beginning of each respective chapter.

Finally, the field of strategy research is a fast-growing and developing field. Relentless researchers, thinkers, and teachers persistently release into our world new and eye-opening methods and approaches, tools and insights, tactics and practices. Some of them support and complement existing methods through a process of natural evolution, and others override them and create huge revolutions.

Thus, I intend to supply my readers constantly with updates and innovations in the field of strategic models and strategy research, via my website, www.captainstrategy.com. You are cordially invited to visit my website and check for available updates.

With all that said, let's now set the sails and weigh our anchors, we are sailing away – ready or not.

I wish you an interesting and productive journey,

Yours, Amos.

Even in his lowest swoop the mountain eagle is still higher than other birds upon the plain, even though they soar.
Herman Melville, Moby Dick

CHAPTER 1: WELCOME ABOARD, CAPTAIN!... OKAY, NOW WHAT??
INTRODUCING THE STRATEGIC MODEL

STRATEGY DEFINED

Welcome aboard. This is your ship, your business. You have just embarked on a journey to success. But, how do you get there? What should you do? In what order? With who's help? These are not simple questions. The seas are vast and swarming with beasts, myriads of other ships… and dangers; your market shores are miles away and the waters are deep, very deep indeed.

With all of these, how can you raise your chances of making it, and making it well? The answer is simple and straightforward, and can be spelled out in one word – Strategy.

The term Strategy is derived from ancient Greek word, 'strategia,' and means office of general, command, and generalship. This word is composed of two parts: 'Stratos' means 'army,' and 'Ago' is the ancient Greek word for guiding and driving something forward. It is military in essence and was used originally to describe the pre-battle maneuvering of troops into the best positions to enable the most efficient tactical implementation of policy in order to achieve desired goals, usually a defeat of an adversary (or, competitor?).

Well, as the Chinese like to say, "The marketplace is a battlefield." They have understood, already ages ago, that the wisdom which guides the general in the battlefield is very similar and could be compared to the wisdom that guides business leaders in the market place (where resources in business constitute the appropriate parallel to the historical troops in military). And so, somewhere along history the term was borrowed and embraced by the business world with two loving and possessing hands.

The concept of strategic planning as we know it today originated in the 1950s, and became popular in large companies by the mid-1970s. During this period, there was an increasing belief that strategic planning could solve any problem, and it became the magic word of the period.

In the 1980s, however, the spotlight was diverted away from strategic planning as a result of the emergence of additional planning theories, but unfortunately, these did not provide better results.

Since the 1990s, the popularity of strategic planning has once again risen, yet at this point it was, and still is, treated with a milder and more realistic approach.

Nevertheless, today, we can still say that the word 'strategy' had morphed in to a widely used business term, and perhaps the most widely used – yet less understood – of all. It is waved freely and respectfully by the full spectrum of management personnel of all practices and disciplines and breathed with awe by every expert standing around every planning board in every organization, big or small.

It constitutes an inspiration for a myriad of researches and studies; it is grinded by the academy and taught in mandatory courses in business schools all over the world. And yet, do we know what its real meaning is? Do we attribute the same significance to the word 'strategy' when we use it in a sentence as we do when we use it in business practice?

In the literature there is no uniformity of opinion regarding the meaning of the term "strategy." Most study books on strategy provide a definition somewhere along the lines of this one:

> **A Popular Definition of the Term Strategy**
>
> **A road-map outlined by senior management for the purpose of using available resources to achieve desired goals in an uncontrollable environment, in harmony with organizational culture, goals, and objectives.**

The core meaning of this statement is that it is a set of rules by which an organization can guide itself toward success, where success is defined as the realization of pre-set goals.

Approaches to strategy range from those who see strategy as a great master plan thought out by great minds, to those who see strategy as no more than a local guideline for decision-making.

Others, like Gary Hamel, see strategy as an "aspiration that creates by design a chasm between ambition and resources,"[1] constituting an inspiration for resource leveraging.

Michael Porter maintains that "the essence of strategy is choosing to perform activities differently than others do."[2]

Other knowledgeable people who have tried to describe the process of strategic thinking and planning have defined it in various ways, which basically includes similar values.

In the box below, you can read various definitions given throughout history by leading thinkers of strategy, each choosing a different critical aspect of strategy formulation and building his definition around it.

---

1 Gary Hamel and C.K. Prahalad, Strategy as Stretch and Leverage: Harvard Business Review, March-April 1993, pg.
2 Michael E. Porter, What is Strategy? The Harvard Business Review, November-December, 1996

THE TERM 'STRATEGY' – FAMOUS DEFINITIONS

Moltke the Elder (1882-1888)
Strategy is a system of ad hoc expedients; it is more than knowledge, it is the application of knowledge to practical life, the *development* of an original idea in accordance with continually changing circumstances. It is the art of action under pressure of the most difficult conditions.

B. H. Liddell Hart (1895-1970)
(Strategy is) "The art of distributing and applying military means to fulfill the ends of policy."

George Steiner (1979)
Strategy is that which top management does that is of great importance to the organization.
    Strategy refers to basic directional decisions, that is, to purposes and missions.
    Strategy consists of the important actions necessary to realize these directions.
    Strategy answers the question: What should the organization be doing?
    Strategy answers the question: What are the ends we seek and how should we achieve them?

Kepner-Tregoe (1983)
Strategy is "the framework which guides those choices that determine the nature and direction of an organization."[3]

Kenneth Andrews (1987)
Corporate strategy is the pattern of decisions in a company that determines and reveals its objectives, purposes, or goals, produces the principal policies and plans for achieving those goals, and defines the range of business the company is to pursue, the kind of economic and human organization it is or intends to be, and the nature of the economic and non-economic contribution it intends to make to its shareholders, employees, customers, and communities.

Michael Peri (1991)
(Strategy is) "A series of decisions, actions, and allocation of resources, which determine the organization's place and the direction of its progress in the environment in which it operates."

Michael Porter (1991)
"Strategy is a direction of activity, or long-term planning, which is designed to fulfill the goals of the organization."
    And in a 1996 *Harvard Business Review* article Porter argues that competitive strategy is "about being different… It means deliberately choosing a different set of activities to deliver a unique mix of value."

---

[3] Top Management Strategy, 1980. Benjamin Tregoe and John Zimmerman. Simon and Schuster.

Gary Hamel (1991)

Hamel distinguishes between the concepts of planning and strategizing. The concept of planning relates to thinking from the present forward, outlining ways to reach the anticipated future, whereas the concept of strategizing relates to thinking from the anticipated future – backward to the present.

Henry Mintzberg (1994)[4]

Strategy is a plan, a "how," a means of getting from here to there.

Strategy is a pattern in actions over time; for example, a company that regularly markets very expensive products is using a "high end" strategy.

Strategy is position; that is, it reflects decisions to offer particular products or services in particular markets.

Strategy is perspective, that is, vision and direction.

Yair Aharoni (1997)

(Strategy is a means to create) "balance between: (1) the opportunities and risks in the environment, (2) the resources and abilities in the firm, and (3) personal values and ambitions."

Today, however, the world has changed considerably. As much as yesterday's world was seen as rigid, predictable, and stable, today's world has become constantly changing, unpredictable, and turbulent.

Things, important things, change extremely from one minute to the next, and the only predictable notion – and you have probably heard this a million times – is that nothing is, or will ever again, be predictable. In light of these developments, the notion of strategy has developed too, and those who fail to update their strategic outlook will not be able to survive in the craziness of the ever-hectic 21st century atmosphere.

According to the old approach, strategy was something to be set and untouched and unchanged for years to come. Just like Seth Godin wrote in his book, *Tribes,* "Corporations might as well have been run by Joseph Stalin – they had unalterable five-year plans, sharply controlled channels of communication, and a royal court surrounding the monarch."[5]

Today, however, strategy must be much more fluid, flexible, and responding to rapidly changing conditions. Therefore, the importance of strategic models has increased considerably since they have to be used constantly, for reassessments of market analysis, conditions, developments, technology, innovations, and what not, which are all data to be inputted in to your company's strategic algorithm, in order to receive constant strategic updating and adjustments, or as I like to call, in: Continuous Strategic Overhaul (CSO).

In other words, what this means is that strategy, in general, is a detailed set of guidelines for making future choices in various arenas of activity within a dynamic and changing environment – using existing, available. or leveraged resources for the purpose of attaining certain pre-defined goals.

These guidelines go as far as setting guidelines for adjusting these same guidelines in light of

---

4   The Rise and Fall of Strategic Planning, 1994. Henry Mintzberg. Basic Books.
5   Seth Godin, Tribes, Portfolio Books, 2008.

certain realities or developments. You see, business strategy is designed to help a company achieve its targets and goals (by the maximum profit for the shareholders, reaching sales volumes or market shares, building awareness, winning public support, etc.), and it generally does so by putting the company in the strongest competitive position possible in its environment.

Since business environments change perpetually, even throughout the entire life cycle of a single product, any business strategy which professes to supply results must also take the form of a dynamic process of real time change and adaptation.

Strategy researchers have indeed begun to refer to strategy as a perpetually ongoing process rather than a given business formula. Already in 1993, Kotler & Armstrong have defined the term business strategy as follows:

(strategy is) "A process to develop and maintain the strategic alignment between an organization's targets and its changing marketing opportunities. It is based on determining a clear task for the company, setting appropriate targets, designing a well-structured business portfolio, and development of adjusted functional strategies."

In light of all of the above, let me, at this point, propose a new and somewhat radical definition of the term strategy, which is more apt for today's business turbulence, and which will constitute our reference in this book:

Captain Strategy's Definition of the Term 'Business Strategy':

A dynamic, operational, target-oriented algorithm set by organizations, designed to analyze regular inputs of relevant information from the ever-changing outer organizational world (markets, technologies, competitors, trend analysis, consumers/customers, innovations, economy, etc.) as well as from the ever-changing inter-organizational world (skills, abilities, strengths, resources, human resources, assets, technologies, constraints, etc.), and to deliver current formulated outputs of updated goals, targets, objectives, and ways of reaching them and beyond, all conditioned to comply with the company's vision and culture.

With this definition, we reach closer to the dynamic – rather than static – nature of the strategic process in organizations today, in the 21st century. Note that the vision becomes much more important to a company and to its strategic process today as compared to the past.

As the outside world becomes more hectic and unpredictable, it forces organizations to constantly readapt, react, innovate, and skip to maintain a position ahead of change. Companies must aim to be where the ball is going to fall when it hits the ground – at the precise time of that fall, and that takes a lot of know-how, especially when you have to work out which forces are going to effect that ball and how, during its flight.

This is what we do with strategy models. Necessity has forced strategy to morph into a constantly developing and changing algorithm rather than a proclamation, thus the company's vision has become the central compass, which points the company in the desired direction.

And yet, it is not enough to articulate an algorithm. Any dynamic strategic process must include several key attributes in order to be applicable and efficient in the 21st century marketplace, just like the Three C's of Branding (Clarity, Consistency, and Constancy). Thus, we have devised an acronym to remember, for your convenience.

INTRODUCING: THE CAPTAIN STRATEGY ACRONYM:

C for Clarity:

A strategic directive must be clear, understandable, and coherent in order to be carried out correctly and effectively by all organizational functions, each in its specific area of activity. Once your strategic directive becomes unclear, is open to multiple interpretations, or not focused enough, the organization will cease to behave like one coordinated being.

Anderson and Lembke compared organizations to cows. In cows, they said, the parts are not aware that they are parts. They have no trouble sharing information, and working in a coordinated manner. This is how you want your organization to work: All the parts, together, naturally and smoothly. A clear, strategic presentment is essential for this to happen.

A for Agility:

Being that our strategy is now a perpetual process, a constantly forming and reforming formula, or as we referred to it earlier, an algorithm, it must be formulated in such a way that will enable the organization to maintain agility, flexibility, and reactivity as top values, in order to be able to synchronize itself with a constantly changing reality.

P for Perpetuity:

While in the past we used to talk about the need for consistency in strategies, today we are no longer expecting constant strategic guidelines but rather a continuous process of ongoing strategic formation and development. A strategy should be able to lead organizations to success throughout their life cycle, in an uncontrollable and unexpectedly changing environment. A good strategy is articulated in such a way that it will be able to correct itself and redirect itself in response to changing conditions.

T for Target:

Every strategy must be built around a clearly defined and strongly pursued vision: A target, purpose, or goal, and be geared toward achieving them, above anything else. No matter what your target or goal are, they must be: (a) Clearly defined, and (b) modifiable in accordance with the ongoing strategic process.

A for Aspiration:

One of the most important papers ever written on Strategy, *Strategy: Stretch and Leverage*, by Hamel and Prahalad, published in 1993, claims that… "Competitiveness is born in the gap between a company's resources and its managers' goals." This paper claims, and rightfully so, that fewer resources will not stand in the way of greater aspirations. Ambitions create visions and visions drive growth. Aspirations are the crucial component your strategy will need if you want your organization to reach the "beyond" part of our definition of strategy. Aspirations separate the phenomenal from the crowds, the outstanding from the average.

I for Implementability:

Implementability is of vital importance. The less implementable a strategy is the less relevant and efficient it will be, and vice versa. The more implementable a strategy is, the better the results are going to be. Better implementation possibilities also means that strategists will have more time at hand to be creative and come up with novel ways to drive the organization foreword and reach better and higher goals, since they will not be needing all their creativity for the sake of implementation itself.

N for Narrative:

A strategy is designed to produce a collective organizational orientation toward certain goals and certain ways of achieving them. It is an integrative organizational "to-do" list, reflecting on all of the organization – from the doorman to the CEO. Dressing strategy with a relevant and compelling narrative will not only improve the remembering capacities of the organization by enriching dull numbers and imperatives with meaning and logic, but will also help make sense of relationships between the multiple factors, contexts, correlations, and parties involved, hence making implementation a much more achievable process.

All scholars agree that a process of formulating strategy is the only process likely to lead the company toward its goal. However, one might note that the concept of strategic planning seems to contain an internal contradiction.

According to Hamel, strategic planning means that an organization must define where it wants to be at the end of a time-defined process, and to plan its steps to reach this future. But on the other hand, as Van Der Heijden (1996) puts it, it is necessary to hone the ability to conduct "strategic conversations," meaning to think about possible scenarios, and to maintain flexibility in the sense of a readiness to change the strategic approach in response to a changing business environment.

Captain Strategy's definition of strategy, offered in this book as an algorithm, solves this contradiction elegantly. It compares the organizational strategy to a homing missile with an active guidance system, seeking and detecting the target (goals, vision) constantly as this target changes its coordinates in space (characteristics). Our homing strategic algorithm constantly calculates to follow its target along its path until interception (success) occurs.

Now, having reached the definition of strategy which will serve us in this book, we can move over to the "how-to" part, and learn what strategy can do for us, and how.

STRATEGIC MANAGEMENT – MANAGING OUR JOURNEY

When we raise the anchor and set out to sail the vast seas safely and efficiently, we have to orchestrate between at least three stages and forms of preparation and planning. We call this process: *The process of Strategic Management.*

Strategic management is usually defined as a process that includes three stages: Strategy formulation, implementation, and evaluation.

Stage 1: Strategy Formulation

The planning and formulation of any business strategy begins with the **gathering of information and the analysis of the business environment**. Only in light of the company's resources and its administrative values, the goals of the company and the horizon of its activity can be set, including products, service, distribution channels, marketing communication, and so on.

According to Dan Galai and Lior Hillel (1989), the company should gather information about: (1) The needs of potential customers, (2) the market potential, (3) customers' characteristics, (4) the competitors and the competitive environment, (5) the technological environment, (6) the funding environment, and (7) the broader environment (i.e., economic, political). This pretty much covers all that is necessary, although we can add today, in light of the internet revolution, that it is important also to collect information about the environment, i.e., relevant electronic or virtual environment, as well as specific information that is industry-unique.

After gathering all information, we can begin with the formulation of our business strategy. By strategy formulation we mean deciding where we are headed and how we are going to get there. This, as previously mentioned, strongly involves the development of our vision.

It also involves repetitive characterizations of our external environments (with a focus on opportunities and threats) and our internal environments (locating the strengths and weaknesses). Then we formulate goals; we locate, identify, and evaluate alternative strategies, and finally we select the chosen one, which seems to best fit our goals and aspirations. I would like to emphasize once again that this is not a one-time project, but an ongoing process, that needs to be performed constantly, as a way of life.

Stage 2: Strategy Implementation

Strategy implementation is carried out in real time, under real and changing conditions, and toward defined goals. There is a wide consensus among business and strategy writers, especially prominent ones, that in order to ensure successful implementation, a strategy should be specific and simple.

For example, Eisenhardt & Sull (2001), wrote that the best strategy is of no value if it is not properly implemented. Proper implementation depends on the ability of the management to introduce the strategy to its employees, and the simplicity of the strategy helps the management do so.

According to Gadish and Gilbert (2001), the way to implement strategy in real time is based on formulating a correct strategic principle, and a correct strategic principle is a simple one.

Simplicity and brevity have become widely accepted as basic requirements for a workable and effective strategy. At this point, I always like to recruit to my aid, as was also done by Wilson back in 1998, a very important principle called the principle of Ockham's Razor, attributed to and named after 14th century English logician and Franciscan friar, William of Ockham. This principle states that whenever there are several acceptable explanations to a phenomenon, the simplest should always be preferable, and is the valid one. In other words, when attempting to explain something, no more assumptions should be made than is necessary.

Drawing on this concept, a strategic model should be kept very simple, and should include a minimal number of rules and assumptions. We will see later in this book how important this is when we begin to discuss the models themselves, including real examples given to demonstrate the impact of those models on our strategy and chances of success.

Stage 3: Strategy Evaluation

Not less important, a strategic model should be clear and measurable. Measurability is crucial for the strategy evaluation stage. The changes that take place in the various environments affect the business strategy over time, and directly influence the functional strategies, including: Marketing, operations, human resources, and management strategies.

In order to lead the organization to success and growth, constant evaluations must be made as to the effectiveness of the selected leading strategy and its relevance. And in order to evaluate efficiently, we need indexes of success.

There are several approaches to strategy, from which it is possible to derive indexes of success to measure our strategy's effectiveness:

a. Efficiency – the deployment of resources in order to produce value around the product or service.
b. Uniqueness – a focus of attraction for customers, one that is hard to compete with, difficult to copy, and sustainable over time.
c. Fitness – the components of the strategy must suit one another, and not cause opposing or clashing interests within the organization.
d. Profit acceleration – a strategy must contain within it a system that increases the company's growth rate. There are four types of profit accelerators:
e. High yields (through the network effect, positive feedback, or learning).
f. Competitor blocks (getting ahead of competitors, creating areas of domination, or attracting customers).
g. Strategic savings (through size, focus, or scope).
h. Strategic flexibility (the ability to innovate and maintain or demonstrate flexibility in operation).

STRATEGIC MODELS

Categorizing Strategic Models

In order to achieve the three stages of the strategic process, we use what are known as Strategic Models. Strategic Models are advanced tools for analyzing, evaluating, measuring, assessing, and examining the relevant factors impacting our strategies.

For the purpose of understanding strategic models in this book, models will be presented visually, in order to make it simpler for readers who are not yet skilled in analyzing strategic models to understand what they must implement during the analysis and the strategic planning. For that purpose, three groups of strategic models will be presented before you in detail, followed by examples and illustrations from the real business world:

A. Descriptive Strategic Models:

Descriptive strategic models provide us with methods of strategic planning through a one-way process of constructing a formal plan as an output of outer and inner environment analysis

B. Market Oriented Strategic Models:

Market oriented strategic models provide us with methods of strategic planning, which are based on current market orientation, dealing with the analysis and mapping of a mix of company products, services, or brands, and an analysis of its portfolio.

C. Focus Driven Strategic Models:

Focus driven strategic models provide us with methods of strategic planning based mainly on dialogues about possible scenarios.

Strategic Models: Our map and Compass

Strategic models are our map and compass, our stars and sails, our wind and current detectors, our GPS electronic aids, binoculars, and weather forecasters. They are our means of formulating our strategies, appreciating their effectiveness, and measuring their success. They are necessary tools for finding our way at sea, toward the market shores of our choice, and fate.

Before we go on, let us better understand what the strategic model looks like. According to Hamel (1991) it includes four bases. I would like to discuss these bases, while taking liberty to bring some information up-to-date in light of the immense revolutions that have taken place since these words were first written, in areas such as technology, communication, retail and internet retail, consumer and customer behavioral patterns, decline of barriers to entry, the strengthening of competition, and the shortening of product life cycles.

Hamel's four bases are as follows:

a. ***Contact with customers*** – meaning points of interface between the organization or the brand – and customers, present, past, and future. Points of contact constitute means and channels of exposure, distribution or provision of the product or service. To name a few: Shelves, service desks, packaging, advertising, correspondence – electronic or hard copy, electronic brand presence, call centers, sales reps, other staff personnel, branded vehicles, stores, signs, logos on products, or any other occurrences of exposure of any type, as well as occurrences in which implementation of service, pricing, and communication policies is carried out.

b. ***The core strategy*** – the main elements around which the business is built. Every business must define its vision and the areas in which it is involved. Our company's or our brand's competitive advantage is the area in which it is better than others – meaning that it supplies an added value competitors do not supply, or in other words, a benefit worth investing in, in the eyes of consumers. Usually, if we manage to turn this benefit into our unique differentiation, we can distinguish our company from its competitors through this differentiation, and make it memorable. Our basket of products and brands should, of course, support our company's mission, vision, and differentiation. The link between our company's core strategy and all points of interface with its customers must be beneficial to those customers, in such a way that benefits are amplified maximally and systematically.

c. ***Strategic resources*** – resources deployed for the purpose of implementing our company's core strategy. Those resources include among others: Core competencies, technologies, strategic assets (both tangible and intangible), processes, and human capital in the organization. The link between a company's core strategy and its strategic resources determines the configuration of the company, which is the way in which it operates in order to achieve its goals.

d. ***The value chain*** – is composed of all external factors with which an organization contacts regularly in order to expand its boundaries. Partnerships and alliances can, for example, add knowledge to the organization and reduce costs, as well as expand the boundaries of the company. The link between a company's strategic resources and its value chain determines the boundaries of the company.

As previously mentioned we will work with four types of strategic models, which we will now describe in more detail.

Descriptive Strategic Models

Descriptive models are methods of strategic planning by means of a one-way process of constructing a formal program. It is parallel to a captain preparing her ship for sail, and the journey: She will examine the ship, its condition, its abilities, its limitations, its capacity, etc. She will study destinations in terms of opportunities and goals, and she will search the maps for the shortest and safest path to get there. Finally, in correlation with all findings, she will devise a strategy which is best fitted to take the ship to its destination.

One of the most well-known descriptive strategic models, designed for assessing an organization's positioning relative to its competitors and environment – is the **SWOT Model**. According to this model, an organization must identify its internal strengths and weaknesses, as well as the threats and opportunities it encounters in the external environment.

In order to analyze the threats and opportunities, the organization must analyze both its distant and immediate external environment. To analyze strengths and weaknesses, the organization must analyze its internal environment. A strategy according to the SWOT model helps us devise a plan which will take advantage of opportunities, neutralize or even leverage (turn around) threats encountered, while basing itself on internal strength and reducing the effect of its weaknesses.

One of the strategic models for analyzing external environments is the **PEST Model** (Porter, 1980), or the more modern PESTEL. According to this model, the external environment should be analyzed according to several factors: The political, economic, social, and technological environments.

Similarly, the environment of the organization can be presented as comprising 10 sectors (Samuel, 1996), the four principal ones being: Technological, economic, human resources, and political. A change in one of them affects the balance of the organization, and obligates it to adjust its strategy.

Porter's Five Forces Model (Porter, 1980) is a strategic model for analyzing the industry in which the organization operates, and it assumes the existence of five main forces that affect the degree of competitiveness in the industry: Barriers to entry and exit, bargaining power of buyers, supplier power, threat of substitutes, and existing competitive rivalry between suppliers in the industry.

Another famous strategic model for analyzing the internal environment of an organization, i.e., the company profile, is the **Value Chain Model** (Porter, 1980). According to this model, one does an in-depth analysis of both the main and the supporting activities in the organization; each activity should affect the value of the product/service provided by the organization.

Market Oriented Strategic Models:

Models with a market orientation are tools for analyzing and mapping the current or future mix and architecture of your company's products, services, or brands, in a portfolio analysis. The results produced by the analysis and the mapping serve in strategic decision-making process in accordance with the situation.

It is parallel to a captain's freight manager computing space storage capacity verses profit assessments. The ship's storage space is a given, much like a company's production capacity or service capacity.

How does the freight manager make sure that this space is taken advantage of in the most profitable mix? For example, storage of small units with a high profit potential will be preferred over large units, which have a small profit potential, but on the other hand, a delicate balance between profitability and serviceability should be maintained by keeping a large enough mix of products or brands, in order to keep customers happy.

These are considerations that need to be taken when planning the storage inventory. In the same manner, a company's mix of products, services, or brands should be composed to ensure maximization of profits, and minimization of customer churn, etc.

A good example of a market-oriented strategic model is the **BCG Matrix**, developed by the Boston Consulting Group already in the 1960s, evaluates the products or services of the company along two dimensions: The company's relative market share and the industry's growth rate in the market.

A product with low growth and high market share is a cash cow, meaning that it is a product the company can generate steady and good cash from, which it invests in other products. A product with a high growth and high market share is a star. Stars use large amounts of cash, but also generate large amounts of cash.

A product with a low market share and a high industry growth rate is a question mark – it may succeed in attaining a market share and become a star, but it may fail. A product with low growth and low market share is what is known as a dog, which constitutes a cash trap because of a problematic, competitive position and a problematic market.

Another famous market oriented strategic model is the **McKinsey Matrix** (Grant, 2001), which classifies the strategic business units in a specific company according to the attractiveness of the industry and their competitive position in the company. In addition, the model presents the size of the business units in the company through a frontal presentation of circles of various sizes, which indicate the size of the product's market share.

A similar model, the **GE Matrix**, presents the business units three-dimensionally, and makes it possible to see where the center of gravity is located, and what strategy is required for each business unit. The GE Matrix presents business units on two dimensions: The competitive strength of the business unit and the market attractiveness over the long term.

In each dimension, the market share of the various business units is illustrated by circles of equivalent size, and in addition, the market share of the company is displayed as a section of the circle, with the angle of the section reflecting the trend in the company.

Another model that examines a company's basket of products or services is the **Core and Environmental Model**, which classifies a company's products in to two main groups: Core products and environmental products (Grant, 2001).

A core product is one from which the company generates revenue. It is the main product from which the company has to make a profit. An environmental product is a by-product of the core product, which helps it to survive, or strengthens it.

Since there is no "black and white," the classification of the products is done sequentially (0-1). The closer the product is to 1 (core product), the greater the expectation that its profit rate will be high.

A complementary product, on the other hand, can also cause losses since it supports the sale of the core products. In the final analysis, the model makes it possible to draw a line of anticipated profitability from any product along the sequence, and to examine which products "fall" below this line, which require improvement, or removal from the basket.

Grant's Variety Model, and **Six Business Departments Model** (2001), on the other hand, classify a company's products into groups according to which they should be promoted or "killed."

Focus Driven Strategic Models

Focus Driven Strategic Models are actually dialogue models, demonstrating focused patterns of relationships and communication occurrences within the organization as well as between the organization and its environment.

It is parallel to a strategy a captain embraces when controlling or driving communication channels and patterns among the ship's crew members, or when engaging in any type of contact with the outer world, with a focus on specific scenarios. For example, how would he handle a situation in which a competitor's ship has anchored in a previously ordered and paid for landing space? How would a rebellion be handled? How would crew members' outstanding performance be rewarded? Etc.

On this line of models, we have Kaplan & Norton (2001), who present strategic models as a dialogue about specific scenarios in the organization, and recommend implementing a system of monitoring and evaluation of the chosen strategy in the organization under study, while adapting it to the changing business environment.

We also have Menipaz (1999), who presents a paradigm for leaders of strategy. This is a graduated process of constructing the strategy according to a formula focused on the specific company, providing precise instructions as to the tasks the leaders of strategy must perform at each stage. According to this researcher, for instance, there are three levels of tasks: Constructing a strategic infrastructure, developing the strategy, and implementing it.

Summary

What is strategy then? Is it simple? The answer is no. Strategy is a complex and integrative concept, but it must be expressed in simple and clear statements. It is a conceptual notion that leads the organizational direction on the one hand, and also a practical integrative "to-do" list on the other.

It is a position taken, an organizationally inclusive state of mind or policy, but also an action orientation, or even specific local sets of imperatives. It is the platform on which tactics are devised, and by which we deploy our means to pursue an end. It may be referred to as a homing device assembled on a company's corporate vision, geared to track its moving and actively changing target. It is a process, a living process, which is vital to any organizational or business success.

In order to formulate a winning strategy, which will be effective over time, we will need advanced analyzing tools. These will be found in a wide array of strategic models, which can be divided in to three main groups:

1. Methods of strategic planning through a one-way process of constructing a formal plan that uses descriptive strategic models.
2. Methods of strategic planning with a market orientation, which deal with the analysis and mappings of a company's mix of products, services, or brands, and an analysis of its portfolio.
3. Methods of strategic planning, which are based on dialogue focusing on possible scenarios.

All the aforementioned strategic models and approaches and much more will be presented in the body of this book, in detail, including explanations, instructions, and examples.

CHAPTER 2 – MODELS
THE BCG MODEL IN CAPTAIN'S EYE VIEW

THE CONNECTION BETWEEN COWS, DOGS, STARS, AND YOUR PRODUCT PORTFOLIO

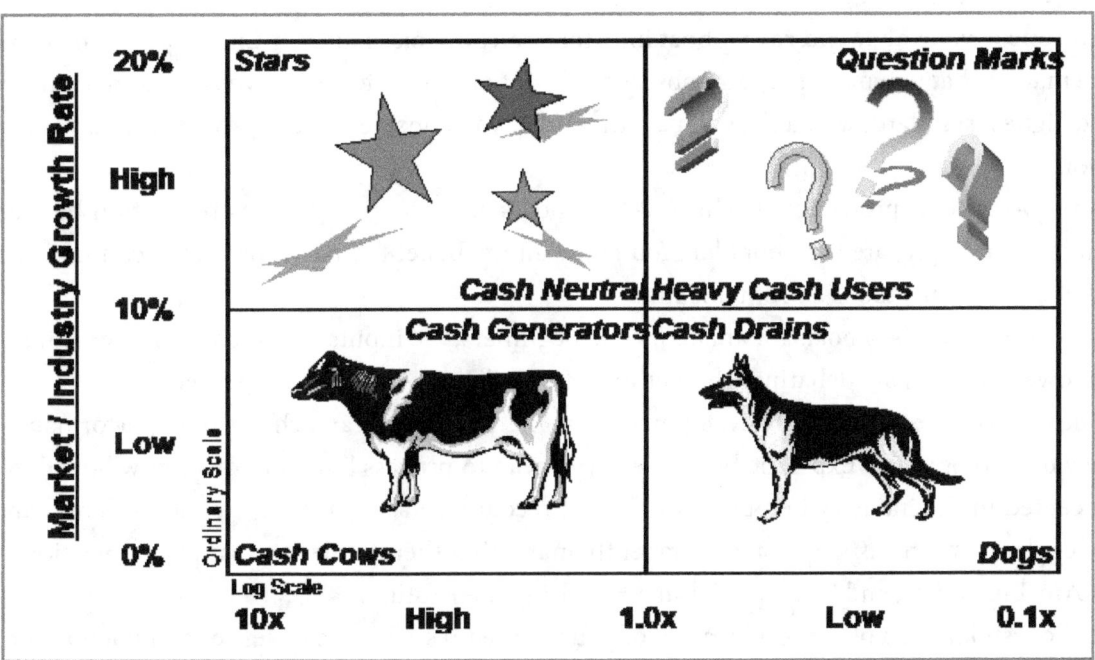

Key Winds in our Sails

The BCG matrix is about using two factors: Market Share and Market Growth, to construct a brand or product portfolio that works.

BCG (named after Bruce Henderson of the Boston Consulting Group, who developed it) is designed for inter-organizational analysis purposes. If other models view the big picture (i.e., the company as a ship floating in the big ocean, which, as unpredictable as it may be, could be crossed successfully if you have those special skills – not forgetting that you are sailing amongst other ships racing you to the same shores), this model highlights the ship's internal decision processes.

Of course, you cannot say that these are not influenced or affected by the great oceans in which the ship is sailing, but inside the ship decisions have to be made, and they have to be smart too.

With this strategic model, we zoom in on the business's brand or product portfolio by placing our brands or products on a matrix that has two dimensions: The vertical axis stands for **market growth** (high and low) as the key factor in industry attractiveness, and the horizontal axis stands for **relative**

market share (high and low), as key factor in competitive advantage. We use the **BCG** matrix as a framework to evaluate the strategic position of our business portfolio, and to help sort out, categorize, and plan ahead the company's brand mix or product mix in such a way that will enable profit maximization and future prosperity.

The most important contribution of this model is the fact that each category comes with its matching set of strategic default choices. It is also very simple to understand and to work with, thereby making it a useful, straightforward tool for every manager.

Let's look at an example.

Imagine that your company manufactures racing boats, and, to simplify our example, let's say you have four product lines.

Line one is your high-end racing boat line, for professionals. This Pro-Line is positioned so high in the market that you may charge an obscene amount of money for it and your customers, in search of the highest standards available, will pay; therefore, you consider it very profitable and your profit anchor.

Line two is semi-professional. The SeP-Line boats enjoy your Pro-Line's reputation but sell for much less; therefore, are very popular. You enjoy all the benefits that accompany economy of scale and believe that this too is a profitable line.

Line three consists of boats for amateurs and beginners, the inputs are far smaller, the selling price is far lower, and you are debating whether or not to kill your Am-Line altogether.

Line four is an experimental development of a smart boat that can achieve high performance due to new technology. The Exp-Line boats are very cheap to process but you don't know how they will be accepted in the industry because they are not recognized as legitimate racing boats by standard race regulations. This is why you are currently marketing them under the same low positioning as your Am-Line boats, and in deep dilemma regarding their future.

So, how should you plan the allocation of your limited resources in order to manufacture the best product mix for your company? Let's begin our analysis with the help of the BCG matrix.

Pro-Line racing boats:

Is charging an obscene price for a product and getting it enough to declare a product profitable? The profitability equation includes many parameters: Inputs in human resources, inputs in materials and capital resources, inputs in marketing resources, etc. Do all the inputs, let's call them – selling costs (all inputs to be invested in a product in order to sell it), balance out the income or does the product generate a cash surplus?

In order to determine your cash-return balance you would have to calculate and quantify the inputs that make up the selling cost of your Pro-Line boats, and so you did. Lo-and-behold, despite the high price you have been charging, you find that profits per boat are not so high after all! Have you been wrong about this line all along?

So, you have determined that Pro-Line's profitability is questionable, now you have to decide where its future lies. According to BCG the factors to consider are: Market growth to assess the industry attractiveness, and relative market share, to determine your competitive advantage.

Let's look at the market growth potential. Is this a growing market? Will tomorrow conjure up a sudden growth of demand in high-end racing boats, thereby compensating for small cash returns by future scale? Take time to think this through – I'll give you a clue. It has to do with stability, conservative industry, regulation, and niche markets.

Let's consider relative market share. Being the finest of the finest of high-end products, you would have to say that although clearly you have an advantage, your market share is relatively small. Two minuses according to BCG, AND low profitability.

Well, you just found out that Pro-Line may be your anchor indeed, but in the negative sense. Is Pro-Line tying you down? Let's leave the answer for later. Right now, we will call the Dog by its name.

Pro-Line is a classic DOG according to the BCG matrix.

> ### The DOG, According to the BCG Model
>
> **The DOG, also referred to as a Cash-Drain, is a product or a brand that holds a low market share and operates in a slowly growing or diminishing market. The Dog generates low or negative cash returns and its maintenance, development, and production take up a large share of your company's resources.**
>
> **Since it does not generate profits, from a pure accounting point of view, the default strategy would be to retrench, liquidate, or, in simple language – get rid of it.**

SeP-Line racing boats:

Analysis confirms that this is indeed a profitable line. Although it operates in a steady market, it enjoys the benefits of economy of scale, and has a high market share thanks to a solid reputation; it has all the makings of a true Cash Cow.

> ### The CASH-COW, According to the BCG Model
>
> **The CASH COW is the most profitable brand or product in your company. Although it operates in a mature and steady market, it occupies a handsome market share; thereby, suggesting that it has a strong competitive advantage and generates high cash returns.**
>
> **It earned its name because the company can and should "milk" it to provide as much cash as possible for as long a time as possible. Usually it is common to determine that Cash-Cows do not deserve R&D or other investments, and should be provided with as little support and maintenance as needed to maintain their high market share.**
>
> **It is also common to determine that the cash returns from the Cows should be invested into making your Stars (soon we will identify them) shine – or in business language – to support their future growth. So, your default strategy would be to do whatever it takes to keep the milk flowing.**

Am-Line racing boats:

As you recall, as chief strategist in your company you are debating whether or not to "kill" the Am-Line altogether. It is a simple product that does not make you proud, it is a low-quality low-priced boat, and truth be told, you are not so sure as to its value for your organization. But, have you considered market share and market growth?

We will begin by analyzing market growth. Amateur boat-racing is a growing trend in beach recreation areas and demand is spreading to include non-private high-wear customer groups such as hotels and recreation beach parks. Due to global warming, new beach areas are joining in on the fun. This information suggests that we are talking about a market with high growth potential, which makes it especially attractive for your company.

Let's look at your market share. Most manufacturers – your competitors – narrow down their production lines to high-quality and high-cost products that make them proud. Your Am-Line raceboats, although relatively simple, are solid, dependable, and affordable, which strongly suggests that you have an especially strong competitive advantage in this market.

Let's add in some production information you managed to dig up from finances: Although Am-Line racing boats are down-priced, you find that due to their simple production they generate the highest cash-returns per product compared to all your other product lines.

Does that change the picture? How? Well, I will tell you how. I think we may have just found ourselves a STAR.

The STAR, According to the BCG Model

The STAR operates in high growth industries, while maintaining high market share. It is both a cash generator, at least in potential, and a cash consumer due to R&D and market share maintenances needs in a growing industry.

The development of Stars, usually financed by Cash-Cows, is crucial to a business' future. The best Stars of all become Cash Cows themselves when they mature, but others incur losses or simply fade away, which gives them a high risk factor.

Of course not all Stars become Cash Cows, but successful Stars generate enough cash surplus to make up for the losses that fallen stars incur. So, if you suspect you have a Star, your default strategy would be to assess its potential of becoming a Cash Cow for your company, and if the potential is high – to invest in it big-time.

Exp-Line racing boats:

The Exp-Line boats' future is decorated by a huge question mark. Do they have a future in the industry? In the company? Is the company able to turn its potential into a real momentum by starting a new racing field? Could it target new markets such as non-professional, or recreational boating? Fishing? Could the new technology to improve the old products in terms of performance or production costs? Can you think of any other strategies to leverage the new technology or the new product?

Let's make this short and sweet. What are QUESTION MARKS according to the BCG matrix?

> **The QUESTION MARK, According to the BCG Model**
>
> The QUESTION MARK, often referred to as the Problem Child, is the trickiest of all. On the one hand, it seems to belong to a high-growth market, but many times we are talking about new markets so that we may be right, but we may be wrong.
>
> On the other hand, it does not perform well in terms of market share. If the reason for this seems to be logical – such as, it is a new product, new technology, new industry, etc., then the strategic decision-making would have to include investment considerations: How much inputs would be needed in order to create a new market, or to penetrate an existing market with a new technology, or to educate the customers, or do whatever it takes to build up a "desire share" that will lead up to market share for your product?
>
> If the reason for its poor performance is not clear, the strategic default would be to analyze your performance: What are you doing wrong and your competition doing right? Could more investment change the map altogether and turn your Question Mark into a big shining Star?
>
> The answers are never ever clear-cut. You have to keep in mind that Question Marks do not always justify the investment, and that revolving doors happen only in the movies.

Remember, an effective portfolio is the basis of success. Cash Cows can substantiate only so many Stars and Question Marks, BUT, they can last only as much as they last so these Stars and Question Marks must be treated like life-lines.

When Cash Cows dry out, they must be ready to take their place. You may find out that in order to maintain your portfolio's health and effectiveness you will have to rebalance it. Have you been putting too many bets on new Problem Children? Is your portfolio too concentrated in Cash Cows and not enough Stars?

Dangerous Murkiness Ahead

The BCG Matrix Overlooks Many Factors in the Equation

Although the two determinants that this model focuses on are indeed valuable and important, there are many other factors to consider that this matrix overlooks.

In order to determine an industry's attractiveness, growth rate is not enough. More references are needed such as reference to market scope and size, to the structure of competition, to barriers to entry and to exit, seasonality, etc.

In order to determine a competitive advantage, market share is not enough. More references are needed such as cross-product learning curve, cross-product distribution channeling, R&D breakthroughs, etc. Moreover, if a company is not traded on the stock exchange market, it is very difficult to find relevant information.

The BCG Matrix Overlooks Product Relationships and Architectures

The BCG Matrix treats each type of product or brand separately, but one must realize that they all have to work together. If you take a flower apart, you can analyze it by observing its stem, its petals, its leaves, its stamen, but this is not the essence of the flower, it becomes an absence of the flower. The essence of the flower is embodied in the way all its parts work together as one. That is why it is not enough to identify and categorize products or brands.

In order to build a good strategy, a healthy working portfolio is needed. Brands and products are mutually affected, and maneuvering your portfolio as if it were a bunch of separate unrelated products or brands would be a mistake.

'Dogs' can, under certain conditions, turn into 'Stars,' or be valuable assets to the company in other ways.

You don't always want to "kill" the Dog. Under changing market conditions, in dynamic markets, a Dog may morph into a Star, or a Cash Cow.

If the Dog provides VALUE, and not only market share, you should think twice about "killing" it. Synergy with other products or brands, a reputation umbrella that other products or brands enjoy, psychological or emotional or social value for your organization, or its customers that only the Dog can provide, etc., are all crucial determinants that should be considered before declaring a Dog useless. The Matrix does not recognize this at all.

If a Dog can be used to undermine or tire the competition, to block penetration of a new entrant, or as any other tool in the market, discarding it would be a mistake.

The BCG Matrix Suffers from an Oversimplified Market Portrayal

Characteristic of models conjured in the 1970's, they portray a market which differs from that of the 21st century in too many ways, and to name them all would be beyond the scope of this book.

For example, back in the 1970's, people did not crave constant change or variation as they do today. The dynamic markets of today resist anything that stays fixed. Everything today is "Drive or Dive," like a bicycle. In order to maintain Cash-Cows, huge investments and R&D have to be allocated for the purposes of constant improvements, variations, niche within niche offers, and new brand and product generation within the Cash Cow segment. This entails some complexity in using the BCG under 21st century conditions.

Categorizing According to BCG is Subjective Rather Than Objective

Determining whether a market or an industry is attractive strongly depends on how you define that market. A brand may dominate a small niche with high growth, but under a wider industry definition it may have a small market share in a steady industry.

Therefore, two strategists can easily come up with contrary recommendations and conclusions – in which the same product or brand will be categorized as a Star or Cash-Cow by one of them, and as a Dog by the other.

All Hands Aboard!

Analysis of Israeli Publishing House APH Using the BCG Matrix

Israeli Publishing House APH was established over 20 years ago, when book publishing was still a profitable industry in the small Israeli market. It tried to penetrate the market in several genres until it finally narrowed down to a very specific niche – non-fiction titles in therapy, coaching, psychology, and other family related issues from before birth until old age.

The publishing house began to import titles written by leading experts from around the world to the Israeli Hebrew-speaking professional and interested public, and to offer a platform for local experts to publish their solutions as well. Soon, as small as it was, it managed to become a market leader in this field in Israel, and also to be meaningful in many ways.

The introduction of important and groundbreaking new titles from the world highlighted new areas of knowledge that were just beginning to make the agendas in therapeutic circles, such as ADHD, autism, learning disabilities, coaching, etc.

As A, the owner of the publishing house used to say, "As long as people have problems I can provide meaningful solutions." The success of these titles and their impact established the publishing house's position in the market and its logo and name became stamps of quality, credibility, and reliability.

However, several crucial changes took place in the market that pose a serious threat on the House's core business. First, new technologies arrived and became established in the content industry – from internet to e-publishing to self-publishing, the availability of content became exceedingly high and barriers to entry became exceedingly low.

In addition to that, printed books – are, in a way, a diminishing industry, taken over by electronic media with all its advantages: No storage space necessity, no reproduction costs, no distribution channels, no transportation, no paper, no… no… no… only nice and clean, dynamic and updatable content. Well, there is a question of reliability, but with low barriers to entry and multiple self-publishing options, this question is industry-crossing.

Second, internal changes in the value-chain, rising cost of paper, scarcity of shelf space in book shops, and bloody price wars between the big competitors, semi-monopoly of distributors, and we did not even say a word about digital printing, and company take-overs yet, all of these made the industry extremely complex to handle, unpredictable, and unprofitable to say the least.

In order to stay on top of the market and to survive, APH widened its product portfolio to include other content products, in the same knowledge fields, as follows:

APH Products Portfolio Includes:

Publishing Products:

Translated Printed Titles with Publishing Rights:
- Targeted customers: Random readers.
- High cost of production (purchase of rights, translation, editing, physical production, transportation,

storage, inventory management, royalties, distributors' discount, retailers' price wars, etc.).
- Low risk – high demand for books by international experts.
- Profit – percentage of income from book sales.

Local Titles with Publishing Rights:
- Targeted customers: Random readers.
- High cost of production – like above.
- High risk – local experts are outshined by internationally renowned titles.
- Profit – percentage of income from book sales.

E-publishing
- Targeted customers: Random readers with e-book devices.
- No cost of production.
- No risk.
- Profit is percentage of books sales.

Self-Publishing (aka vanity publishing) Platform for Local Experts:
- Targeted customers: Writers.
- No cost of production – all production costs are covered by the writers.
- Low risk – profit is achieved by the production process, and there is no need to appeal to readers. The selling of the books is only a bonus and not the main profit-generating activity.
- Profit by production – mainly for investment of time and knowhow, connections and publishing expertise, and for the use of the publisher's brand reputation, for which the writers pay fees to the publishing house on top of the production costs.

Other Non-publishing Info-products and Services:

Professional Conferences Covering the Same Knowledge Fields:
- Targeted customers: the same customers who purchase the House's books, who are interested in acquiring professional content on treatment, therapy, coaching, etc.
- High cost of production in a highly competitive marketplace.
- High risk since the activity is based on random registration.
- Profit by registration fees.

New Content Services – in Development
On-line content delivery to the same customers who purchase APH products.

- High cost of R&D.
- High risk.
- Profit model to be determined.

APH now needs to reevaluate its core business and product portfolio. Let us help A. from APH decide how to rebalance his product portfolio for maximal financial achievement, using the BCG matrix:

The DOG:

Obviously APH is feeding *two* DOGS: Translated titles with publishing rights, and local titles with publishing rights. These two product lines are total cash drains, requiring high investments of money and HR, and generating low to negative cash returns.

Problem is, the firm's reputation and appeal to professionals has been established and based on this product line's success; therefore, in order to develop its business in all other activities the House will need to maintain some market presence in that area, at least in terms of selling existing titles.

Low Market Growth Rate:
The demand for professional books is steady. Any growth due to a growing number of therapeutic professions and professionals will be cancelled out by the whopping availability of information on the web, and new e-learning options.

Low Relative Market Share:
The House's market share has been declining due to multiple penetrations of existing publishers with titles in the same genre, while the House has been reducing activities in this area and has not been publishing new titles. Also, due to the domination of distribution channels by the huge competitors in the market.

A straightforward BCG analysis would definitely recommend that these product lines be "killed" immediately. However, in our analysis, we must also consider the model's weaknesses and inaccuracies as discussed above. Since the House's high reputation has been achieved solely due to the publishing of renowned foreign titles as well as meaningful local titles, the brand may seriously be weakened should these product lines be diminished.

Accordingly, our BCG analysis will recommend that activity in these segments be set to operate with minimal resource drainage – i.e., only as much as is required in order to nourish the brand's strength and to ensure that the more attractive business segments maintain their attractiveness.

The CASH COW

According to this analysis, the company has two CASH COWS to milk and protect: The self-publishing segment (of printed books) and the professional conferences segment. Let's analyze why this is so.

Self-Publishing:

Low Market Growth Rate:
The high cost of production and the long process of writing are demand killers in the self-publishing industry of serious, heavy, non-fiction. Those who do publish their books are usually experts who believe in their writing skills, at least, as much as they believe in their professional skills.

The titles are published for purposes of professional leverage; therefore, are not considered direct profit generators. All of the above amounts to a low market growth rate.

High Relative Market Share:
Thanks to the high reputation and the strong brand that the House enjoys in the market, it attracts the best and most proficient writers of family-care related titles. Therefore, it would be fair to say that the House's relative market share in self-publishing is unaffected by the changes in the book publishing segment.

Professional Conferences

Low Market Growth Rate:
 Frontal learning has been a declining segment for years. Online learning and content have been chewing away at this segment continuously ever since the digital era began.
 Transportation, time drainage, absence from home and work, the inconvenience of public places, parking, are all factors that contribute to the decline of the frontal learning market. However, they still maintain an appeal of being there, belonging, meeting, and mingling. All of this amounts to a steady, non-growing yet existing market – for now.

High Relative Market Share:
 Conferences provide good business for the firm due to the brand's strength and professional appeal, as well as the company's high standard delivery of content in this segment.
 Under the BCG matrix, these two segments should be categorized as Cash Cows and should enjoy the company's maintenance attention for as long as they are able to deliver the cash.

The QUESTION MARK

Let's look at the segment of e-publishing.

High Market Growth Rate:
 The market is definitely growing and is potentially promising. The world is moving toward e-books: first and foremost, technology enables this transition. All of the other advantages that follow, as discussed above, constitute serious and significant motivations for publishers as well as customers to go forward with this transition. It is the future.

Low Relative Market Share:
 House's current position in this segment is weak, due to low activity as well as due to it being a new market with relatively few users as of this time.
 Under the BCG matrix, this segment will definitely be located in the Question Mark zone. The House needs to decide whether to invest heavily in customer education and promotional activities in this area, realizing that this is a risk that may be just a little ahead of its time. Otherwise there is no

logic in continuing this activity because it does not deliver any cash returns at all.

The STAR

This analysis determines that new online content services in development should be titled as the Stars under the BCG matrix:

High Market Growth Rate:
The market of e-content is booming. From e-learning to webinars, to apps, people are finding information on the net more than anywhere else. If a company manages to construct an informational source with a good profit model, the sky's the limit.

High Relative Market Share:
The brand's strength and professional appeal, as well as the company's high standard delivery of content across all of its activity, will enable it to gain a high relative market share in the segment of online content delivery in family-care matters.
According to the BCG matrix, our recommendation to A.; therefore, would be to invest in this Star with every resource he could allocate, so that he could be there and expand together with this expanding market from the very beginning and achieve the highest market share possible.

PORTER'S FIVE FORCES MODEL IN CAPTAIN'S EYE VIEW

Finding the Right Strategy by Understanding the 5 Pillars of Every Market

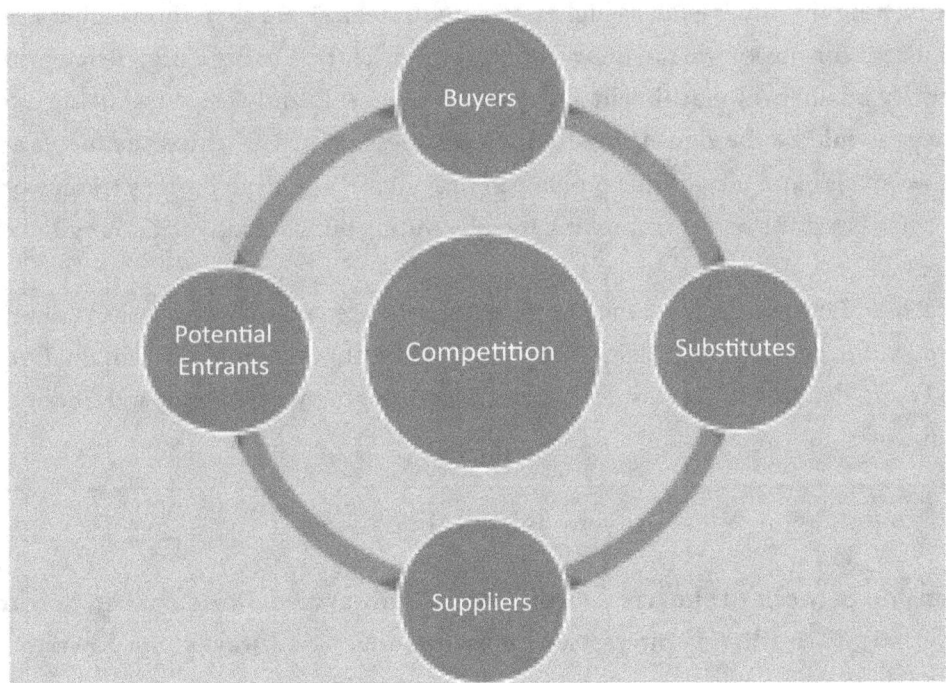

Key Winds in our Sails

Porter's Five Forces Model is one of the most important and central strategic models ever. It describes the impact of five major market forces on the company's external and internal environments.

A company needs Porter's Five Forces Model in order to analyze the competitive forces at work in the industry in which it operates. In order to develop a strategy that can deliver a competitive edge in any industry, one needs to analyze and understand the industry profoundly, in terms of forces, context, structure, and players.

For instance, why would one industry be captive to low margin and low profitability, and another could be enjoying the opposite? Why is one industry dominated by few large players and the other seems like a huge outdoor marketplace? Good answers to questions like these are a product of intensive analysis.

Porter's Five Forces Model is designed to help any executive or CEO draw a clear picture of the industry structure in order to identify opportunities, threats, and potential resources of power.

The model aims to do so by unveiling three crucial yet unknown variables: First, how the different forces in the company's business environment impact the overall level of profitability in the industry, second, the degree of attractiveness of the products in the market, and third, the nature of the Industry's inner dynamics.

According to Porter's model, we can identify five major forces at work as follows: Buyers' bargaining power, suppliers' bargaining power, threats of entry by potential competitors, threats of entry by potential substitutes, and the intensity of competition and rivalry among industry players.

You will see that this model determines that the stronger the five forces become, the harder it will be to maximize profitability by raising prices. Therefore, we can say that strong forces depress high pricing. Weakening the forces enables higher pricing strategies, and therefore, higher profitability.

The first useful conclusion we can draw from this model, is that **using a high price profit strategy should identify business arenas in which the forces are weak**, and vice versa, **using a low pricing profit strategy would be the right thing to do in business arenas in which the forces are strong.**

To see how much more insight this model can provide, let's analyze Porter's framework of forces and how it impacts a firm's strategic thinking by substituting our company with our good old familiar "brand-ship."

This time, in order to understand the model better, let's pretend that we are the captain of a transportation vessel for people, much like a ferry boat. Using this example, we will analyze the forces in the market and determine our business strategy. Let's begin by describing and understanding the five forces at work:

Buyers' Bargaining Power

The relationship between the buyers and the sellers is always a delicate trial and error song and dance of mutual and conflicting interests, which when analyzed always come down to the bottom

> line: Costs and benefits.
>
> **The buyer wants to buy and the seller wants to sell, both sides need each other, but the buyer always wants to pay less for more value, and the seller always wants to be compensated better for less value. Whoever pulls harder at this tug-of-war gets the better deal.**

How do we define costs and compensations? Two words: Money and value. How do we generate money? Income minus expenses. How do we generate value? Now that's a far trickier stunt to pull. First and foremost, we will have to understand what value means for our customers. There are several forms of value as follows:

There is what we call **functional value** – for instance, if people must get from one side of the canal to the other, and there are no bridges, then the functional value is to provide people with a means of crossing the canal.

Functional values can include things like technological superiority, aesthetic superiority, ease of use, precision, etc. There is **complementary value** – for instance, if our ferry can haul vehicles to the other side, or if the two-way ticket is cheaper than two one-way tickets, then we have a complementary value for our customers giving them an extra something for their money.

We also can identify a **user experience value** – for instance, if our ferry serves expensive Champagne in beautiful and branded champagne glasses that passengers can take home, while the competitors serve soda in disposable plastic cups, then we got ourselves an experience enrichment booster, which can certainly have valid value for our passengers.

It is not linked directly to the product or service, but it gives the buyer's experience a certain glow, a special memorable, extra bonus. Put all these values together and get your brand differentiation.

All of this is nice and fine but there is one little, or more so, major problem. Values as described above, even though they are very commonly distributed under conditions of market competition, are easily copied by competitors, and have the potential of becoming the standard in less than no time; thereby, compelling all players to reinvent themselves time and again and go overboard with unnecessary expenses that have one purpose – to cater to the buyers' whims in order to win their hearts... uh... and their dollars.

The thing with whims is that they have no limit, and they tend to develop creatively at our expense, becoming industry standards, sending us like a guided missile directly back to square one, i.e., at a "tie" with our competition, and in search of a new, sustainable, hard-to-replicate, unique, and desirable **differentiation**, or **competitive advantage**. This strategy often turns out to be a hollow, bottomless pit for the industry as a whole.

The even darker side of it all is that strategies like these keep us running after buyers; thereby, leaving all the bargaining power in their hands. So, how do we turn it around, and reclaim our power? How do we make them come searching for us, choosing us in advance over our competition, and making us their default preference? Or, in the terms of this model, how do we make sure that the Buyers' Bargaining Power stays weak?

We do it by providing value that sticks and is difficult to copy. The psychological value. The strongest value of all is the **psychological value**, which means that we manage to create a sense of belonging to a coveted group, status, or feeling – through ownership or purchase of our product or service.

Psychological value is the strongest value you can deliver. It is created by differentation and branding. The stronger the differentation – the stronger the psychological value. For instance – an Executive Ferry that targets CEOs, middle and upper managers and "status-wannahaves," will provide, in addition to conference rooms, secretarial services, and a refined atmosphere – a psychological value for people who want to feel important and/or make good use of their time, in the exact same manner that a Rolex watch provides – besides the time and aesthetics, a feeling of extravagance, status, or show-off for the owner.

So, if your company operates in an environment that empowers buyers, or in other words, if your buyers' bargaining power is strong, the best way to turn it around and reclaim the power would be by **differentiation** that will link a strong psychological value to your brand in the eyes of your buyers. Otherwise, you would have to use a bargain-oriented pricing strategy.

Now, in order to see the big picture, we would also have to distinguish between several types of buyers. There are what we call – the end-users, who buy for their own use, consumption, or service, and there are what we call – resellers, those include retailers, wholesalers, or any type of agents, mediators, and other sorts of middle-people.

Usually (but not always), resellers enjoy a stronger bargaining power than end-users, thanks to advantage of scale of course, which is sometimes manipulated to generate an even stronger impact on the industry by formal or non-formal unions and agreements between groups of resellers. To exercise your brain, try to come up with situations where end-buyers can impose an impactful bargaining power.

Let's now speak in more general terms. To evaluate your buyers' bargaining power, the company should map and characterize the identity of its clients and formulate a client profile. They should map market segments, assess the market's scope and its growth rate.

After having read all of the above, you can now see how strong buyers' bargaining power can impact the price, the quality, and time of delivery of your company's products. The size and consolidation of the customer group is also significant. A bigger and more consolidated group of buyers will have a stronger bargaining power than a smaller, more diverse group. Brand and product differentiation are business tools that can balance back the buyer's bargaining power.

When your products and brands are not strongly differentiated the buyer's bargaining power strengthens. When the cost of switching brands is low, customer churning is high. When you provide value nobody else provides in the market – your customers' bargaining power weakens. This is how it works.

Suppliers' Bargaining Power

We had already said that the relationship between the buyers and the sellers is always a delicate trial and error song and dance of mutual and conflicting interests, which, when analyzed, always comes down to the bottom line: Costs and benefits. When talking about suppliers' bargaining power, it is no different, only our role has turned around. Now, we are buyers.

As buyers, we want to own the bargaining power. We want to break our suppliers' differentiation, overtake the psychological value they've been providing us with, and get higher value for less money – either from them or from other players in the market. But things are never simple, are they?

You see, we also need our suppliers to stay healthy, business-wise, because our business success depends upon them too. They are a significant link in our value chain. If they are good suppliers, we do not want to lose them; therefore, this time we have to control OUR whims for the sake of our business and find the silver lining.

So, our suppliers' bargaining power is composed of several factors. Our business's dependency on their service is one of them. We also have to deal with the extent of supplier centralization and power in the market, the strength of our suppliers' brand, and the uniqueness of their products.

Our company should continuously be examining the costs of switching to competitors, and the cost of switching to alternative products or services. At the same time, we should never ever forget that they can switch too and supply our competition over us. If our competition demands to be exclusive, and they are bigger and provide more business than us, then our suppliers have more bargaining power.

For example, a popular beer brand will not supply our ferry if we dare sell another brand of beer on board. They can turn against us in other ways as well.

Another example. When the prospect of our suppliers' becoming competitors can be used as a threat against us, then their bargaining power increases.

In addition, the bargaining process between us and our suppliers is affected by the excellence and quality they provide: When they provide higher value, their bargaining power increases and vise-verse. When the value they provide is not unique, their bargaining power decreases.

We still haven't said a word about binding contracts, ownership of non-sellable assets, managerial stagnation, or technological industry-changing breakthroughs. All of those, and more, are crucial parameters which affect our suppliers' bargaining power, and by natural order, our business as well.

Going back to our Executives' Ferry, let's say that our suppliers are ticket vendors. Take time to do an exercise now, and dive deep into their bargaining power. What do we, as CEOs of our ferry, need to analyze? What should we be looking out for? What should we consider? What are our options? Where is our alertness needed? What insights will the analysis of our suppliers' bargaining power give us?

Remember: Our profitability is weakened in direct correlation with the strengthening or our suppliers' bargaining power.

Threats of Entry by Potential Competitors

According to Porter's model, potential competitors are factors which are currently not considered threats but could penetrate the market and become threats sometime in the future.

The threat of entry to the market by new players depends on barriers to entry and on the reaction taken by the current players in the market. When barriers to entry are very low, new competitors can oftentimes bring new spirits to a market, turning conventions upside-down, and setting new rules altogether.

In order to evaluate the seriousness of threats of entry by potential competitors we would need a complicated formula, which includes many variables. For example, let's look at two parameters: Economy of scale, and technological superiority.

If our business activities enjoy economy of scale, we can be attractive to our clients, more than a newcomer who is fighting over the crumbs we leave behind. However, if this newbie can boast with superior technology, and technology is a strong component of our product's value in the eyes of our customers, then we might be in more trouble than we had anticipated.

If our product is strongly differentiated, and our customers/clients associate a strong psychological value to having or using it, then we can assume that their loyalty would stick longer, and we will be less affected by the forces of threats of entry by potential competition.

More advantages that can balance out the threat of entry are live patents, high cost of switching, or a strong learning component that may serve as a barrier to switching, IT systems, owning or controlling exclusive distribution channels, good connections in the industry, national policy and regulations, safety measures, environmental considerations, etc.

As technology sinks in and deteriorates barriers to entry, we will be always worried by the prospect of our suppliers executing forward integration, using our information, knowhow, and expertise, our connections and business ties we've actually handed over on a silver platter as a basis for our cooperation, in order to become our competitors in the market.

On the other hand, we may choose to execute backward integration and own our suppliers if we can. But wherever there is a value-chain, there will always be another link behind us. We are doomed to live forever in the buyers' shoes, and dilemmas, no matter how far backward we integrate.

For example, if we run the Executives' Ferry, and the company which markets our services is looking for a business investment, they might become a threat of entry by potential competitors if they invest in a ferry larger and more modern than ours, and are currently looking to purchase a more central docking spot.

If we wait until they begin to market tickets to their own ship (while using all OUR knowhow, ties, and connections), docking in a more strategic location than ours, we might be too late. Thus, when we perform our Five Forces analysis according to Porter's model, we would have to foresee this option and formulate a potential course of action to balance out the threat – or pose a counterthreat while we still can. In this model's terminology, we would have to make sure that the forces by threats of entry by potential competitors – stay at their weakest.

Threats of Entry by Potential Substitutes

Potential substitutes are products, services, or solutions which answer the same need – usually on better terms. When the costs of switching are low, these substitutes may have a significant impact on the industry – locally and sometimes on much larger scales. Potential substitutes may draw a significant market share and cause existing players to lose business.

The threat of potential substitutes is influenced by variables such as client loyalty, the strength of your brand, the nature of your customer relationship strategy, customer inclination to try new things, etc.

Now, let's imagine that our Executive's Ferry is situated in a crossing where a bridge or an underwater transportation tunnel is being constructed, threatening to render our ferry services unnecessary; or to push us down from a "must" category to a "nice to have."

For instance, compelling us to change our category from vital transportation solutions to maybe – tourism attractions.

This is not improbable. For example, in many places around the world, where water transportation has been the only option to cross a large body of water such as a river or a strait, too wide for a bridge but not wide enough to justify flights, technology now enables construction of roads and railroads.

The world's deepest underwater railway tunnel in Istanbul is only one of many instances. At the time, Prof Murat Güvenç, head of the Urban Studies Institute at Sehir University, Istanbul, said about the Marmaray project, "We have no idea how it will affect the city…" referring to the demographic map, development of commerce and the prices of property. "Increased overall accessibility – access to transport, shopping, culture, etc. – will cause rents in formerly cheaper areas to rise quickly. It will substantially change the social strata of the city. With the opening of the Marmaray line, the Bosphorus Strait will cease to be an obstacle. It means the end of Istanbul as we know it."

Erdogan himself said that the Marmaray rail line would, "Connect London to Beijing," reviving the ancient trade routes across Asia to Europe! So, we can see that we are talking about a substitute transportation solution, but it carries a potential to make an overwhelming effect on the area, the nation, and even on the continent as a whole – tourism, commerce, regulation, import and export, housing, and what not.

We will look at one aspect a little bit closer: The local ferry industry, which is right in the eye of the storm.

The Bosphorus Strait has been, for hundreds of years, and still is, one of the busiest sea crossings in the world. In an article published by Lykke an van de Kerk on 2005, it was claimed that at the time, approximately 50,000 major commercial ships used to pass through the strait every year.

In addition, hundreds of smaller commercial ferries used to carry passengers and cars across the Bosphorus every day. And then, the Marmaray underwater tunnels, opened on 2013, with the ability to carry up to 75,000 people an hour in either direction across the Bosphorus straits.

The Turkish government estimates that today, 1.5 million people cross the straits every day on the Marmaray lines. The subway crossing lasts the incomprehensible duration of four to five minutes; only a fraction of the time needed to cross by ferries.

What was the effect on the local ferry industry? What happened to the very same ferries which, for hundreds of years, have been crisscrossing the Bosphorus being the only transportation option between the European and the Asian parts of Istanbul? How were they affected?

One example is enough to show the impact. The City Lines Ferries, which is the public sea transportation subsidy of Istanbul Metropolitan Municipality, posted a 28 million Turkish-Lira (equal to U.S. $11.4 million) loss in 2014, mainly due to a decrease in work post launch of the Marmaray train line. Many lines had to be discontinued, and improvements needed to be made in all areas, including financial management, maintenance and modernization of the vessels, user experience, and economical attention.[6]

---

6   http://www.hurriyetdailynews.com/istanbul-ferries-budget-hit-by-mismanagement-marmaray-78426

So, we see that sometimes, the threat of entry by potential substitutes may have a much stronger and wider impact on the world as we knew it. You may say now, well, what does THAT have to do with my company? Well, let me tell you. If a threat of entry by potential substitutes may change the world as YOU know it, you'd better be prepared to reinvent yourself too or you will find yourself stuck with an old-fashioned unattractive offer to customers who are already mesmerized by a far better solution.

Do you want another example? Let's talk about the print industry. Digital printing – a direct substitute, and electronic media – an indirect substitute, both took their toll on offset printing. Not only did they grab away huge chunks from the market, but they also changed the industry and the world of information altogether.

Some might argue that they have blown the market into a previously unimaginable size and scope, thus creating more work for everyone – newcomers, as well as old-school solutions. It all depends on your point of view.

Sometimes the change comes in one blow. Other times it is gradual process like in the printing industry. But change, substitutes, and threats will always be there and you'd better be watchful and prepare as best as you can.

Accordingly, when you analyze your company's future using Porter's Five Forces Model, you would have to conduct serious research to find prospects of potential substitutes in your industry and business, and consider your findings with the utmost seriousness, and make sure you never underestimate the force of threats of entry by potential substitutes.

Intensity of Competition and Rivalry Among Industry Players

The fifth and final force you would have to analyze is really a summation of the previous four. It is a product of the buyer's bargaining power: When the buyers have more power the competition becomes more fierce.

This means that your competitive edge is not so sustainable; therefore, potential customers have trouble differentiating you from the others on the basis of your product or service and are just looking for the better deal. It is a product of your suppliers' bargaining power: When the suppliers have more power that's when competition becomes less fierce because suppliers become a barrier to entry; thereby, "cleaning" up the market, leaving only the strong players.

It is a product of threats and opportunities in the market: More opportunities mean more competitors and intense rivalry. More threats mean higher barriers to entry, thus more moderate competition.

When analyzing your company according to Porter's Five Forces Model, you should identify your present and potential competitors, your existing and potential substitute threats, and the overall player-map of the industry. The intensity of competition and rivalry among industry players affects the company's ability to raise prices, and to compromise on quality. It effects your company's motivation and willingness to invest in R&D, and to improve or develop better products and better manufacturing processes. It effects the company's freedom to choose how much to invest in promotion, advertising, marketing, and indeed all critical success factors for the industry.

The competition will rise when there are many competitors in the market, when barriers to exit are high (contract violation, non-sellable assets, etc.), and when competitors are not highly differentiated. Under these conditions a company would experience difficulties maintaining high profit margins and might find itself forced to use high-cost promotional tools and to utilize non-price oriented competitive weapons.

When the competitors are highly differentiated, they create mini-markets inside a larger industry and those mini-markets sometimes may act as niches with less intensive rivalry, like family cars versus sports cars. The rivalry in the industry may be very high but the mini-markets enable companies to operate in less comprehensive territories; thereby, providing more freedom and flexibility to choose their promotional strategies.

Dangerous Murkiness Ahead

Porter's model was developed in the early 1980s. Back then, the four revolutions: Technology, information, transportation, and communications, were only just beginning to envelope.

The huge globalization process was just beginning to see the light of day. The power of e-commerce was not even a fraction of what it is now. Most industries were not as dynamic as today. Business models were built and developed more in office boardrooms and less out in the streets. So, mostly this model's weaknesses result from the fact that it does not complement today's dynamic, unpredictable, crazy world:

- The model cannot deliver meaningful insights if you are operating in a regulated market.
- The model cannot deliver meaningful insights if you are operating in an e-commerce market.
- The model cannot be implemented in the complex multi-national, multi-segment, no boundary markets that the 21st century offers.
- The model cannot be implemented in the complex multi-national, multi-segment, multi-form, or multi-model companies that the 21st century has bred.
- The model is static and cannot provide business insights for highly dynamic environments, or for unbalanced environments.
- The model is not able to provide insights as to the scope of influence of the different forces or what measures need to be taken by the company in each case
- Targeting new markets instead of operating within existing ones is not in the scope of this model.

All Hands Aboard!

Analysis of Starbucks Using Porter's Five Forces Model

Howard Schultz founded his first specialty coffee store in Seattle, Washington, in 1986. He offered, besides premium coffee – a new concept he coined as, "the third place" (with home and work being first and second), where people can take some time-off, have coffee and meet the "regulars" from their community.

Following an ambitious expansion plan and its success, Starbucks penetrated the U.S. and then other countries across the world, until it became a global empire.

Let's analyze Starbucks according to Porter's Five Forces Model:

Buyers' Bargaining Power – Low

On first impression, buyer's bargaining power is very high. Offers exceed demand, service is very local, and proportions, friends, a good cup of coffee, after all, for most people, falls under what we call: Nice to have, not a must.

Buyers are end-users, who love the brand, or who are located at a geographical convenience, but hey, they can get coffee anywhere. They are not organized in any way, but they are mostly regulars, which makes them more significant than random customers, and increases their bargaining power even more. The buyers' bargaining power is mostly characterized by their ability to switch to other competitors.

Switching costs to other companies are zero, and also switching efforts are zero. Sometimes, special efforts are even needed in order to sustain brand loyalty (leaving home earlier, standing in line, paying more, etc.). The only value that other companies cannot deliver is the psychological value that Starbucks offers – the brand itself – the "third place" concept, which, next to the quality and diversity of products, creates a brand differentiation with real significance to its customers. This is where Starbucks won and turned around the force-relationships between the buyers and the brand, to its benefit.

In the U.S., for instance, where the "third place" concept was conceived, the buyers' bargaining power dropped to an all-time low, because no other place provided them with an intentionally warm welcoming atmosphere like Starbucks.

In America's big cities, where urban loneliness is a growing phenomenon due to a growth in single occupant households, a strengthening tendency to see homes as more and more private, and maximal dedication to work and careers at the expense of community participation and family time, the third place was a genius idea, and sure enough it caught like fire. it provided informal opportunities for people to have neutral and social interactions, or at least to feel like they do since real social interactions involve commitment of some kind.

But here, they knew they were welcome to sit there whenever they please, and to go whenever they please, no commitment, no strings attached, no extra privacy-compromising burden, just the sound and sight of other human beings minding their own business, and an occasional chat.

Nevertheless, note that the things that lead to low bargaining power for customers can be very culture oriented and are definitely not absolute truths. There were territories in which this concept did not necessarily work.

In Israel for instance, where people are very socially oriented, in big cities too, singles too, with very close (on a daily basis) bonds with biological families as well as families of choice (lifelong very strongly connected groups of friends – not related to work), the third-place concept was greeted with utter indifference. People did not need it. Their homes are always open to friends and family members. They consider their homes to be much less private than is customary in America. If they want to feel welcomed, they pop into the neighbor's house for a chat and a coffee, that is, when their friends or family members are not popping in themselves.

Non-work-related socializing is simply a very big part of their culture, and they had no need for that third place in their daily routine. All they required was good enough coffee. As it turned out, the coffee itself, without the psychological value, was not enough to sustain business there. We will briefly return to this later too.

Suppliers' Bargaining Power – Moderate

The suppliers' bargaining power is very high, if Starbucks wants to maintain the high quality of their raw materials. The most significant raw material – coffee beans – can be purchased from specific regions in the world only and are extremely delicate and sensitive. The yield is dependent on general weather and climate conditions, labor shortages, price fluctuations, and many other challenges, uncertainty being the strongest one.

Same suppliers provide coffee to all coffee manufacturers and brands across the world, including mega brands of instant coffee, who use the same raw material, and enjoy economy of scale, in comparison with Starbucks. Not easy.

Nevertheless, there are conditions that balance out the suppliers bargaining power and pretty nicely too. Coffee cultivation is a very challenging industry. From the many risks inherent in coffee farming, to unpredictable weather, pest control, and regulations, coffee producers are probably the most poorly paid link in this rich industry's supply chain. So, they sell what they can, and they value each customer.

Generally, what we can say about the suppliers' bargaining power in the case of Starbucks, is that it is moderate.

Threats of Entry by Potential Competitors – Potentially High but Market is Saturated

It depends on the local market in which Starbucks operates. In the UK, for instance, this threat is low due to a saturated coffee-chain market and high capital requirements for new businesses.

In Israel, the chain itself posed a threat of entry to other local chains and ended up clearing out. In New York, where there exists a strong coffee-chain culture, and the habit of stopping for coffee on the way to the office or for an afternoon break is very rooted, the threat of entry by new competitors may seem higher at first, but the market is mature, and growth is moderate so maybe not so much.

Threats of Entry by Potential Substitutes – low

Coffee-wise: The threat of entry by potential substitutes is insignificant. Despite the increasing range of energy drinks, anti-dairy trends, and substitutes made of mixtures of rye, barley, chicory, sugar beet, dandelion root, and other stuff, none of those ever seem to weaken the human craving for this wonderful morning wake-up potion.

Coffee has become culture and an art-form, a craving, a self-defining choice, a passion, and a desire. We know who we are by the coffee we drink. We know who YOU are by the coffee YOU drink. Non-dairy creams, caffeine-free alternatives, variety of aromas, and intensities of flavor have become popular and available. No substitute has yet managed to rise up to the level of coffee as a pillar of culture, not even close.

Third-place-wise: Here is where Starbucks won all its stars. The concept is not so deeply identified with the brand, that no other brand can actually take it away. Other brands can offer other concepts, but not this one. It is theirs, and only theirs.

Intensity of Competition and Rivalry Among Industry Players – Extremely High

The intensity of rivalry among coffee chains in the market is very high, and the numbers of branded coffee shops have been increasing across the world – brands, as well as shops.

The indirect competition is also significant and fierce and is composed of coffee brands and products targeting homes, ranging from simple instant coffee to more complex and high-end coffee machines and blends.

To Conclude:

We did not find a definite orientation. We have a strong force of buyers' and suppliers' bargaining power, and weaker forces of threats. We have a fierce and complex competition in the market and we have to decide what to recommend.

Lowering prices would be suicide since the quality of raw material is hard to come by and is the flag of this brand. Competition is fierce but people won't give up on their coffee, so the best thing to do would be to pull them into Starbucks coffee shops and expand market share by way of branding – strengthening the psychological promise of benefit to customers, leading them to believe in the brand and what it has to offer them. This is the core of customer loyalty.

Secondly, they should formulate a strategy that attracts customers by way of extending the service, i.e., by catering further to their needs instead of lowering prices. And indeed, the Starbucks strategy does not include price wars. Instead, they maintain a growing selection of complementary food products, a continued selection of premium coffee drinks for people who are not prepared to settle for less than Starbucks' blends and willing to pay slightly higher prices for their cup, and new high-end blends and individualized brews for people who swear by their coffee and also willing to extend more dollars for their special taste.

Third, in addition to all of the above, Starbucks maintains its position under the media spotlight by delighting and surprising their customers with new and exciting endeavors, like the Starbucks Reserve Roastery and Tasting Room in Seattle, thus coming up with a premium blend of branding – the love of coffee and fun in just the right amount.

PORTER'S DIAMOND IN CAPTAIN'S EYE VIEW

Creating a Competitive Advantage Through National Leverage

National Competitive Advantage

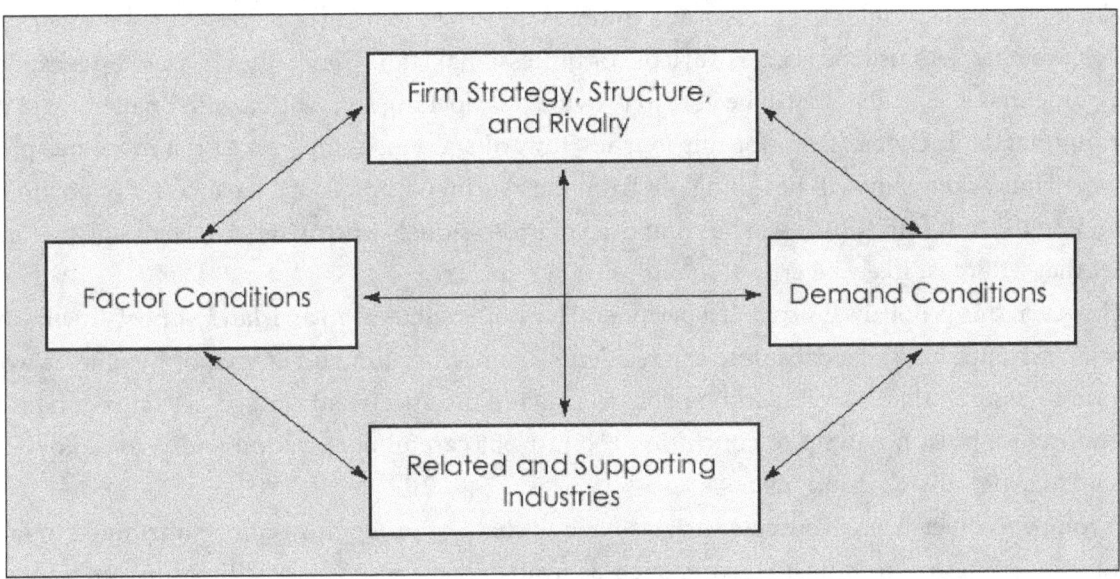

Figure 11.1 The Porter Diamond

Key Winds in our Sails

Porter's Diamond is about competitive advantages derived from national conditions. Our clue for understanding the logic behind this model, which led Porter in his research, is the clustering of successful industries or companies in specific countries, despite globalization. For example, the automotive industry cluster located in Japan and Korea, the chemical industry cluster located in central Germany, or the timepiece industry cluster in Switzerland. This clustering suggests that each of these countries must be doing something which positively impacts its industries' competitive position in global markets. What is that something?

Porter has identified four attributes, which any national environment can provide, that have the power to sustain and empower global competitiveness for businesses located in that nation. Porter positioned these four attributes in a diamond-like model known today as Porter's Diamond.

In order to make it easier to remember, let's refer to the theme of this book, our "Brand Ship." We can say that Porter's Diamond determines that a ship's (a company's) competitive advantage is stronger when its home-port provides support, i.e., the more able the port (or nation) to provide it with an environment that leverages its efforts, the better its competitive position will be.

This environment has four facets, like a diamond, as follows:

> **Factor Conditions**
>
> **Porter describes Factor Conditions as the nation's ability to favorably impact factors of production, such as the skilled labor or infrastructure necessary to compete and succeed in a given industry.**

For illustration purposes, let's conduct a simple comparison between a central and a peripheral docking port and consider the plusses and minuses of using them for our ship.

For example, let's use the success variable of professional staff. Generally, it would be reasonable to assume that a central port will be able to provide our docking ship with a wider gallery of skilled working hands to choose from for our journey toward success, compared to the more peripheral harbor. Thus, if our ship will be sailing out from the central harbor, it will have better opportunities of finding the best staff, which will be composed of professionals who own the special skills we need, a fact that will most likely be crucial to our journey's success.

However, this is not always true. If a peripheral harbor is situated on an island or port-town, where sailing and shipping skills constitute the residents' major vocation and source of income, it would be safe to assume that it would still be able to provide the special advantage of factor conditions. Therefore, we must not jump to conclusion too fast but careful observation and prior analysis are crucial to avoid mistaken judgments.

A long and diverse list of success variables in any chain of production can be attributed to factor conditions, ranging from basic factors such as availability and cost of skilled human resources, through physical given conditions and availability of raw materials, to sophisticated resources such as technology, innovation, infrastructure, etc.

The quality, availability, cost, and competitiveness of local golden links in the production chain are like national treasure chests: They are major determinants which have a power to boost the competitive advantage that nations can offer certain industries operating within them.

Let's look at an example from marketing fields. Swedish craftsmanship has been celebrated for many years before the rise of IKEA furniture. Glass, ceramics, and textiles have long been major factors in the Swedish basket of global commerce.

Sweden can showcase a glorious history of design appreciation, brought into the present with the growing and developing modern concept of "beauty in the home," which has become that national industry's motto.

Craftsmanship and knowhow at such high levels constitute fertile grounds on which to base an international success story like IKEA. The factor conditions Sweden offers are based on years of experience and excellence achieved by generations of relevant professional craftspeople, including textile designers, carpenters, home planners, raw material manufacturers, etc.

Availability of raw materials needed for production of furniture, as well as developed wood and textile industries and high reputation in areas of home design and craftsmanship all constitute a solid gallery of factor conditions supporting IKEA's global success.

> **Local Demand Conditions**
>
> **Porter defines demand conditions as the nature of home-market demand for the industry's product or service.**

We've all heard the saying that a good salesman can sell ice to an Eskimo. But what if the marketer *is* an Eskimo and he wants to market ice, say, to Africans?

In "EskimoLand" there is no demand for ice, simply due to over-abundance. Our marketer could pack his ship with ice to the roof and take off for Africa. Will he be able to profit from his ice? Not likely. Even if he conducted all the research in the world, he would have no hands-on experience selling it at all, and especially not under the very different climactic and cultural conditions he is going to encounter there.

On the other hand, high local demand provides grounds for stimulating any industry to reach high standards of product quality – companies learn how to walk their talk, including: Upgrading, specialization, innovation, identification of trends, shifts, and directions, and even developing the capability to set and create trends and fashions.

Companies learn how to see their customers, to identify their needs, and to provide high quality solutions to those needs.

High local demand is like an especially powerful pair of binoculars with which a company can see its customers' needs in remote markets, after having perfected its performance based on its local markets' needs.

Why did Israeli Gottex Swimwear do so well in the world? As an Israeli company, Gottex had ample opportunity and time to test and hone its product at home, being that Israel is a country with a long summer, long beaches, and lots of long-legged, good looking, young people who love summer and beaches, not to mention strong summer tourism and everything (and everyone) that comes with it.

With immense demand at home for quality fashion swimwear, Gottex had become true pros of swimwear fashion and by the time they went global – they were experts, they knew what people liked, they knew all about swimwear fashion, they knew how to make material that would withstand extreme usage conditions such as constant exposure to salt, water, sand, sun, etc., and they knew how to sell and market their brand effectively.

All their knowledge was accumulated thanks to extensive experience gained while providing for high home demand and competition. They took this extensive experience and translated it to many foreign markets and languages, and they were very successful.

The same can be said about the Japanese auto industry, American fast food, and German appliances, among many others.

> **Competitiveness of Related and Supporting Industries**
>
> **Porter defines this facet as the presence or absence in the nation of supplier industries and other related industries that are internationally competitive.**

Say we are a company which manufactures heavy duty vessels, and our home country is also renowned for producing top-rated military vessels or luxury yachts, will that reputation spill over to our freight ships as well? Most probably, yes.

If there is an internationally successful industry of large and powerful engine technology, would that impact our chances of success with our ships in world markets? Also, yes.

Porter has discovered that the presence of local, internationally competitive, related and/or supplier industries constitutes a direct impact for empowering strong competitive advantages globally. These advantages can range from the creation of high barriers to entry on the global level, down to local collaborations and synergic cooperation.

The presence of highly competitive related and supporting industries in a company's local marketing arena could be compared to an underwater support squad, offering below-the-level cooperation and empowerment.

For example, when it comes to Japanese auto industry, past research conducted by a study group at the University of Michigan proved that the Japanese success in this area could be attributed to lower material costs, a result of Japan's tight network of suppliers. High-end Swiss watches enjoy synergic benefits derived from the developed high-end jewelry industry there.

Firm Strategy, Structure, and Rivalry

According to Porter this facet of the diamond is composed of two related factors: Firm strategy and structure as a result of the national business culture and policies governing how companies are created, organized, and ideologically managed.

The nature of industrial rivalry is key to a company's power to develop a globally sustainable advantage.

So, has the rigorousness of domestic rivalry driven your company to upgrade its all-around business conduct to the utmost possible level, providing it with margins big enough to withstand the risk of going global? Or has your company been "spoiled" by the convenience of a soft competitive environment?

And more, does your home port favor your ship to strange ships which have come to do business? Does it provide you with apt financial aids? Does it provide training and enrichment to your staff? Can you trust it to provide prompt services?

A nation's ideologies and policies are like a lighthouse guiding its brands at sea, illuminating their way. Import export policies, international commerce agreements, management ideologies, financial leverage options, taxing regulations, and even international politics may have an outstanding impact on global competitive advantages of companies.

There is no limit to what a nation could do to promote its industries worldwide. Take, for example, Switzerland, a very small country which has become a branding empire: Many of its top brands appear regularly on the Interbrand Best Global Brands lists.

The country has branded the value "Swiss Made" too well… so well that it began to backfire. The value of "Swiss Made" has become so high and sought-after that it has become subject to excessive exploitation and abuse, putting the Swiss brand's legendary reputation at risk.

"The Legislation of Project Swissness" is a movement launched in Switzerland, in order to protect "Swiss Made" label from misuse and exploitation. The result: Every company which will legally win the right to showcase the "Swiss Made" label will immediately be the owner of a huge and sustainable competitive advantage in global markets.

Dangerous Murkiness Ahead

Criticism of Porter's Diamond revolves around several core issues of which the main points are: Its dependence on the existence of solid boundaries between nations, its disregard of electronic commerce and the global revolution, and its incompatibility with small nations' economies.

The looser the boundaries – the looser the theory

Porter's choice of the nation as the unit of analysis may not be relevant to the world of the 21st century. Economies today do not have completely defined and solid boundaries; therefore, Diamonds of National Advantage may not be analyzed independently any longer.

Firms today may choose to enjoy selected determinants from their national economies as well as neighboring ones, and at the same time, are involuntarily affected by National Diamonds of other nations.

Furthermore, many companies today maintain several headquarters situated in several locations around the world, where they conduct all, or several, of their value-chain activities: Acquisition, production, R&D, marketing, management, and so forth, and from where deliveries are dispatched, whether domestic or international.

The diamond analysis needed in cases such as this is very complex and must take into the formula several national diamonds and the relationships they have with one another, forming extremely complex matrixes which are impossible to analyze.

And we have still not even mentioned multinational joint ventures or mergers of multinational companies.

One of the results of the breaking down of economic boundaries in the 21st century is the 'Born Global' companies in general, and especially Knowledge Intensive Born Global firms (KIBoGs).

These are companies which strategically view their market from the very beginning as the international global market, skipping the phase in which domestic market is targeted as main market, learned from, and benefited by.

The KIBoGs, which constitute a new phenomenon of the 21st century, are completely ignored by Porter's Diamond of National Advantage and cannot be satisfactorily analyzed by it.

Virtual Grounds do not Stick

Porter's Diamond is not applicable for analysis of e-commerce success or failure.

Online shopping is a different world which operated under different rules and logic. Content and musical products, or tickets that could be printed upon payment anywhere anytime regardless of their location, online shopping of financial services, education, news and other knowledge based products, software, videos, databases, etc., are all products and services which can be delivered immediately upon order completion, they are not characterized by any physical existence, they do not require shipping or international commerce agreements, and consequently they are not subject to national borders of any kind, nor regulations, or any other nationality-based determinant.

Some marketing thinkers go as far as treating the internet as a separate "national" unit with rules and industrial structures of its own, that do not abide by the logic under which Porter created his Diamond.

The National Advantage of Largeness

Finally, Porter's Diamond of National Advantage grants by definition higher advantages to companies originating from bigger economies, whereas businesses from small and minute economies suffer disadvantage from the very outset.

The diamond usually does not explain business successes generated from small economies; therefore, we can carefully determine that it is limited in scope.

All Hands Aboard!

Analysis of IKEA Using Porter's Diamond of National Advantages

IKEA was founded in 1943, in Sweden, by 17-year-old Ingvar Kamprad. It specializes in home furnishing, décor, and textiles.

As of January 2008, it is the world's largest furniture retailer, with over 300 stores in over 35 countries and still growing. Kamprad was listed as one of the world's richest people in 2013.

How could Porter's Diamond of National Advantages have forecasted this success?

Factor Conditions:

The reputation of Swedish furniture is world-renowned. Almost 70% of its production is sold internationally, making Sweden the 7th largest European furniture exporter. This means availability of professional hands, including carpentry, textile manufacturing, marketing expertise, and a strong infrastructure for export.

The Swedish design industry has grown quite a reputation in itself. Since 1993, the number of firms in the Swedish design industry has risen by more than 300%. At the same time, the number of full time students studying for design diplomas in third level institutions has expanded by more than 350%. This means an abundance of professional designers. It is interesting to note that during those years IKEA's turnover has grown by the same percentages exactly.

Combined with Sweden's long and glorious history of design appreciation and guided by its home design concept manifested today by the industry's motto: "Beauty in the home," we have a sound and strong foundation of factor conditions supporting IKEA's chances of success in global markets.

Demand Conditions

The Swedish traditional home lifestyle is family-centered and child-friendly. The majority of the Swedish population in the area where IKEA was first founded consisted of hard-working and modest, family-oriented people, experts at making the best of limited resources, including in-home spaces. Their typical climate, being cold and dark – drove them to introduce bright colors into the interiors of their homes.

Smart use of limited space, maximal functionalism, fresh and raw (minimally treated) wood, textiles in bright colors, and avoidance of extravagance and lavishness (in style and in pricing policy) – are all reflected in IKEA's design concept. Although IKEA's design and marketing concepts were initially targeted for typical Swedish demand, as it turns out, this concept mix was extremely attractive for millions of homeowners around the world.

IKEA's deep and profound understanding of its local markets' demand turned out, as often happens, to be the key to its global success.

Competitiveness of Related and Supporting Industries

The presence of related and supporting competitive industries in Sweden also constitute a major determinant of success for IKEA.

For example, the wood industry has been one of the most important Swedish industries throughout the 19th century until today, thanks to the vastness of forests there.

Being the third largest wood producer in Europe, Sweden is a world leader in wood industry making it a classic globally competitive industry. Being that wood is a major raw material for IKEA's produce helps IKEA's competitive edge in several ways: Local abundance of wood suppliers promises regular supply of raw materials, and the locality of this industry enables IKEA to save on the cost of delivery and storage.

Although most of IKEA's production is outsourced, wooden components are produced in Sweden by Swedwood, a production group under IKEA.

Swedish home textile industry is another very strong and competitive industry in Sweden. The industry's growth rates have fluctuated up and down in recent years, but the Swedish home textile and décor markets is still one of the most rapidly growing retail sectors there. Even though home textiles account for a limited share of total sales in IKEA, it is important to consider two facts: First, furniture production requires textiles as raw materials (from upholstery to storage solutions). Second, in absolute terms, home textiles carry a meaningful significance with regards to total sales.

Firm Strategy, Structure, and Rivalry

The Scandinavian management style leans toward informality and cooperation in areas such as clothing, colleague mutual conduct within and across managerial levels, and with customers.

The IKEA customer experience is enhanced by these Scandinavian core values, which are suited for a retail industry targeted at people who seek satisfaction in expenditure results, personal service, and quality.

IKEA has formulated a deal with its customers: A low pricing strategy, but in return, the customers give up a link in the production chain and serve as this link themselves. IKEA's customer policy dictates mutuality by making its customers not only deliver but also work to assemble most products. As it turns out, this is a trade millions of people are willing to make. Not only are they getting better prices without compromising quality, but also, they end up gaining the advantage of satisfaction from their own accomplishment.

All in all, we can say that the business context as is manifested in the Swedish culture is very much in agreement with the values of IKEA and constitute a core factor driving consumer satisfaction.

To conclude, if we were IKEA's strategists, asked to determine whether or not IKEA would succeed as a worldwide business, we would have to say that analysis by Porter's Diamond of National Advantage determines strong presence and positive impact of all four determinants, which supports IKEA's high chances of global success.

PEST MODEL IN IN CAPTAIN'S EYE VIEW

Seeing the big picture, getting the big achievements

PEST Analysis Layout
Enter your subhead line here

POLITIC FACTORS
1. This is a sample text. You simply add your own text here.
2. This text is fully editable. It can be replaced with your own style.

SOCIAL FACTORS
1. This is a sample text. You simply add your own text here.
2. This text is fully editable. It can be replaced with your own style.

ECONOMIC FACTORS
1. This is a sample text. You simply add your own text here.
2. This text is fully editable. It can be replaced with your own style.

TECHNOLOGY FACTORS
1. This is a sample text. You simply add your own text here.
2. This text is fully editable. It can be replaced with your own style.

Key Winds in our Sails

If you are a surfer, a great curled wave soaring right at you can be a great opportunity, if you are ready for it; however, the very same wave may pose a dangerous threat if you are not. If you are a sailor, a strong north wind can be a great opportunity if you are prepared to ride it; however, the very same wind may be deadly if you are not. The environment changes on us constantly, just like winds, waves, seasons, temperature, and other conditions in the open sea.

The forces are bigger and stronger than us. No matter the size of our vessel, if we are not prepared, the waters will toss and hurl us around as if we were the littlest of aunts. We cannot control the marketing environment in which we are operating just like a sailor cannot control the open sea. New technologies often behave like forceful waves. Shifts in attitudes or trends can have an impact on our "boat" like strong winds.

As skillful, careful, and ambitious business leaders, we could really use a chopper that would take us up, hovering in mid-atmosphere where we can see what's coming and what's going. PEST Analysis can be that chopper. If we use it correctly, it will help us see the big picture, assessing and predicting opportunities and threats, which our environment is "cooking" for us somewhere in the future: Below, above, and all around. The implications are clear. Threats will be identified and avoided as much as possible, or at least you will be prepared for them, while more importantly, opportunities will be identified, foreseen, or even created self-handedly at best, and then taken advantage of to create a sustainable competitive advantage and to make a profit.

The PEST model, also known as PESTEL or STEP or several other prominent variations, is a simple and very popular tool for intelligently analyzing the political, economic, socio-cultural, and technological waves and winds that dominate the environment in which our business operates; revealing opportunities, threats, directions of change, and the big picture in general.

Note that the forces should not only be identified but also assessed to give us an idea of their impact on our business activities. Once done right, they could very well be the points we will put inside our SWOT table.

A few Words About the External Environment we are Seeking to Analyze

Our external environment exists on three levels:

Level one is the industry you are a part of, for example – Over-the-counter (OTC) health products.
Level two is your nation of origin, for example – England.
Level three consists of foreign target markets, for example – Africa (if you are originally from Europe or America).

Note: Defining foreign markets has become more complex and difficult today as e-commerce is booming, and the world has become one small island in the vast seas of the universe; however, we will have to simplify our discussion in order to understand the basic concepts.

So, before we begin to widen our view and talk about borders and their significance in marketing; and before we begin to examine the eighth continent, after Africa, Europe, Asia, the two Americas, Australia, and Antarctica, that very same new continent that was bravely created, discovered, uncovered, and developed by the Columbuses of this era. The continent that we are all a part of, no matter where we are stationed – and I mean the Internet – we will, at this stage, focus our discussion on physical markets, as they are our key to understanding.

Note also, that in order to understand foreign target markets we will need to analyze them on two levels: The local industry level, for example – OTC market in Africa, and the national level – for example, cultural regulatory, legal, import-export policies, etc., in Africa.

P is for Political Factors

Or… let's make this easy to remember and understand, and let the **P** stand for a simpler term to remember it by… the **P**ower of the winds in mid sea: Are the winds blowing east? West? Are you heading downwind or windward? Are there storms on the way? Are the winds stable or are they whirling, and how will all of that affect your ship? How can those air currents be used to your benefit?

And in business language: Political Factors may be things like government regulations, legal factors, political stability, war and peace, taxes, governmental policies regarding everything from trade regulations through environmental policies to import and export, international affiliations, and so on – often act like winds in our sails.

We'd be better equipped to handle them and even benefit from them if we have a good idea of where they are coming from, which way they are heading, and predict how they will behave when they do arrive.

E is for Economic Factors

Or… your ship's **E**nergy source: Are you drawing energy from the winds? Currents? Do you have solar energy solutions onboard? Do you have a gasoline engine? Is your Energy source expensive? Sustainable? Are you getting the most out of it? How far does it let you go?

And in business language: Economic factors may be all economic issues that impact your organization, from inflation to interest rates, from economic growth to government policies and leverage opportunities, credit, capital, loans and investments, bank policies, mergers and acquisitions, privatization, etc.

S is for Social and Cultural Factors

Or… the **S**eagull effect – what can you do that would lure the seagull and convince her to honor you with her presence on deck? What type of fish does she like? What type of atmosphere will make her stay longer? Does the direction of your motion affect her willingness to stay? Does the time of day? Does the time of year? Is the seagull the only bird that you are able to attract or are there more species making friends with you?

And in business language: Social and cultural factors refer to the demographic, cultural, and social characteristics of your organization's target market: Customer needs, purchase triggers, decision factors, repeat purchasing patterns, social changes, habits, trends and fashions, lifestyle, religion, etc.

T is for Technological Factors

Or – **T**ides in the open sea and how they affect our boat. High tides and low tides change the way we progress and move. They are accompanied by waves and underwater currents, they are expected and predictable but only to a certain extent, they are perpetual and eternal but every time they seem different. If we are prepared and knowledgeable, we can use them to gain a sustainable competitive advantage. If we are not – they will pose a serious threat.

And in business language: Technological factors can impact our business to a great extent – positively as well as negatively, just like the tide. It can pick us up soaring, racing, and leaving everyone behind to breathe the sprinkles sprayed by our speeding engine, or it can swallow us up or cause serious delays in our schedule.

Technological advancements can be a huge threat or a great opportunity depending on our skills and capabilities, on our awareness and on our readiness. So are technological breakthroughs, fashions, patents, lifecycles, user friendliness, imitations and limitations, etc.

More Letters are Often Added to the Acronym

E is for Environmental Factors

Environmental factors refer to the influence of and on the surrounding environment, and to ecological considerations. They may include waste management, recycling procedures, sustainability, pollution, carbon footprint, climate and seasons, restrictions and limitations of environmental characteristics, earth-friendly choice of raw materials and degradable products, etc. The term corporate sustainability responsibility (CSR) might come to mind as the environmental awareness to global warming and to the devastating effect of human-made pollution has on ocean wildlife in particular, and on the whole planet – eventually also on human beings – becomes common knowledge rather than some extremist activists' apocalyptic prophecy.

L is for Legal Factors

In every territory in which an organization is active, there are legal considerations to understand and to be aware of. How legislation may impact your business activities, consumer laws and protection, safety and health issues, regulations and restrictions, from employment laws to licensing, copyright and patents, compliance with industry standards, import and export, and so on.

One must also keep a tight watch on any changes that occur and may impact the business operations: New laws, amended laws, seasonal changes (for instance hunting – allowed or not), international relationships, etc.

Note that political factors do tend to cross over with legal factors; however, the difference is that political factors are initiated by governments and policies, whereas legal factors must always be complied with.

Common Acronyms Based on the PESTEL Model Include:

PESTLE / PESTEL; PESTLIED; STEEPLE; SLEPT; LONGPESTEL

Now, once we have understood the basics, you are welcome to look them up and see what they stand for. It will be much easier now.

Captain Strategy's PESTEL Breakwater Matrix

This is a whole lot if information to gather and it may seem confusing at first. The best way to organize your data so that it will make sense and be useful is with Captain Strategy's **PESTEL Breakwater Matrix**:

	Factor	Threat	Opportunity
Political			
Economic			
Social			
Technological			
Environmental			
Legal			

And so on.

Note that the opportunity row is widest and farthest to your right. This is intentional. Although threats are indeed important to consider, I always feel that the opportunities are much more important. Oftentimes they cancel out threats, overrule them, and outpower them.

Basically – they constitute your vision, your promise, your future. Therefore, they should be the most dominant part of your matrix. Always give them more space and always place them on the far side of your table, where your eyes can find them automatically, without searching.

Dangerous Murkiness Ahead

PEST or PESTEL analysis is one of the basic tools available today to understand and predict the external factors and forces pushing and pulling, swaying and hurling your organization in the environment in which it operates. Nevertheless, it does have its limitations, as we shall soon find out:

1. Identifying opportunities may be a tricky feat to pull if you fail to consider your organization's internal factors in your analysis. A growing market may be considered an opportunity only if you have the skills to compete and profit there. The best way to overcome this limitation is to use PEST with other basic models present in this book, which will provide the necessary linkage between the crucial factors external to your organization and the crucial factors internal. This link is vital for your insights relevant to your decision-making processes.

2. Too much information may lead you to what we call paralysis by analysis – therefore, make sure you narrow down the information you gather to critical, operational, and doable categories.

3. On the other hand, too much narrowing down may oversimplify your insights and conclusions; thus, you might scrape away value and significance from your analysis and make it a one big fat waste of time and resources.

4. Methods of collecting, updating, and trimming down the necessary information are beyond the scope of this model; however, the accuracy of the data is critical for its effectiveness.

5. This tool analyzes the external environment, and the environment changes constantly. It is so dynamic that sometimes the changes are daily. It is so unpredictable and tricky that sometimes the changes are unnoticeable or misleading at their initial stages. Sometimes a soft wind is just a soft wind, but other times it may be a warning sign of a huge storm. Therefore, PEST analysis must be a regular process in the organization, otherwise, it will not only lose its effectiveness, but it may also lead you to making wrong and devastating planning and strategic choices.

6. In order to be effective, this model has to draw in a good chunk of information from positions in the organization which are most exposed to the environment, and are aligned along the organization's interface with its surroundings on all its faces. This may be a time-consuming and costly process; therefore. it is not always regarded as first choice due to budget and schedule considerations.

7. Because this model is based on an enormous amount of details that need to be gathered, processed, cross-referenced, filtered, and sorted, there is a tendency to base the analysis on unverified assumptions in order to avoid all the trouble. Beware – assumptions may lead to planning disasters.

All Hands Aboard!

Analysis of Amazon, Using the PEST Model

Amazon is an e-commerce company that began as an online bookstore and diversified its focus to an everything-sellable-ever-on-the-face-of-this-earth online store. It offers a simplified e-commerce platform, and a satisfying shopping experience to consumers, which includes at-home shopping, an ask-your-friends even though you do not know them evaluation and rating system, and an endless selection of stuff to choose from.

It works really well also because it offers a convenient and supportive selling platform for sellers, who can reach worldwide audiences without paying rent on geographically limited brick and mortar facilities.

It was founded by Jeff Bezos in 1994. The legend behind its name is that Bezos was taking a road trip when his accountant called him and asked him to name his new company. Bezos said, 'Abracadabra.'

Phone lines were not a big hit back then, and reception was not so good.

The accountant asked him – why on earth did he want to call his new company Cadaver... Bezos tried to shout the real name and when reception got even worse, he said, 'Whatever, call it Amazonas then.'

Accountant heard Amazon. And, the rest is history.

Anyway, being an international supplier, we can use the PEST model to analyze this company as we know it today, at the time of writing this book.

Political Factors

The political stability of the countries they operate in, influences expansion opportunities there. On the one hand, in Australia, the stability enabled the company to expand its business, but on the other hand, in Europe, possible breaches in regulatory compliance may have a negative consequence on its growth.

In India, Amazon was not allowed to sell products of companies in which they have equity stakes because it is non-compliant with governmental laws and regulations.

In China, the government favors and supports Chinese e-commerce companies, at the expense of foreign companies such as Amazon.

Economic Factors

Positive economic conditions foster growth and development. With a company like Amazon, the better the economy, the higher the sales.

When consumers' disposable income is in an increase, opportunities for companies such as Amazon rise, and the company can expand and increase its market share, but also opportunities for competitors rise, so the company needs to focus its growth on its competitive edge.

Usually, overall negative economic conditions of potential customers will have a slowing effect on the company's growth except for factors such as high pricing in non-electronic brick and mortar stores, due to high taxing, skyrocketing rent, or heavily regulated employee costs. When the prices are high, people find ways to consume at lower costs, and one of these ways is by ordering online.

When there is an economic recession, or a huge pandemic like the coronavirus, it might affect the company either way depending on the context. Recession means that people have less to spend. However, they may be more open to cheaper online purchases, which are less immediate and dependent on mail services. A pandemic means that people will be less inclined to leave their house. However, they may also be less trustful of goods' origins.

Social Factors

Social factors that may contribute to Amazon's threat versus opportunity balance are multiple, we will focus on two of them:

Online buying trend – is an opportunity. More and more people join in on the fun, all over the world. Special calendar dates for e-commerce promotion have become celebrations such as Black Friday, Cyber Monday, and holiday-related occasions.

Save the Earth trend – is a threat. People all over the world have come to realize that their overconsumption of products they have no use for, is ruining the planet by creating access pollution, by endorsing unfair employment, and by development of environment-unfriendly materials and disposal challenges. Environmental sensitive people may be buying less products made of materials such as plastic, paper, cheap fabric, etc.

Technological Factors

Technology is so quick to progress that no big business can keep up with the pace. Technological advances have a direct effect on technology-dependent companies such as Amazon. The more central the technology for the company, the higher the threat of technological obsolescence, and cybercrime. A strong emphasis on technological edge is, however, an opportunity to be first, unique, and fun.

CANEZ'S MAKE-OR-BUY IN CAPTAIN'S EYE VIEW

Making the Best of Costs – Through Backwards and Forward Integration

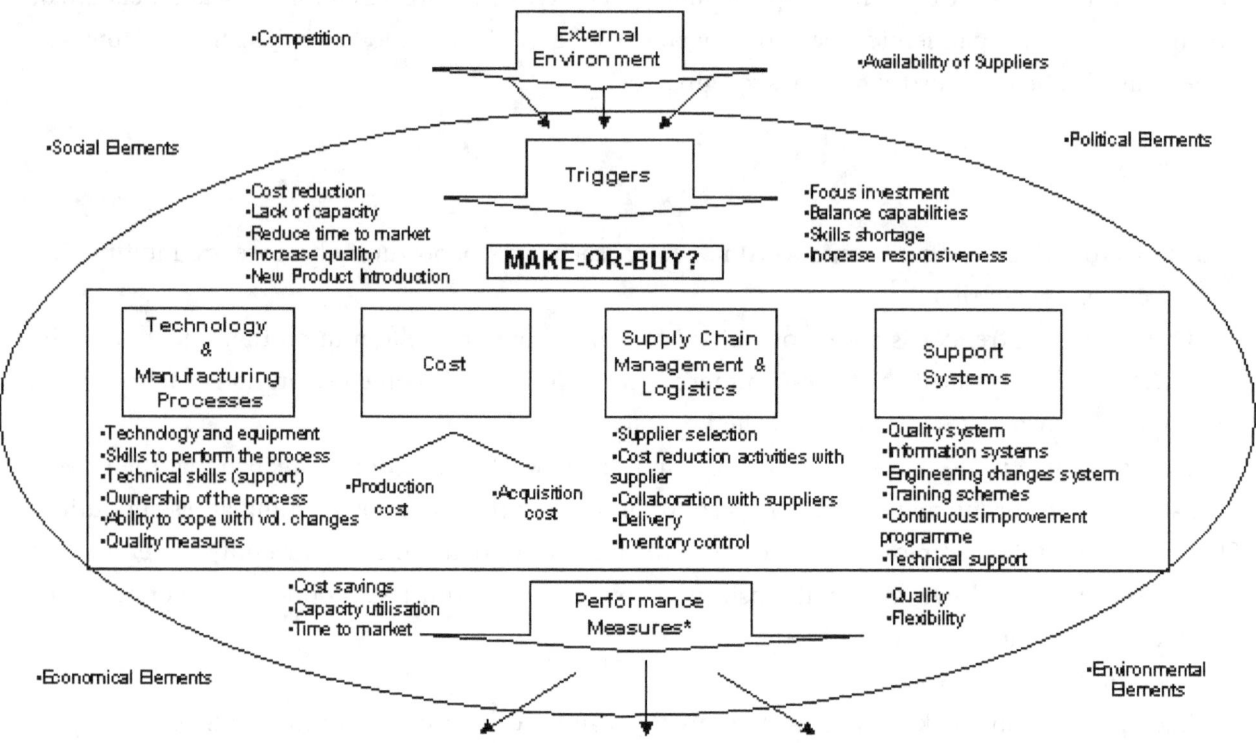

Key Winds in our Sails

I would like to tell you a story, taken from my other book: ***Living My FantaSea, Downwind Encounters and Messages of Wisdom, Inspired by My Worldwide Travels on a Yacht.***

It is a book about people who take journeys, any kind of journeys. I humbly recommend that you read it, as it is as entertaining as it is inspiring, and if you like it or not, as a student, you are now on a journey to your future, so this book was written for you, about you, and with you in mind. Anyway, there is a chapter in the book which is relevant to this model.

In chapter 27, called: *From Living in a Mail-Delivery Van… to Sailing on a Yacht; And about deciding which is better: Catching a huge fish that lasts, or catching a fresh small one every day*, I discuss a dilemma which is parallel to – make-or-buy, and it goes like this (abridged):

One of the more interesting aspects of round the world sailing trips is the aspect of food management. Since the storage volume is very limited, and very small, and the food preparation needs to be managed on a minimal working space, it is of outmost importance to plan your culinary program meticulously. Take only what you cannot do without, and calculate your volumes carefully. For instance, you need to figure out how much food each person may need every day, multiply it by the number of days you plan to be sailing (in our case, approximately three weeks), and multiply this by the number of people you have on board (in our case – four). Then, you translate this information into actual food, breaking down your quantities into vegetables, fruits, meat, fish, flour for baking bread, and grains. You must be prepared for long-term storage that will keep the food fresh and safe to eat. Also, remember that it is a long time, and everyone will appreciate variation. Keep in mind that some people may have specialized needs (like vegan or vegetarian, kosher, possible allergies, etc.), and make sure you add ten percent on all your quantities, just in case. Okay, here's the question that you are wrestling with right now, right? What If you manage to catch some fish on the way? Wouldn't that allow you to be more flexible? Well, sure! that would be great, but you cannot rely on this possibility because there is no guarantee that you will succeed. And by the way, for all you entrepreneurs out there, here's a challenge you might find intriguing: Although by now I am quite the competent dietary planner, I sure could use an application! I challenge you to create one!

So, what's the story with my specialty bread? On one of my previous outings a friend taught me how to make a special kind of bread from sourdough culture that is prepared in advance. The sourdough is kept in the refrigerator, and should be fed a little bit of flour every day, like a pet. Once you get the hang of it, you can do it rather easily. I took his recipe, improved and upgraded it, and made it my art. Therefore, usually, I am the official bread baker on my boat. As we were sailing away from the docks, to justify this reputation, I baked two loaves of this gourmet bread and added in some walnuts. The bread was so delicious that by evening time, it was all gone. Then it happened again on the following day, and on the following. On the third morning, I heard my friend, Rann, making a comment about it to Claud and Goa (our help). He said, "Guys, if you keep on eating all the bread that the captain makes, at this rate, he will never have time to navigate or sleep."

I was relieved and embarrassed at the same time. I felt that it was important to explain the rationale to my co-sailors, so that they will not be offended, and to win their full cooperation. I explained to them that the bread had to be sliced in to very thin slices, as thin as can be, so that every loaf can be cut in to as many slices as possible, otherwise, we might not have enough flour to last the whole trip. The two understood quickly and learned to manage their craving. On the following morning I already saw that the slices were cut thinner, and that fresh salads were prepared by Goa, to go with the bread. Thus, gradually, we all learned the new lifestyle, by which everyone of us must show consideration to each other's needs, eat wisely and plan the next day through a clear vision of the big picture, i.e., with the whole expedition in view. And, of course, I taught them how to make the bread so that they will never have to control their cravings again, after we reached land and moved on.

One day, after a few days of cruising, we managed to catch a huge fish, which was, apparently, eight feet long. It was indeed a great celebration; however, such an occasion certainly requires preparation. We cut the fish into small portions and wrapped each one in a nylon wrap. Each portion was calculated in *such a way as to provide the four of us a day's serving of protein. On the first couple of days we prepared ceviche, which is uncooked fish marinated for a half an hour in virgin olive oil, lemon juice, and onions. It was indeed a true delight. We stored the rest of the fish in the freezer and prepared our daily meals from it, every day a little differently. Sometimes we cooked it, sometimes we baked it, and at other times, we enjoyed it fried. It lasted almost throughout the whole trip, and made us a bit plumper in all the right places… of course, it freed us from our fishing chores, and most importantly, it provided us with class-A proteins, and deliciously so…*

And now, let's deal with the ever-daunting question: which is better, one big fish that can provide you with food for many days, but needs logistic resources, or a fresh, new, small fish every day, which will free you from logistics, but will require investment in fishing? This is not just an arbitrary question to deal with on board a boat, but can be crossed over to many areas in our life. For instance, in business: which is better, one big project, or a series of small ones? One big client, or a bunch of small ones? And on a personal level, which is better, one big loan or a collection of small loans? One long, life-lasting marriage, or several relationships with a beginning and an end? One long trip around the world, or several short ones, with a geographic or a thematic focus?

I'm sure you are aware that there is no one right answer, although this is certainly a question worth stretching your mind about. Every choice has its price. So, can you choose? A lot of the time, you do not have the luxury of choosing. Sometimes, your path chooses you and there is nothing really that you can do about it, but settle for what life and destiny sends up our fishing rod, and acquire the resources to make the most of it.

So, how is it related to our model?

Make or Buy – each has its logistics, and its pros and cons.

Example one: Food

If you are out for a long boat trip, how will you plan your nutrition?

For instance: Let's talk about bread. Will you buy quantities of baked bread and store it on board? What logistical solutions will you need to do that? Or, will you buy an oven, flour, grains, and prepare the bread on board? Are you prepared with electric power to do that?

If you decide to bake, can you or do you want to turn it into a profit channel? Are you prepared to bake and sell, in terms of quantities, storage, logistics? And how about the flour and grains, will you buy those off a supplier, or do you own the production line? Are you equipped to store them? For how long? How much storage space can you handle? How long can your maximal storage volume sustain your needs? In other words, how far will you integrate your business backward? What will be your considerations?

Or, another kind of food – that you can process on the go. For instance – fish: Will you buy a heap of frozen, protein-rich food in advance and store in a heavy-duty freezer (AND buy the equipment) or will you buy a fishing rod or net and fish for food out of the ocean? If you decide to fish, what will be your fishing plan? Meaning, will you fish a large quantity and store the access for future use, or will you limit yourself to fresh daily catch? Do you plan to sell your excess catch? Are you equipped for your choice? Are you skilled for your choice? Are you manned for your choice? Have you done the math and calculated your options money-wise?

Example two: Water

Will you buy bottled water and store them for the whole trip, or will you buy a freshwater generator or a water-desalinating solution and make your own water? Which is wiser? Which is safer? Which is more economic? Under which conditions? And if you generate the water, will you turn it into a sellable product and if so, do you have the means to market it?

Example three: Electric power

Gasoline empowered generator or engine (buy)? Or, sun/wind powered generator (make)? And, when you "make," do not forget that you must be equipped, that means also – buying technology, being able to work it, and maintain its working power as well as its working condition, and keeping someone on board that is knowledgeable enough to push the right buttons. So, that makes it a different kind of 'buy,' right? Much more expensive, much more knowledgeable, yet much less frequent, AND it may require more hands on board, as well as frequent technological upgrading. Is it worth the trouble? Is the investment a smart one?

Now, let's look closely at our three simple examples, through the make-or-buy, and work out the break down. Afterwards you can do the same with the more complex systems you are analyzing.

External Environment and Triggers

First, the model directs us to examine the external environment. The particular environment of our example has two unique characteristics: a – scarcity of suppliers when off-land, and b – abundance of natural resources if you know how to take advantage of them.

Triggers rely on the balance between worthiness of equipping and manning your ship to harvest natural resources, and the worthiness of equipping and manning your ship to rely on off-shore services and supplies.

This balance should be calculated using short-term as well as long-term considerations (long trip or short trip? Single trip or multiple trips?), storage options, space solutions, route characteristics (distance between stops, distance from land in case of emergency, route traffic, climate and weather conditions, season, fish distribution, etc.), and also parameters such as regulations, and so on.

To demonstrate why this is so important, let's discuss one of the above – fish distribution mid-ocean. Fishing mid-ocean is like trying to hunt in mid-desert. You need to be lucky to catch something. Water conditions mid-ocean include poor nutrients, vast currents, and other conditions that only very big fish can survive in. So, if you were planning to cast out a medium-sized fishing rod every day and pluck your daily meal out of the ocean, you'd better think again. The other side of it is that if you do manage to catch a very big fish, what do you do with it, so that you would be able to use it and not have to throw it back overboard?

Let's examine the four key winds in our sails:

1. Technology and Manufacturing Processes

Do you have the necessary equipment? Do you know how to work it and produce whatever it is you need to produce? Do you have the technological knowhow? Is the equipment owned by you? Leased? Who is responsible for maintenance? How do you maintain high quality at all times? Is the equipment flexible in terms of volumes and quantities? Does it fit your needs?

2. Costs

All of the options discussed above should be calculated for costs and not only necessity. Also, potential profit channels should be considered and the costs needed to generate these profits. So, we have production costs versus acquisition costs, all should be calculated.

3. Supply-chain Management

All options require consideration of the supply chain – will you own the supply chain? What is considered supply chain: If you decide to produce water for instance, does that make you a supply chain? Is the company which sells you the equipment? Will it be more reasonable and profitable to buy bottled water or to produce bottled water? Equipment is costly, so, what are your prospects of covering purchase, maintenance, and current upgrading costs? What will be your turning point? Maybe you will have to integrate both options just to be safe?

4. Support Systems

In keeping your functionality intact, you need to cultivate and maintain support systems that will provide you with constant information, quality measures, engineering solutions, training programs, technological support and upgrade, and so on.

So many questions to answer! Yes, it is time-consuming. You will need to invest a lot of time, which is your most precious and limited resource. Keep in mind that this investment now, will serve you very well in the future. Yes, these questions are hard to manage, but they are crucial to your business conduct. You will now be given some tools with which to analyze and make a right choice.

The question, "make-or-buy" represents the basic dilemma that many companies face: Should the company keep the technologies and processes in-house or purchase from an outside provider? Today's global competition and cost-reduction efforts force companies to re-evaluate existing processes in the company, the technology the company uses, manufacturing and services, all in order to focus on the strategic and core activities.

Many companies have limited resources, which do not allow performing all tasks in-house. The decision of "make-or-buy" is a matter of comparative advantage to the company. Ability to make such decisions in a structured and rational way may improve the overall performance of the company.

According to the make-or-Buy model by Canez et al., 2000, the original decision-making method to make-or buy were mainly based on cost-reduction in manufacturing.

Since the beginning of the millennium, more research was done on the subject that introduced different approaches. The approaches represented structured ways for making the decision to "make-or-buy," and included many parameters that were not considered before.

The main findings from the interviews made with the academic staff who conducted the research were as follows: The suggested approaches were easy to understand and simple to implement within models in non-complex organizational situations. These included step-by-step processes for making the best decision. In 2000, Canez developed a model illustrating a flow-chart that combined some of the different research outcomes and added parameters of cost, control level, and prior knowledge of market demands.

The analysis of the interviews with the industry staff exhibited different issues. They added parameters of competition cost, lack of space, lack of knowledge, need to increase the company's response capability, need to increase quality, and the need to reduce time-to-market. In addition, parameters such as purchase price, complexity, competencies, and technology were also taken into account. Canez (2000) combined the academic and industry people's suggestions in his flow chart that offers a graphical representation framework for making the decision to "make-or-buy." See below framework illustration:

Unlike previous approaches, the goal of Canez's framework was to provide the flow for decision-making in a holistic way and to integrate the main and most important points into the process in order to make the best decision possible in the given time and circumstances.

Furthermore, this framework represents a first step toward providing performance measures to assess business benefits for each decision of "make-or-buy." The external environment, on which the company usually has a very minor effect (except for cases of big and leading market changers), usually triggers the process of analyzing the decision to "make-or-buy." For example: Increased cost-competition in the market – requires the company to reduce costs. In this case, the aspect of cost reduction is the focus which triggers the start of the analysis process.

The relevant factors under examination are divided in to four areas:

- Technology and manufacturing processes.
- Cost.
- Supply chain management and logistics.
- Support systems.

Performance measures are closely tied to the factors above and kick-start the process, providing criteria to evaluate how the goals are achieved. For example: If the trigger is cost reduction, cost savings would be the main performance measure, but must take into account other criteria, such as flexibility and quality. This process is not static. Performance indicators in the decision are fed back to the external environment and may trigger other factors that raise the question again to "make-or-buy."

The model has several distinct advantages. As indicated, the model manages to successfully integrate the different approaches academically and per the industry, which enables it to be more realistic, relevant, and applicable, and not only theoretical.

The four parameters included in the framework are the correct main parameters that should be considered in order to make the right decision. They cover the main aspects in the key significant processes in a company in a holistic and simple way.

The model also details the sub-factors in each of the parameters, which assist in defining the key performance measures. It is extremely important to put together the right measures that will enable the company to monitor and examine the decisions made, and if needed, adjust the factors/processes accordingly.

Dangerous Murkiness Ahead

Costly adjustment may be needed

Even though the framework comprises the main processes and enables measurement and monitoring of the decisions made, at this point, the adjustments may be costly. Companies may feel that they have already made an investment toward the change and, therefore, changing or going back to the way it was before may be too costly at this time, or make no sense because it will put the framework into a loop of recurring change and adjustment. The company may get more experience and insight for the next decision to be made, but it may be too late for the ones already made.

In most cases, the cost factor becomes the most significant one; therefore, the other parameters are neglected or considered in a subjective way. The full analysis is reviewed but is not completely objective.

All Hands Aboard!

Analysis of Carnival UK Using the Make-or-buy Model

The cruise industry has moved to outsourcing in many of their non-core activities. For example, the UK's largest and most popular cruise provider, Carnival UK, was keen to respond to a growing demand for cruise holidays in conjunction with air travel. However, expanding their offer was not possible without improving their overall business efficiency.

Carnival UK uses two different in-house booking systems, one for their customers' cruises and the other for their crew deployments. This meant that many activities were handled manually, which was time-consuming and prone to errors. In addition, Carnival UK was planning to make changes in Amadeus, its Global Distribution System (GDS) used to book their customers' and crew's flights to join their ships.

As such, Carnival UK looked to Amadeus for a way to have more control over, and to automate the entire process, as well as to bring Bank Settlement Plan (BSP) reconciliation in-house. To add to the challenge, Carnival UK was working to a very short timescale for the GDS implementation: 8 weeks from start of supplier selection to going live. Another key issue was the interdependency of the various project teams: In parallel to the GDS switch, Amadeus had to specify mid-office business needs as well as build and deliver a front-to-back solution integrating their primary accounting system.

The Solution:
Amadeus consultants developed the scripts and Carnival UK developed the direct interfaces between

the Amadeus GDS and its four key internal systems – reservations, crew management, finance general ledger, and mid-office. Amadeus built a customized point of sale solution with a clearly defined service package based around Amadeus Selling Platform. Amadeus optimizes Carnival UK's booking process.

Analysis of BMC Software Using the Make-or-buy Model

Outsourcing at BMC Software

BMC software was founded in 1980, and has offices worldwide. The International headquarters located in Amsterdam, The Netherlands, and Singapore. Geographic sales centers divided into Europe/Middle East/Africa (EMEA), Asia-Pacific (AP), and Americas regions.

They operate international offices in Australia, Austria, Belgium, Brazil, Canada, China, Denmark, England, Finland, France, Germany, Hong Kong, Hungary, India, Indonesia, Ireland, Israel, Italy, Japan, Korea, Malaysia, Mexico, The Netherlands, New Zealand, Norway, The Philippines, Portugal, Scotland, Singapore, South Africa, Spain, Sweden, Switzerland, Taiwan, Thailand, Turkey, and United Arab Emirates (true to the time of writing this chapter). All in all, they have market coverage in more than 115 countries.

The Research and Development offices located in Houston and Austin, TX; San Jose, CA; Atlanta, GA; Waltham, MA; Herndon, VA; Aix-en-Provence, France; Singapore, Singapore; Tel Aviv, Israel; and Pune, India.

BMC's main expertise is to help business organizations optimize their IT infrastructure by reducing costs and increasing productivity.

The company mission was formulated as to be the leading provider of enterprise management software solutions by helping customers align their IT infrastructure with their business.

BMC pioneered the concept Business Service Management (BSM) and has approximately 6,000 employees.

Ninety-nine percent of the Fortune 500 and over 15,000 companies worldwide rely on BMC to control increasing IT complexity, improve service quality, and more quickly meet the needs of their businesses.

In BMC's efforts to be the leading provider of enterprise management and keep the profitability high, especially during the past several years, the company has decided to focus on cost-effectiveness. The senior management has brought in Mackenzie Consulting to conduct a comprehensive analysis reviewing their main processes. The analysis included the 4 main parameters as per Canez framework, taking in to account the cost-effectiveness as the main trigger for the process.

Mackenzie's analysis contained many recommendations, which most of them BMC's senior management decided to implement. For the purposes of this work, I would like to point out 2 of the recommendations that specify outsourcing decisions:

1. BMC's Headquarters campus in Houston, Texas. was owned by the company. The campus included several buildings, restaurants, fitness center, and a large audio room. Some of the floors in the building were rented out by BMC to other companies and the restaurants and fitness centers employees

were BMC employees. As per Mackenzie's analysis and the company's review, it was clear that BMC's activities as real estate and restaurant owners were not close to BMC's core activities of developing and selling IT software. In order to focus on the strategic core activities, it was obvious that BMC needed to change the way this was handled. Therefore, BMC has decided to sell out the campus and only lease the necessary space for its offices. The fitness center and restaurants were owned by the new owner, and BMC employees used the facilities as part of an agreement made with the new owners. This settlement enabled BMC employees to continue using the facilities as before, but also reduced a lot of activities BMC employees handled internally. These employees could focus now on the strategic activities that can help BMC achieve their business goals. If we look at the model, here they decided to "buy" rather than "make" and changed their holdings accordingly.

2. The R&D customer support organization included employees worldwide in order to be able to support the many customers in the different countries. To provide customized and high-quality support, it was necessary to hire local employees who know the local language and culture. The analysis showed that hiring the employees in each major location/country would be expensive, and the management efforts for each group would be complex. Therefore, BMC management reviewed several alternatives and found that for APAC, the best solution would be to outsource the support activities to a local company located in Dali, China. The outsourcing company employees have the right technical and language skills needed for the different countries in APAC, not only Chinese. But, as being Chinese employees, the salary rates were much lower than hiring employees in Australia, Singapore, and the other countries. In addition, the management efforts were mainly handled locally with specific guidance of BMC personnel.

This solution enabled BMC to keep the main core activities of the R&D (development & QA) as well as the sales in-house, and "buy" the other non-core activities outside the organization.

BMC also put measurement criteria's in place for both solutions/changes. The cost-effectiveness was significant in both cases, but the full implementation of the China team until full independency took much longer than planned. This incurred extra expenses for BMC, such as travel expenses of BMC employees/managers to train the China team, which were not considered originally. In addition, the statistics of the customer support satisfaction level in APAC was reduced, which jeopardized the relationship with the APAC customers and future revenues. In order to minimize this effect, BMC's decision was to continue in the same model and put in the extra cost and effort to full integration.

Conclusion and Insight:

The Canez model integrated the relevant parameters in order to make the right decision of "make-or-buy." In addition, the constant performance monitoring is crucial in such processes. From the examples I have indicated above, we can see that following the steps according to the model enabled to review the organization internal processes, taking in to account the main strategic goals. The core strategic activities always remained within the company, but the non-core activities are reviewed across the 4 parameters to determine if they should continue in-house or "buy" externally. The examination is done to ensure quality control, security, effective flow of the processes within the company, as well as to put together the correct performance measures and act upon them.

Make-or-buy is a matter of reviewing the bottom line but not only. Although the examples brought to you above discuss "buy" through outsourcing, the same type of analysis could be done with "make" and integration.

In business administration, like in every other realm, there are fashions, and also market trends, technological developments, price and cost fluctuations of every aspect that may have an effect (like property – as described in the example above), and also the very debatable subject of control, and keeping all your cards close and hidden. All of these and more, pose legitimate considerations when deciding to make-or-buy.

For instance, if "make" is more expensive than "buy," but it is imperative to keep technologies, or marketing channels, or, in fact, any other part of the production, service or marketing chains, in-house for whatever reason, than the least cost-effective choice may very well be the right choice.

What I am saying really is, do not look only at the trivial stuff. In order to make the right decision creatively, one must look at the bigger picture, consider short-term as well as long-term, and integrate that in to the decision formula of Make-or-Buy parameters, which are indirectly correlated, but may be crucial to the outcome.

SERVQUAL MODEL IN CAPTAIN'S EYE VIEW

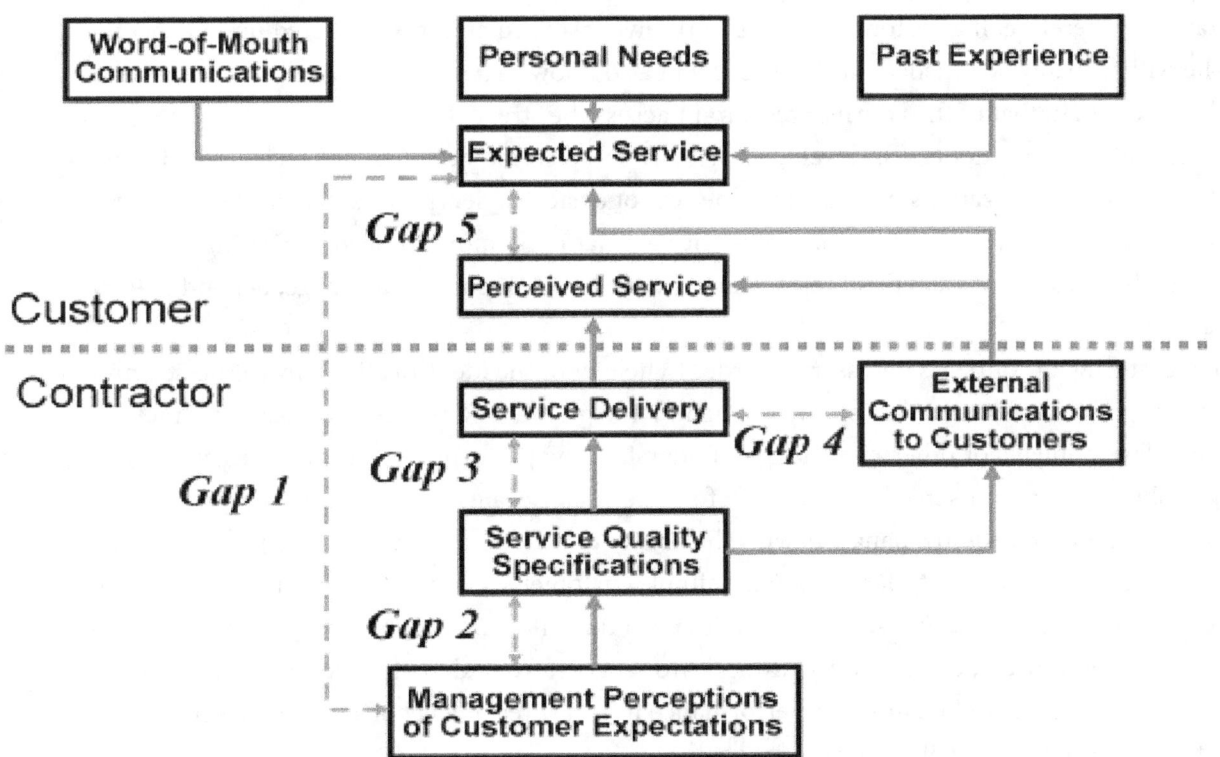

Key Winds in our Sails

ServQual model is a model developed in 1988, by Zeithaml et al to measure the quality of service in organizations. The name of the model consists of the two words: Service and Quality, combined.

The model serves as a technique used to analyze the gap between two seemingly parallel parameters: **Enterprise performance** and **customer satisfaction**, meaning the degree to which the company meets its consumers' requirements for quality of service, as it is perceived by them.

Although they might be wrongly perceived as parallel, these two parameters: Enterprise performance and customer satisfaction, are actually very different and usually not even correlated. Let me explain:

Customer satisfaction is determined by the correlation between customer expectation of the service, and the service delivery in reality. The larger the gap between customer expectations and the service provided (i.e., customers get less than what they expected – we like to call it with a bit of humor – the "Oy-Vey factor") – the lower their satisfaction would be.

An opposite gap will, of course, leverage customer satisfaction (we often like to name it – the "WOW factor," when organizations decide to provide customers with more than what they bargained for).

Enterprise performance, however, is determined by the quality of service relative to the competition, or relative to the company's promises, whichever is the main factor influencing customer expectations. Therefore, if a customer expects to receive fast food and it is delivered upon expectation, she will probably be satisfied; however, she will also know that this enterprise's performance is probably lesser than that of the gourmet restaurant across the street.

Understandably, this model was developed primarily for service-oriented, or service-core industries. While most organizations do provide some sort of customer service as a part of their delivery package to their clients, the service-core industries are naturally more in need of finding a way to measure their service quality, as their performance, as well as their competitive edge, depend mainly on this factor.

The measuring, of course, is necessary in order to help with the identification of weaknesses, and the designing and implementation of improvement strategies. It also serves as a means of tracking over-time developments or otherwise changes, understanding performance benchmarks, and identifying problems or fall-outs in service areas, before they deteriorate and leave their mark.

ServQual, therefore, equips managers with the ability to achieve a broad perspective and a deep understanding of service quality, far beyond the simple customer service that we are all familiar with.

One of the reasons why service-core companies need this information so badly, is that the unique characteristics of services, compared to physical products, make it almost impossible for a firm to follow, assess, compare, and quantify its performance in measures of level of service, as well as connect it to overall success or failure to achieve goals.

Characteristics such as intangibility, personalization, heterogeneity, flexibility, and the lack of any physical traits, make this task very difficult. The model solves this difficulty by providing a structured approach that uses a set of factors, which have been determined as crucial in influencing customers' perception of service quality.

Before we go on, we must know what we are measuring. So, let's provide a definition of service quality, so that you, our customer, should be fully satisfied with our delivery:

Service quality is defined in this book as the degree to which the company (or brand) stands up to its own standards of delivery of its service (as is determined internally by policy makers) as well as the degree to which it stands up to its customers' expectations (as is influenced externally by market norms, trends, and shifts, and by the significant competition).

In order to help companies to measure their service quality, researchers divided the broad term into five dimensions.

ServQual's Five Dimensions of Service Quality

We like to think of our firm as a large ship sailing the oceans. This is why we are all "Captain Strategy." So, let's go through ServQual's five dimensions of service quality and explain what they are. The five dimensions of the ServQual's model are – Reliability, Assurance, Tangibles, Empathy, and Responsiveness. They are often summed up as RATER, which is why this model is also sometimes referred to as the RATER model.

Reliability – is the ability to provide the promised service with credibility and accuracy. It is a measure of dependability and trustworthiness.

When our ship offers Reliability, there are multiple parameters combined that are all a part of that reliability. For example: Reaching the exact destination we stated in our sailing (selling?) pitch. This means that if you, as captain of this ship, advertised your intent to reach the Richmond Port in California, U.S.A., you will not end up at the Alameda Port, even though both ports are equally close to the San Francisco or Oakland container terminals.

It also means that you stand up to the timeframe you originally stated, and that you provide the storage space as well as settings you promised. It means that your onboard staff will receive living conditions as promised, and so on. Any failure to provide those parameters will create a breach in your reliability.

Note, that it does NOT mean that you can and should promise that there will be no weather outbreaks during the trip. Conditions that are not under your control, cannot serve as reliability breakers, **unless** you are not prepared to deal with them professionally; in which case, they are inclined to become reliability breakers very rapidly and turn in to huge deals.

Assurance – stands for the organizational culture of interacting with the customers. How knowledgeable are employees? How courteous are they? Do they inspire trust and confidence? Do the customers feel that they are "in good hands?"

Assurance also refers to the measure of protectiveness that customers feel when they are being provided with the service.

Imagine being on a ship, really worried about something, asking a staff member for information regarding the subject that is bothering you, for which the answer is an impatient shrug, or an in your face, "I dunno."

Imagine on the other hand, a patient answer, specific details, and a fully satisfying interaction; and all from a junior employee. How would that make you feel? Safe? Secure? When your customers are getting answers, when they do not feel that you are trying to hide something from them, when you are able to provide them with details and a smile, and especially, when they can see the confidence in your eyes, that is assurance.

Note, that **telling lies with confidence does NOT fall under assurance**. No matter how good an actor you are, lies are detectable by most. It is usually more assuring for customers, to receive unpleasant truths, as well as a list of professional measures you intend to take in order to deal with them, rather than to receive well-acted lies and fables.

Tangibles – refer to all the visible and useable stuff. All elements that make up the physical environment are included: Equipment and relevant accessories, level of maintenance, interior design (structure, furniture, lighting, room temperature and airing, music, etc.) as well as the employees appearance code.

It matters not which level of positioning you seek to achieve, your tangibles ought to be at their best appearance as well as at their finest functionality. Whether the company is pushing to base its competitive advantage on price or on quality, whether the service has been designed to appeal to low – or to high-end customers, whether it is personalized, or mass marketed, etc., investing in tangibles is always a good business decision.

There is no greater turn-off for customers than poor, outdated, out of style, out of order, out of context – service spaces and equipment. It is like putting them on a ship, ready to sail away from the shore, and that ship is not equipped or maintained for the ride and not ready to meet passengers' needs of accommodation.

Note, that if there is a need to prioritize with tangibles, it will always be more effective to put hospitality, functionality, and serviceability before luxuriousness. Simple but well-kept, will always do a better job than luxury that hides dysfunctionality of any sort. So, when attempting to reach a true ServQual analysis, remember what can and cannot cover up for what, in your customers' eyes.

Empathy – relates to the service provider's ability to provide personal attention to its customers, when needed, to think from inside their customers' shoes, to find their customers' position inside themselves and to relate to it.

Lack of empathy is like inviting seasick passengers on a cruise ship, to join a buffet dinner, served on a table a mile long, when their guts are almost exploding through their eyes. It matters not how much gourmet yummies you will organize colorfully on that buffet table, and to what measures you went to in order to put them there. Your seasick passengers will not acknowledge the gesture, they will not be able to appreciate it, nor will they want to have any of it. Being that their faces would probably be going green as they become sick to their stomachs, some might even consider the invitation a rude laugh at their expense.

So, in order to maintain good service to customers, a company needs to consider scenarios, through an empathic outlook toward its customers, and then to be prepared to provide personal attention to those customers, in accordance with their situation and the circumstances. That takes sensitivity, compassion, and care. Or in one word – empathy.

Note, empathy does NOT mean turning against your own company out of sheer identification with an unsatisfied customer, it just means meeting your customers' feelings, and providing solutions in the frame of the company's abilities.

Responsiveness – is the willingness and readiness of employees to provide customer service, when asked to do so. But before that, it is the willingness and readiness of a business to realize the importance of responsiveness, and in accordance, to hire staff, to provide resources, and to set rules and regulations that put responsiveness in the front.

Have you ever searched for a service attendant and did not find one? Have you ever asked for any type of customer service and found yourself waiting hopelessly, or having to fight your way to receiving it? Well, we know that responsiveness is actually a part of a business' organizational culture. Rules and regulations should be set from above and not left to the representative to decide. The responsiveness of a single representative cannot constitute apt measurement of, but rather a clear policy that is being religiously implemented.

We can look at this model in a reverse way too. We can say that there are five gaps that organizations need to measure, manage, and minimize:

Reliability, Assurance, Tangibles, Empathy, and Responsiveness:

1. **Reliability gap** is a gap of expectation: Between the promises made before closing the deal, and the actual service provided after (influenced by how fully the management chooses to answer to customer expectations).
2. **Assurance gap** is a gap of understanding: Understanding customer psychological needs as the receiving side, versus providing them in reality (influenced by how deeply the management chooses to answer to customer needs).
3. **Tangibles gap** is a gap of comfort: Customers' comfort needs include things like cleanliness, functionality, and appearance. These needs are often met only partially in reality (depending on how the management prioritizes the upkeep, maintenance and care of the premises, personnel, and technical equipment).
4. **Empathy gap** is the gap of feeling: Between how the customer wants to feel, as the receiving side of the service, and reality (influenced by how the company chooses to "shape" the humane side of the service through staff training).
5. **Responsiveness gap** is a gap of patience: Customers tend to be impatient, whereas companies tend to be swamped, or over-regulated, or efficiency prioritized, which may cause a conflict of interest between the two sides.

Dangerous Murkiness Ahead

Criticism of the ServQual model is mainly due to the fact that it relies mostly on objective opinions and perceptions and less on subjective facts and figures:

- There are several researches that have cast serious doubt about the credibility of the five indices measured in this model.
- Careful consideration must be enabled when using the results for fear of inaccuracy of the ServQual reliability research.
- Customer specimens do not necessarily represent all customers.
- Expectations and perceptions of clients are subject to frequent changes, fashion, trends, developments, and even seasons; therefore, they may not stand up to time.
- This tool only checks the quality of the service, and does not take into account other important indices that may influence perception of service quality but do not belong in the category.

All Hands Aboard!

Analysis of Holms Place, Sports Club Chain, Using the ServQual model

Background:
The Holmes Place Sports Club chain was established in 1980, by seven British investors. They were fed up with fitness clubs that offered poor quality service. They came up with the concept of an elite sports club, designed to offer high quality service to a wide range of customers. The idea was – meeting the needs of high-end customers, and providing that standard to everyone.

The first club opened on Homes Street in London, just as Jane Fonda initiated the fitness-as-lifestyle trend. Leaning on this new development, the club was soon singled out at the right place for the right people to be in, and managed to win the hearts (and sweat drops) of members from all walks of society, including celebrities such as Princess Diana and Hugh Grant.

Today, Holmes Place is an international sports club chain, which maintains its value of high-end service globally, in many countries.

Using the ServQual model, we will analyze the five indices of quality of service, based on a questionnaire that was used by the company for that end.

Five dimensions of service quality as expressed in testing the quality of service to customers Holmes Place chain:

1. Reliability – (or credibility): The chain will examine whether branches provide the promised services, and whether the physical trainers display a sincere interest in providing the training and customer service needs as they are expected to, without delay and as promised.
2. Assurance – (or security): The chain will examine the degree of trust that the physical trainers and

other staff manage to achieve with the trainees, the sense of security of the communication between them, as well as the level of knowledge instructors and staff possess and share whilst meeting the needs of their customers and providing answers to their questions and/or requests.

3. Tangibles – The chain will review the facilities and the existing equipment, will explore technological innovation within branch facilities, and will test the appearance of the equipment, of the premises, and of the staff.

4. Empathy – The chain will examine the degree of readiness by physical trainers and other staff to provide personal attention to the trainees: How important are the trainees' interests in their eyes, and how well they understand special and personalized needs as well.

5. Responsiveness – The chain will observe the staff's attitude toward the trainees during training periods, even when not asked for help, as well as the immediacy of the availability of their service when approached.

ServQual Satisfaction Questionnaire, Adapted to Holmes Place Sports Clubs

Rate your expectations from the service and satisfaction by rating:

5 = Excellent
4 = Good,
3 = Good
2 = Moderate
1 = Bad

#	Parameter analyzed	Question reviewed	Customer expectation	Customer testimony about real situations
1	Reliability	Does the club actually provide all the promised services?		
2		Do staff members and physical trainers show a sincere interest in the needs of all the trainees and customers?		
3		Is service provided promptly and without delay?		
4		Is service provided as promised by the club?		
5		Does the club provide proper tracking of trainees' achievements and progress?		

6	Assurance	Do the physical trainers and other staff members induce confidence?		
7		Do I feel confident whilst communicating with staff members?		
8		Are physical trainers and other staff members always courteous and pleasant?		
9		Are physical trainers and other staff members knowledgeable when answering my questions?		
10	Tangibles	Is the equipment modern?		
11		Are the facilities pleasing?		
12		Does the appearance of physical trainers and other staff members create a pleasant atmosphere?		
13		Are the activities offered beneficial and do they meet the trainees' needs?		

14	Empathy	Do physical trainers provide trainees with detailed directions and training plans?		
15		Are the opening hours convenient for my schedule?		
16		Do staff members provide me with sufficient personal attention?		
17		Do staff members give me the feeling that they care about my most important interests?		
18		Do staff members understand my special needs?		
19	Responsiveness	Is detailed information provided regarding times and schedules of service?		
20		Can service be obtained immediately?		
21		Are staff members always ready to help and provide service?		
22		Are staff members always free to provide service, and not too busy or occupied?		

Please provide details regarding any aspect of service which contributed particularly to your satisfaction.

_____

_____

Please provide details regarding any aspect of service which you found particularly disturbing and possibly lowered your level of satisfaction.

_____

_____

After completing the questionnaire, and analyzing it according to the ServQual model, the chain found several possible gaps corresponding with the five parameters, as follows:

1. A gap between how administrators perceive expectations of trainees from them, and how trainees perceive their actual expectations.
2. A gap between what physical trainers think trainees need in terms of training instruction, and how trainees see their own needs.
3. A gap between how physical trainers perceive themselves, and how trainees perceive them.
4. A gap between advertising and marketing material distributed by the Holmes Place chain and the delivery of promises made in the material.
5. A gap between how the chain perceives overall training services they provide, and how the trainees experience them.

Example to gaps model of ServQual in Holmes Place chain:

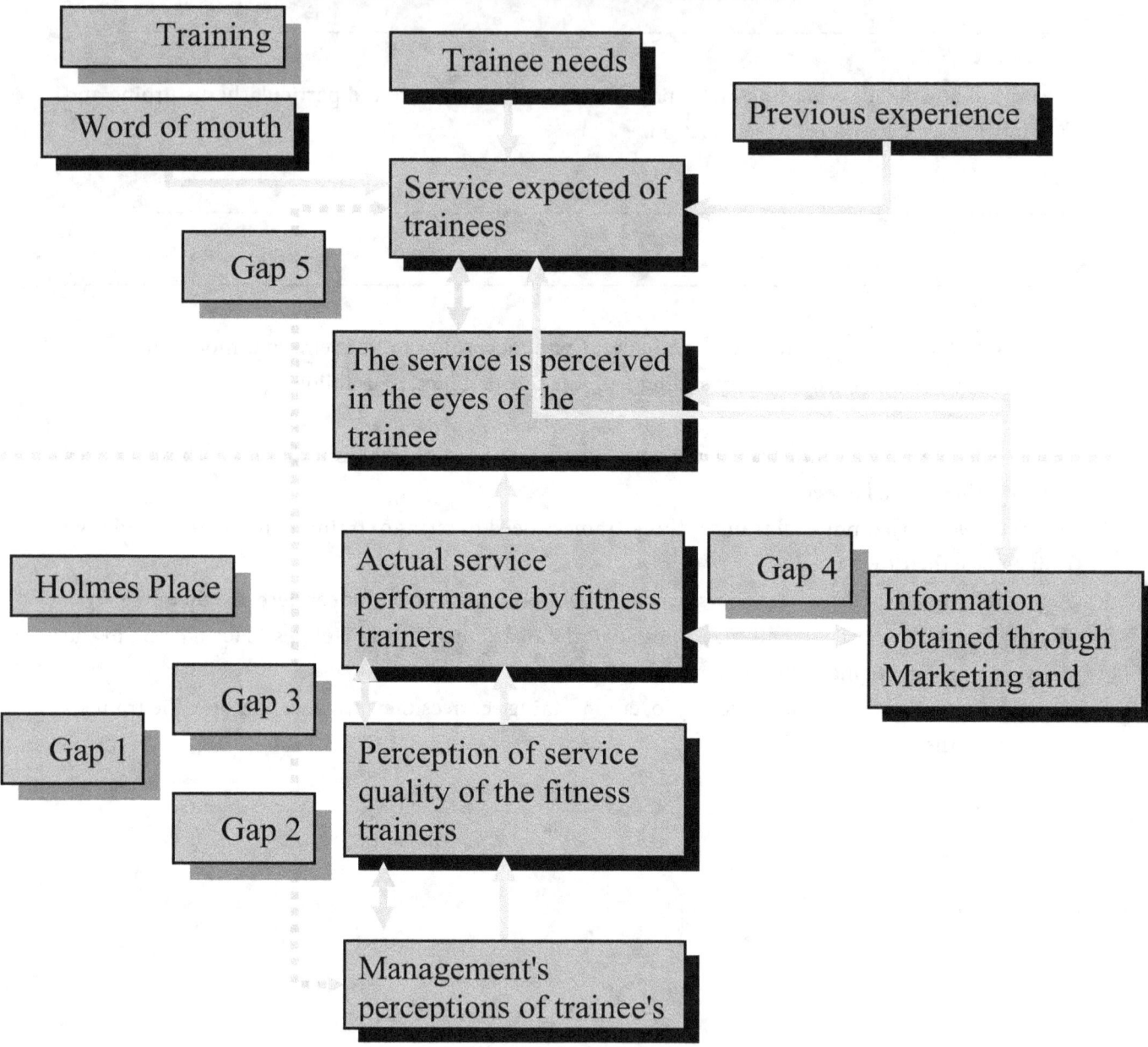

With those important insights, Holmes Place could analyze the quality of their service in such a way that would allow them to perform specific improvements in a cost-effective way, that would influence the overall service performance of the chain.

THE MSD – MONEY-SPENDING-DETERMINATION MODEL IN CAPTAIN'S EYE VIEW, BASED ON SASSER'S CUSTOMER VALUE MODEL

MSD = Money Spending Determination
Q = Quality
I = Image
TCO = Total Cost of Ownership
MSD = (Q+I) / TCO

Key Winds in our Sails

What is MSD (Money Spending Determination)?

The short answer is – how strongly does your customer crave your value offering, which comes down to how powerful is her determination to accept your offer, i.e., to spend money in order to own the value of whatever it is that you are offering.

The 'owning' drive to aim for most, is not on the basis of 'need,' but on the basis of 'want.' Although the line between the two is not distinct, we can say that the craving for emotional value (that can indeed be based on, or generated by other forms of value) is the strongest MSD there is. However, most of the time, purchase choices made on the basis of 'need' also means that brands must overshadow the competition – direct and indirect, in order to be chosen.

First, let me explain to you why I prefer to use the term Customer MSD instead of the term Customer Value (CV) as is usually accepted. When we talk about Customer MSD it is clear that we are measuring the customer's attitude toward your company and not the other way around. The term Customer Value is elusive and may be confusing, especially since it is very similar to the term Customer Lifetime Value, which means, a prediction of the net profit attributed to the entire future relationship with a customer.

Obviously, this is not the same term and we want to use terminology that is clear and not confusing. MSD is a value that we need in order to understand what we, as a company, need to do, in order to have customers wanting to purchase our product or service, and willing to take the measures needed in order to turn their want into a need.

Customer MSD can be calculated by ascribing value to these three parameters: Q (quality), I (Image/Impress), & TCO (Total Cost of Ownership).

Q – stands for Quality: The customer's perception of the quality of the company's service, product, or brand, and of the value of ownership, in terms of direct advantages (technological, functional, experiential, economical, etc.), and indirect advantages (psychological, image oriented, social affiliation. etc.).

I – stands for Image (and also, for Impress – whether you choose to impress yourself or others, image perception is one of the major basics): When we talk about image, we have two aspects to consider. The first one is the image that the brand earned for itself. For instance, Stanford University is considered as one of the top five universities of the world. That is a high brand image. The second one is the image that a customer can gain by owning the brand. For instance, if I am a student at Stanford University, this ownership of service will add to my image, and earn me, as a customer, respect and appreciation among my friends, acquaintances, and most importantly, future employers. So, in this case, the overall image score will be high. On the other hand, if we were talking about prisons instead of universities, we can have a high-end prison, but if I were a "customer," it would not be contributing much to my image, would it? In other words, if I put my 'I' value into the equation, my resulting MSD in this case, could not be high, regardless of the service provider's image.

TCO, or Total Cost of Ownership, is made up of the sum that a company charges for a product or a service, PLUS things like cost of switching from another brand (cable TV), or product (mobile phone), investment of other resources such as time, personal energy, learning efforts, complementary products (toner to a printer), etc.

So, if you take Quality multiplied by Image, and divide it all by TCO, you will get a figure that represents your customer's MSD. Playing with the numbers, and your strengths as a company, using methods of comparison to your direct and indirect competition in the market, you could raise the MSD in a way that is feasible, effective, and competitive.

One needs to remember, however, that there are further factors to be considered. Usually, high image pairs with high TCOs (more than Quality, by the way), and this equation lacks any reference to financial ability, which could be usually (but not always) very relevant. What that means really is that you have to identify your target customers first, maybe group them on the basis of financial ability, and then for every group figure out how to reach a desired MSD figure.

When one buys music lessons, for instance, one embarks on some type of a musical journey. When one purchases a loan, there is also a journey in mind, which the loan would somehow influence. People become attached to products and services they purchase, so much so that sometimes, additional purchases are made just for the purpose of justifying the first choice.

I believe that every purchase is a journey. The higher the cost – the more significant the journey. Now, you must have understood by now that the journeys I crave most are at sea, so let's make this insight more perceptible.

Let's say that your potential target customer is standing on the platform. Every boat she sees, stands for a product or service offered. The marina stands for your marketplace. Now, assume that your potential customer needs to reach some other coast. How will you make your value offering more attractive than the others'? How would you raise the overall figure of your MSD?

Offer Quality – for instance, level of maintenance, hour or intervals of departure, speed of boat, extras on board, etc.

Offer Image – for instance, better docking spot, PR and famous guests, etc.

Plan your TCO – the higher the Quality and Image, the higher your TCO can be and still maintain an attractive MSD.

When you do your homework, it will be worth your while to consider also those potential customers who are not seeking "transportation," but rather recreation, or amusement. The Q and I that you want to offer them differ in the sense that you want to make them seek your service or product even when they do not really need it, but rather – want to own it and willing to spend in order to achieve this ownership. They might need a different formula with differently assessed values of Q, I, and TCO.

When your customer's MSD is strong enough to outpower any barrier (price?) or deterrent (competing options, or – non usage) – the chances of transactions happening are high.

Dangerous Murkiness Ahead

Customer value models can be fairly simple, but that doesn't mean they are always easy to build or used in a significant manner. There are at least two major difficulties that may arise in the way of approaching these models.

First, it is very difficult to attribute meaningful values to the indicators used, for they are based on impressions and not on quantified variables. For instance, how do you measure Quality? Is there an absolute "grade" to Image? Attribution of numbers, or "grades" to the indicators rely on intuition, appreciation and estimation, comparison work, personal taste, and subjective interpretation.

Therefore, any attempt to work this model will usually tend to rely on vague, intuitive beliefs about what the customer wants or feels. This makes it almost impossible to use this model as a tool that would enable comparisons, process analysis, or any common usage that will carry forth one meaning and one significance for all, throughout the organization, throughout communication with other external parties, or even for same persons or organizations at different times or situations.

Second, is what we call the Aristotelian Thinking: A great many people who use explicit customer value criteria fail to exercise validation of their beliefs via solid customer research. They think or believe that they know what is important to their customers. On the basis of this belief, they conjure up lists of factors to work with, only they never stop to actually verify their guess work.

All Hands Aboard!

True Purpose

Let's look at an example. Let's say that we want to create a high-end service, like for instance business or personal consulting. So, in our mind's eye, we predetermine that TCO should be high. Therefore, if we want the MSD to also be high, we need to work very hard on the quality and image factor, with respect to our competition. But, what if we rendered our competition irrelevant?

While we are all aware of the fact that in our world, blue oceans are very scarce, it is reasonable to assume that if we want to find one, our only chance to do so is if we conjure it up ourselves. That means, making competition irrelevant by creating a whole new market segment, assuming that it manages to provide actual value to the customers we seek.

So, a very accomplished and talented man by the name of Tim Kelley creates a new personal development plan, aimed at extremely high-end customer segments: Business and political leaders.

He labels himself a Global Change Agent, constructs the True Purpose leadership methodology, and goes on to "work with top leaders in many fields and countries to transform human institutions and evolve society. He helps executives, politicians, and organizations to become potent and capable creators of change."

What he did was, he gave the personal development goal that his customers seek, an added value for his customers. He gave them something bigger than himself, and bigger than themselves – a higher purpose of doing good for society whilst developing themselves personally and professionally – by finding their true purpose. And, it worked.

First, how did he make competition irrelevant? He invented a new field of consulting – a blue ocean – therefore, he is the only expert in the world (except his students) who knows how to provide it. Why do people want to pay him high sums of money in order to own his ideas? He has proven his services valuable: He worked very hard on his Quality factor (not only are you going to do good to yourself, but you are also going to benefit society); he also worked very hard on his Image factor (if you seek my advice, this means that you can see yourself as belonging to an elite group of leaders, and agents of change who impact the world).

So, if his Q and his I factors are high, he can keep his TCO high and still achieve a very high MSD.

British Airways:
When British Airways launched a major customer-research project in the early 1980's, they asked their passengers to grade the importance of on-time take-off, as a decision-maker or deal-break factor, when making travel plans. Shortly before that, Scandinavian Airlines had managed to build a significant competitive advantage in the market, out of on-time take-off commitment, and achieved the position of the most punctual airline in Europe.

However, very soon following, punctuality became a standard expectation, and could no longer be used as anything but a basic component of the service. No airline deserved extra credit just for taking off on time, or for delivering service as advertised. On-time take-off had moved downwards in the hierarchy of customer-valued features from desired to basic expectation.

What happened really was that customer expectations were reconditioned by the rising competition in the industry, and performance standards skyrocketed as a result of SAS's competitive strategy.

Customer value research, however, came up with a new emerging factor that may be the current leader in CVM (Customer Value Maximization efforts) for airlines. I am talking about on-board air quality. Many people find that after flights, longer than several hours, they feel foggy, tired, and overall uncomfortable in ways that cannot be explained by the magic word – jetlag. Some frequent fliers have even begun to wear surgical face masks to filter out the germs and dust particles from the air that they are inhaling.

New studies reveal that stale air on board airplanes during long flights may be making flight attendants and passengers ill due to the increased concentrations of airborne germs, dust, and carbon dioxide. Not only that. In high altitudes, air pressure does not allow humans to breathe independently. To overcome this obstacle, hot, compressed air is drawn in from the plane's engine, cooled and then directed into the cabin to supply breathable air. This air is known as "bleed air."

Faults in engine seals and faulty maintenance may result in air contamination by lubrication and hydraulic fluids, as well as other harmful chemicals. The negative health effect is known as "aerotoxic syndrome." It may lead to wide ranging health symptoms such as migraines, extreme fatigue, aching muscles and joints, breathing difficulties, cancer, and even thinking difficulties.

These days, newer aircraft designs and innovative air conditioning systems, like in the new Boing 787, have actually managed to develop "bleed free" technology, reducing the amount of external air needed in order to refresh the internal air supply. In addition to improving air quality inside the aircraft, it is also a way of reducing energy costs needed to process bleed air.

We also know that since cabin air is normally dry, many people suffer from injuries to the delicate membranes in their nasal passages. The dryness may cause tiny cracks in nasal tissue, making people more susceptible to infections and nosebleeds.

The question that should be popped in to the air, so to speak, is: Why does the air on an aircraft worth thirty million dollars have to be dry, and why are passengers expected to travel in a cabin in which air is pressurized at the equivalent of an altitude of five thousand feet, while breathing rarefied air for many hours? Have you ever noticed how many people fall asleep on airplanes, within a few minutes of the wheels leaving the ground? It is not because they are tired, or groggy due to insufficient oxygen. Could it be a version of altitude sickness, aggravated by breathing bad air? Could the onboard environment be conspiring to make passengers groggy on purpose, and therefore, more compliant, mellow, and easy to manage?

Actually, this issue could very well become one of the most important differentiating elements of customer value, in an industry where customers perceive very little difference between suppliers. Could you see how air quality on board aircraft could raise the MSD significantly? I certainly can. Is air quality a factor used often to create a competitive edge? Aristotelian Thinking.

Hospitals

Hospitals have an interesting customer value proposition. Research into perceptions of patients in hospitals clearly shows two value factors to be critical in the patients' willingness to return to a particular hospital and to recommend it to others. Yet, probably less than twenty percent of the hospitals regularly measure these factors or do anything with the findings.

The first key factor is whether or not patients feel empowered. It is very common to see patients being considered helpless, powerless, and unable to participate in their own health decisions. They are often treated like children who have no authority over themselves, are provided with minimal information regarding their own conditions, and encouraged to be excluded from the decision-making processes.

However, including patients in decision-making processes, and providing them with relevant in-depth information, has clearly been shown to reinforce their satisfaction from the service and their inclination to return upon need.

The second key factor is building trust through perceived teamwork and continuity of treatment. Contradictory treatments and diagnoses given by different staff members (doctors, nurses, specialists), treatment mistakes (wrong medication, mix-ups, etc) cause doubt and distrust. Incidents like these are very common with hospitals, and many hospital managers have no idea how frequent they are. Staff requesting specific information before operations, for example ("which eye did you say needs the surgery?") is not uncommon, but it sure kills patient confidence.

The complex nature of health care organizations virtually guarantees ample opportunities for things to go wrong, for miscommunications, and for cases falling between the cracks or departments. The patients' perception of trust, teamwork, and continuity cannot be left up to randomness. It must, and should, be well managed at all times. Yet very few hospitals explicitly make it their business to explore and manage this aspect. It is remarkable how many executives discover, through open-minded and creative customer research, that their most firmly held beliefs about their customers' feelings are way off mark.

One of the most strategically effective things any manager or leader of any enterprise can do is to set aside established beliefs about what their customers think, believe, want, or need, and take the question directly to them. By listening in an open minded, innocent way, they might very well discover truths that have been invisible to them, and that have a power to provide them with huge strategic insights, especially if they are invisible to their competition as well. Of course, knowing is not enough, doing and implementing are necessary to make a difference.

Services Marketing mix Strategy Model in Captain's eye View

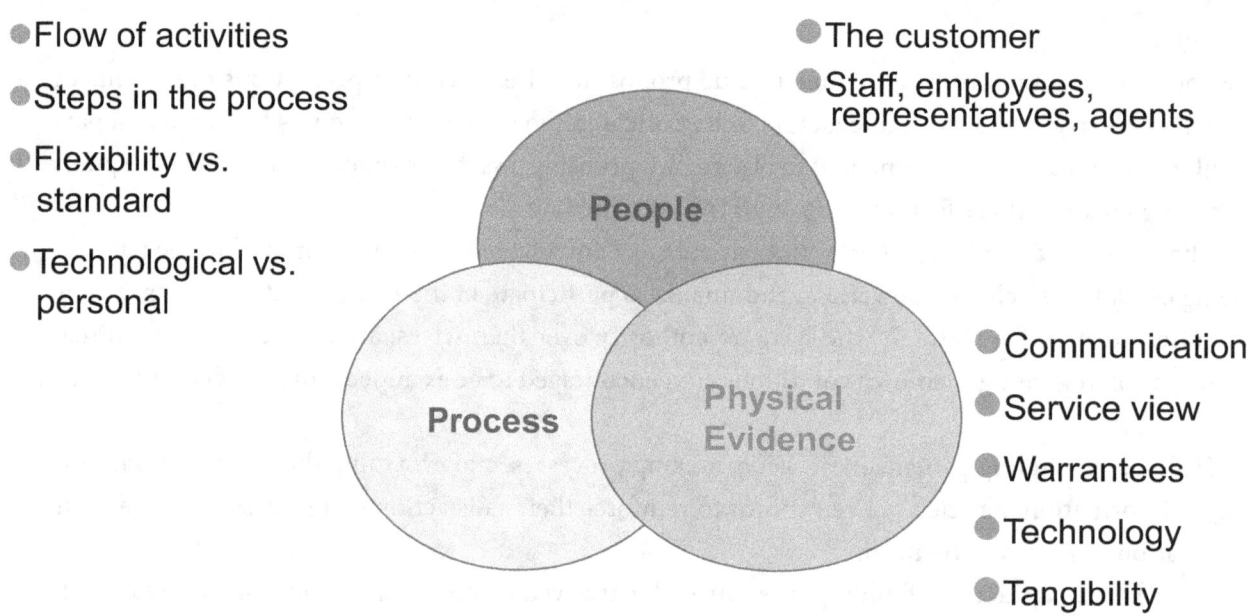

Key Winds in our Sails

The 4-Ps model was developed primarily for products. The set of differences between products and services, however, require that we make adaptations should we wish to consider this model for analyzing a service. Today, sometimes there is a very thin line between services and products; therefore, let's, before we begin, remind ourselves of the nature of services, and also that sometimes we will have to deal with the fact that services and products (goods) are not always absolute in nature.

According to Wolak, Kalaftis and Harris, the characteristics of services are:

Intangibility – a service cannot be felt, viewed, or touched. One should be very precise in defining the service down to the finest details so that customers know what they are getting and what they are not.

Simultaneity – you cannot separate a production of a service from its consumption. They happen at the same time and are interdependent. A service is being produced at the same time that it is supplied.

Customizability – basically it means that a service can be personalized and adapted to a specific need or requirement; therefore, it will rarely take on an exact reproduction from one customer to another.

Perishability – you cannot store a service for future use.

Now, that we understand more about services, the first thing we can do, is redefine the first Ps, in a way that will make sense with services. Then, we shall extend the 4 Ps to 7 Ps to allow for a more thorough analysis of the marketing elements and framework necessary for marketing services. While doing so, we will understand the rationale behind this new concept designed to achieve the insights we need out of this model.

First, let's see how we deal with the traditional 4 P's in services.

Re-Definition: Product → Plan Toward Value

While products provide promised value upon purchase, we can say that every service is a plan, at the end of which, or in the process of which, the customer comes to own or gain a promised value. Unlike most products, the attainment of value requires a timeframe of specific action and interaction, and a certain level of ongoing communication between the providing and the receiving ends.

This small modification may seem self-evident to you at first glance, but in a captain's eye view it is vital to the understanding of this model's added P's.

For example, a ship is a product, a very large and expensive one, of course, but nevertheless, a product. A sailing expedition would be a service, and so would be a docking agreement. Services are plans of action taken in order to achieve the value, and we can see how an expedition or a traveling itinerary falls under this category: they require a timeframe of action, interaction, and communication, in order that the customer comes to own or gain the value.

When we talk about a plan toward value, it allows us to resolve the conflict between standardization and customizability. The scope for customizing the offer becomes wider and the concept more comfortable. Under this concept it is possible to design the service offering it in a way that will be both (just like light acts, both like waves as well as particles).

Re-Orientation: Place → Platform (Integrated Place) / Presence

Place is described traditionally as the location where a product (or service) is marketed or delivered. Since the delivery of a service is concurrent with its production, the place assumes crucial importance, and requires special attention from service providers.

Nevertheless, in the era of technology and internet, the concept of place has morphed beyond our wildest imagination. Today, 'place' can be our very own home, on the couch with our laptop, on the train while commuting to work with our smartphone, and by the time you will be reading this chapter, surely there might be an even newer concept of place. We can say, then, that one type of 'place' can be named simply – an e-connection. Many services can be fulfilled to completion with nothing more than an e-connection and an apparatus with a screen, from banking through some types of therapy to business consulting, etc.

Now, let's take this insight one step further. When we are online, the 'place,' which used to be one physical unit, is surgically divided in to two separate entities that must intercommunicate well with each other although they are fundamentally different:

The first, is the place where a customer or client is physically stationed and it needs, more than anything else, an electronic connection and device. The second, is a virtual non-space, which is a place without coordinates or physical traits. According to traditional understanding, it does not exist physically but rather it is a programmed platform that must be tidy, friendly, updated, designed, and intact.

The first is not fixed, it can be anywhere as long as the human customer has a way to operate it (by touch or voice, or even eye movements). The second – needs (at least still needs) a screen surface in order to be expressed, and manipulated – by a human, and is more often than not, powered – by a machine, that is monitored by a human on a regular schedule.

Hence, now we can redefine the traditional notion of place, and treat it as an have an integrated 'place' made of several forms of spaces which need to work with one another without fail, in order to produce any business activity. In the new language – we call it – Platform.

Another philosophical discussion that needs to be introduced when we talk about this new notion of integrated place, or platform, has to do with presence and the interaction between the 'place' and the people who use it. When I walk in to a bank for a monetary service, obviously I am present, noticed, dressed for the occasion – my appearance matters, my behavior matters, my language matters (speech and body language), and also the time that I choose to appear or stay or leave – matters.

For example, if I appear two minutes before the bank closes and I want to sit with a teller for half an hour, that would not be appropriate. On the other hand, when I 'walk in to' a virtual bank, I am not bound by physical limitations, but… am I present? Am I noticed? Does my appearance take on a different shape or form altogether? Am I alone or am I in a crowd? What would I prefer? And what effect do these revelations have on the 'place's design and features in the realm of e-services?

Of course, the old traditional notion of 'place' is still relevant and when service has to be given in a 'place' of a traditional sort, like a hairdresser, a massage parlor or a gym for example, then everything that has been determined in the past still holds.

That is why I chose to divide the 'place P' in to 2 new P's: Platform and Presence

Re-Volution: Promotion → Public Individuals / Presenters

Promotion in the 21st century: It is a whole ball game on its own, way beyond the scope of this book. However, it needs to take in to account the social media revolution that has changed the world of promotion altogether, when it comes to marketing products and services. This notion becomes more extreme when we talk about services, but it is relevant to both services and products.

Promotion used to be articulated, designed, and staged for people to view, in an artificially pre-formulated way, usually not natural (but pretending to be), and portrayed as bigger than life. These materials were staged, produced, posted, plastered, showed, and played on surfaces such as screens, billboards, televisions, signs and posters, trucks, etc. A lot of guessing and calculation were needed to figure out where, when, and for how long. You needed to figure out where your customers are spending their time anyway, and be there with your promotional material.

Today, promotion is designed for people to experience through other people whose opinions they value. While promotion used to portray characters in the process of consuming, staged as bigger than life, today, promotion has morphed into real people publicly exposing themselves in the process of consuming, in real life situations.

The huge consequential development is the who-is-chasing-whom direction. While yesterday, at the time these P's were conceived, brands were compelled to be following target customers, in order to be "flashing" them with temptations, today, customers are FOLLOWING the brands out of their own enthusiastic will.

We do not need to guess where our target customers spend their time, but rather we have to give them a good reason to follow US around. We do it through opinion leaders.

These people are usually referred to as presenters, or as I like to call them: public individuals. They are individuals who have willfully compromised their privacy in return for public attention, for the purpose of promoting services and products by opinion leadership (an entrepreneurship that ultimately earns them money, and lots of it).

Today, models, actors, players, bloggers, social media celebrities, and other opinion leaders are selected and paid to do promotional activities. They own one skill in particular, and that is a pretty new skill indeed: The social media skill.

Re-Formulating: Price → Partnership Arrangement

Pricing of a service is more complex than pricing of goods and products. In the case of services, there are a lot of factors which are unknown, and costs which are hard to figure out in reference to a single customer, such as overhead, attendant costs, labor, time and range costs that have to be factored in.

When we talk about services today, we have to let go of the old, traditional concept of a simple price, because we want to engage our customers to join us in a partnership arrangement that is far more significant to them than paying the price for accepting a service and walking away.

So, we talk about a new type of partnership. Customers are expected and encouraged to be more involved in the construction of their plan toward value. This is not the traditional form of partnership as we used to know it; however, definitely a lot more than service provider against service customer.

It seems that we are all in this quest for value together. Service providers call themselves "family" and "home," they talk about togetherness and dedication, and they foster mutuality, in efforts, decision-making as well as in risks associated with them.

One other significant characteristic of a service is that it is much more customizable than a product; therefore, it is more flexible in terms of ability to adapt to customer requirement. Hence, the customer encounter also assumes particular significance.

Now that we have adapted the 4 Ps to services and to this era, let's analyze the extra P-parameters that we will be looking at, in order that we can use the Ps model for understanding services. These extra Ps are: People, physical evidence, and process. Let's elaborate on each one of them:

People:

On the part of the service provider, when we say people, we mean not only the employees themselves but all matters concerning them. We should consider matters such as recruiting, training, motivation models, success reward models, cooperation culture (teamwork versus Individual work), training, skills, education, etc.

On the part of customers, we can look at the relationship between customers and the firm – for instance, is it personal or digital? Or we can map the customers and understand who they are and what are their expectations?

All human participants who take part in the service, in the transactions, and in the delivery, influence the people's P, and should be considered when analyzing forms of communication throughout the service interaction.

Since we are talking about "partnership arrangement" (see above) and "plan toward value," and other forms of long-term engagement, the people's P, especially when it comes to communication, becomes even more crucial than ever before.

However, some will feel that this is not true because of the simple fact that people have been excluded by computer interfaces in numerous points of what would have otherwise been some type of contact. Nevertheless, exclusion of people in so many stages and past points of contact, only makes them more important and significant in the few places that they have been still allowed to be present. That is because, first and foremost, service is people and people are service.

Physical Evidence:

Physical evidence is the environment in which the service is delivered and all points of contact where the firm and customer meet and interact.

We should also include under physical evidence any tangible components that facilitate performance or communication of the service, such as facility design, equipment, signage, employee dress, other tangibles, reports, business cards, statements, guarantees, any other paperwork, any assisting gear, premises lighting, etc.

Physical evidence cues provide opportunities for firms to send consistent and strong messages regarding the organization's purpose, intended market segments, and the nature of the services; therefore, we can say that they play an integral part in the marketing and promotional processes as well.

Process:

In services, more than products, a process is an integral part of everything, and all the Ps participate. It includes the flow of activities and its nature: Is it standardized or customized? Is it short or long term? How many procedures does it entail? Is it simple or complex? What is the customer's level of involvement? Is it pleasant or unpleasant? Etc.

The operational flow of the service provides customers with evidence by which they can judge the service, and upon this judgement, base future decisions regarding that service.

Dangerous Murkiness Ahead

A major drawback of the 7-Ps marketing mix is that it fails to address the topic of productivity, with regards to profitability, quality, output, efficiency, duration, etc.

In service, like in production management, improving productivity, efficiency, and profitability are crucial elements that need to be on the agenda.

On the other hand, quality of service as the customer understands it and as the market defines it, as well as achievement of the value offered at the other end of the plan toward value, are also essential. Sometimes, there may be a conflict between those two goals, and a company will need a strategy to optimize the trade-off between them.

A second downside is that the service Ps cannot be analyzed uniformly on a global level. Services are very much affected by culture, language, traditions, habits, regulations, and other variables that change from country to country and require adaptation. Therefore, if a service providing firm is global, it would have to use a separate region-adapted Ps analysis for every country or culture, which makes overall strategizing much more complex.

A third weakness is that it is difficult to turn this model into an algorithm that can analyze the plan-toward-value in all its variations, especially when the variations are infinite.

All Hands Aboard!

The 7 Ps of Service Marketing in the Cruise Industry

Cruise lines today have articulated unique offers of adventure, relaxation, luxury, and travel, all in one. They are essentially floating hotels, that reach diverse destinations, while offering onboard facilities, remarkable itineraries, endless fun, specialty dining/ great food, gambling, and all you can ever dream about.

A cruise fits the four characteristics of services: It is intangible, it cannot be felt or touched but only experienced. It is simultaneous with the production of it, you cannot separate the production from the consumption. It is customizable like any vacation, and you cannot store it for future use; therefore, once you take a cruise, it is over.

Let's begin with the first 4 Ps of services:

Product → Plan Toward Value – depending on the emphasis of the service, whether it is reaching exotic destinations or gambling on board, or enjoying the company of celebrities, each cruise has its unique itinerary, route, and onboard services.

Place → Platform (Integrated Place) / Presence – in the case of cruises, we are still talking about the traditional place, as this type of service cannot be provided online, except the process of ordering it, where the platform concept is valid. Like with many travel services, the 'place' is mobile, although the cruise ship usually can be analyzed under this definition. In looking at the bigger picture, we do have an integrated place, which is comprised of the ordering platform and the place of consumption.

Promotion → Public Individuals / Presenters – are recruited to create a buzz and promote cruises. They are offered free cruises, where they serve as marketing magnets. Regular paying customers are encouraged to go on social media with pictures and experiences, and spread their excitement among their followers.

Price → Partnership Arrangement – on multiday cruises, alongside the regular services offered to passengers, many times they are encouraged to participate in ways that make them more partners than just passengers, such as participating in the scheduling and itinerary setting.

People – are of the utmost importance on cruise ships, where there is continuous close contact between staff and passengers, from the cleaning crew to the captain of the ship.

Physical evidence – consists of everything from maintenance to uniforms. Like in the hotel industry, physical evidence is a crucial factor in determining the satisfaction of customers.

Process – a vacation is a process. Like most services, it has a timespan – a beginning and an end, in the midst of which there are developments, changes, routines, and a path from the beginning point to the final point.

Note that all the downsides mentioned above are relevant to be considered in this analysis.

CHAPTER 3:
GUIDELINES FOR UNDERSTANDING ALL STRATEGIC MODELS IN CAPTAIN'S EYE VIEW

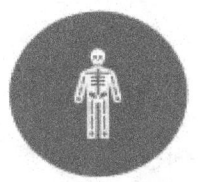

1. The world of business strategies is characterized by multiple and varied strategic models, which were developed by researchers throughout decades of business thinking and development.

2. The generic models propose analytic thinking directions for businesses on the levels of Marco, Micro and Implementation.

3. These models are scattered and diverse, and when CEOs of business firms are required to use them, they may encounter difficulties in finding the right model to solve the business dilemmas or situations that exist in their company.

4. This niche is where we come in with a new integrative model, that is easy to grasp and implement by CEOs of business firms, by students of management professions, and by business consultants. These constitute our target audience, and this model has been designed for their use and advantage.

INTRODUCING: CAPTAIN STRATEGY

The world of business and marketing strategic models is growing and developing by the hour. While some models are flexible and relevant through time, others may need adaptations, and new models are being developed with relevance to the world as we know it today, which is far different from the world that we knew back when Porter and his respectful colleagues revolutionized the world of management.

In order for us to be able to make effective use and to arrive at a clear understanding of most models available today, Captain Strategy has developed a method of breaking down each model to an integrative model that fits all and is easy to understand and put into effective use.

Some of the information you are about to see will be a repetition of some of the things I said in the first chapter of this book. However, now, having read chapter 1 and 2, I am most certain that this revision and summation is worth your while, as now you will be able to see it and understand it through the Captain's eye View.

Goals and Definitions:

The Captain Strategy Approach: Goals and Definitions

- The Captain Strategy Model integrates existing strategic models using a new analytic outlook

- The model offers a new strategic analysis, which is inspired by the world of sailing, boating, oceans and the relationship between man and nature at sea

- The model was designed to offer a new integrative solution to manage the diversity of strategic models, and to provide a new integrative model which can be easily used by our target audiences, i.e. CEOs of business firms, students of management professions, and business consultants.

- The model was designed in an integrative systematic manner and in reference to the needs of any business, no matter what stage it is in, in order to drive it to profitability, in a quick and efficient manner

- The model was designed to be easily implementable on any existing business model, to make it more approachable, categorizable and tangible, in a way that enables efficient tackling of ad-hoc business challenges by choosing not only the right strategic model, but also the right sequence of analyses

To use the model, several basic definitions should be established:

- The definition of strategy
- The definition of a strategic model
- The definition of Captain Strategy's strategy
- The definition of Clear Wind Strategy
- The definition of the Sea to Gulf to Harbour methodology
- The C.A.P.T.A.I.N Strategy's Acronym
- Model Template
- Implementation of the Captain Strategy model on a real company

The term **Strategy** was derived from an ancient Greek word:

'Strategia', means office of general, command and generalship.

This word is composed of two parts:

'Stratos' means 'army', and

'Ago' is the ancient Greek word for guiding and driving something foreword.

A popular definition of the term 'Business Strategy'

A road-map outlined by senior management for the purpose of using available resources to achieve desired goals in an uncontrollable environment, in harmony with organizational culture, goals and objectives.

The problem with this definition today is, that no map can be sustainable and relevant over time, in a crazy world, which undergoes multiple revolutions one after the other. Those revolutions change the world, make it more complex and very unstable. This definition was concocted at a time when the world was a more stable and predictable environment. Imagine a road map for reaching desired goals, in an environment in which the roads change by the minute, and not only the roads, but also the concept of roads changes. Before the roadmap is completed, it is already obsolete.

That is why Captain Strategy has come up with a new definition of the term Business Strategy, as follows:

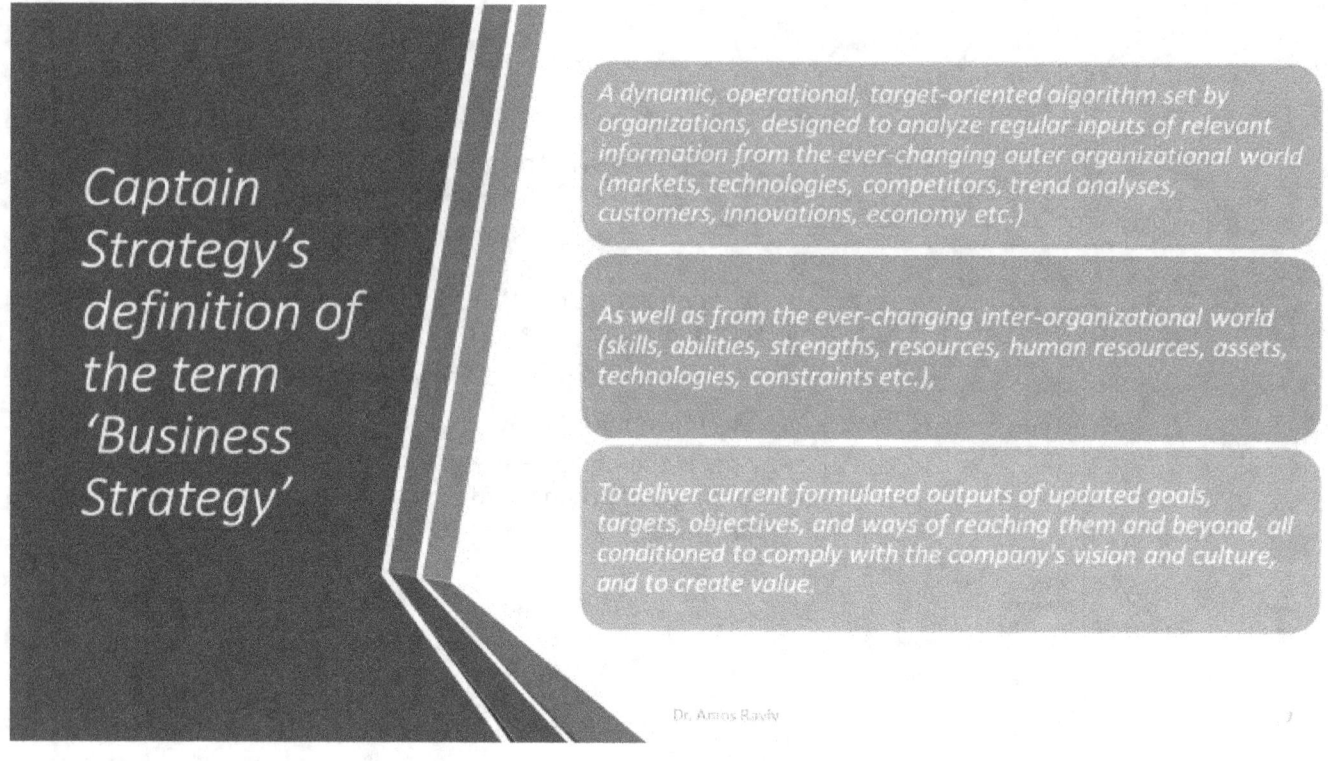

In order to formulate a business strategy, serious and deep analysis need to be conducted, and the tools to conduct them are business and marketing models:

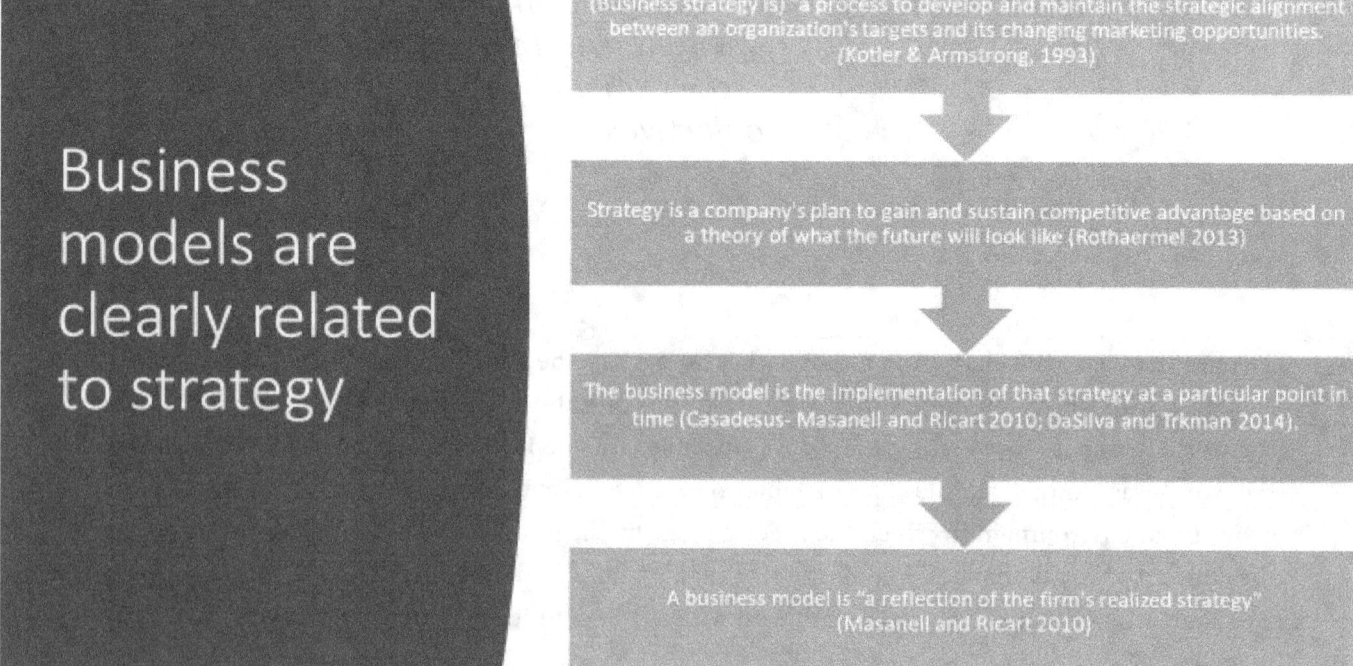

Business Model Canvas

 The key resources, key activities, and key partners that generate value for the company

 Revenue streams minus cost structure and its customers.

 Value proposition and customer relationships for customer segments through transactions channels.

A business model is??

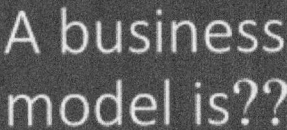 While strategy is about developing valuable resources that can lead to competitive advantage

 (Barney 1991; Wernerfelt 1984).

 The business model is about how to deploy those resources optimally.

Dr. Amos Raviv

Clear Wind Strategy

CAPTAIN STRATEGY's CLEAR WIND STRATEGY

This Strategy is based on the six ancient principles of competitive sailing:

It gives a relative advantage to companies and CEOs, and is based on the Clear Wind Strategy

Action Principle 1: Always be in motion, at the speed that suits YOU

Action Principle 2: Be at the right place, in the right time

Action Principle 3: Stay balanced in all circumstances, including in profit turn points

Action Principle 4: Be the first to Jump-Start, but don't get disqualified

Action Principle 5: During the race, watch your primary competitors, when you are above wind and they are below wind

Action Principle 6: Even when you are not at the lead, do not despair and try to find clear wind through leveraging your relative advantages

A new and simple funnel methodology for categorization of strategic models:

1. One of the main issues of the Captain Strategy project is a methodology for categorization of strategic models using an analytic funnel that is based on activity environments

2. The methodology begins with the **Sea**, which stands for the Macro environment (vast and far): a country, state, continent etc.

it proceeds to the **Gulf**, which stands for the specific industry's environment (internal competition). It is connected to the sea yet separated by a narrow opening and consists of separate "marine" habitats.

Finally, it reaches the **Harbour** (the company itself and its differentiation)

3. **Sea to Gulf to Harbour methodology:**

An analytical method for business companies using generic strategic models in an educated manner.

After gaining a deep understanding of every model by itself, we define, using this methodology, which models will be used to analyse the company

TAXONOMY OF BUSINESS MODELS

1. Descriptive Strategic Models
The first model will relate to the Sea environment, and will give us an understanding of the macro environment in which the company is active

e.g. PESTEL

2. Market Oriented Strategic Models
The second model to be used will be a Gulf model, and will provide us an understanding of the industry with orientation towards the specific line of activity of the company in that industry

e.g. McKinsey

3. Focus Driven Strategic Models
The third model will be a Harbour model, and will focus specifically on the company and its performance against its competitors in the market, in the same line of business

e.g. Porter's Value Chain

4. Integrated Industry Oriented Strategic Models
It is possible to integrate models in different fields of activities with strategic models that are oriented towards focused differentiation

e.g. Industry specific integrated strategic model like my Marina model

TAXONOMY OF STRATEGIC BUSINESS MODELS

Analysis by Environmental Orientation Funnel

Analysis of the vast and far environment

P.E.S.T.E.L

Macro Environment Analysis (external, country, state, continent etc)
Analysis of a country's national advantage using Porter's Diamond Model

Sea

Analysis of a specific business industry

Porter's Five Forces Model

Ansoff Market analysis

Blue Ocean Analysis of Innovativeness

Gulf

Analysis of a company's internal environment

ABELLE   S.W.O.T

Porter's Value Chain

Porter's Strategic Competition Strategy

Marina Model Analysis

Harbour

The C.A.P.T.A.I.N. Strategy Acronym

An **acronym**

 Is a word or name formed as a type of abbreviation formed from the initial components of the words of a longer content such as of a name or phrase, often with individual initial letters, as in NATO (North Atlantic Treaty Organization).

 Acronyms result from a word formation process known as blending, in which parts of two or more words are combined to form a new word.

An **acronym**

C.A.P.T.A.I.N

THE CAPTAIN STRATEGY ACRONYM

Any dynamic strategic process must include several key attributes in order to be applicable and efficient in the 21st century marketplace, just like the Three C's of Branding (Clarity, Consistency and Constancy). Thus, we have devised an acronym to remember, for your convenience.

THE CAPTAIN Strategy acronym : C

C for Clarity

- A strategic directive must be clear, understandable and coherent in order to be carried out correctly and effectively by all organizational functions, each in its specific area of activity.

- Once your strategic directive becomes unclear, open to multiple interpretations, and not focused enough, the organization will cease to behave like one coordinated being.

THE CAPTAIN Strategy acronym : C+A

• A for Agility

- Being that our strategy is now a perpetual process, a constantly forming and reforming formula, or as an algorithm, it must be formulated in such a way that will enable the organization to maintain agility, flexibility and reactivity as top values, in order to be able to synchronize itself with a constantly changing reality.

THE CAPTAIN Strategy acronym : C+A+P

• P for Perpetualness

- While in the past we used to talk about the need for consistency in strategies, today we are no longer expecting constant strategic guidelines but rather a continuous process of ongoing strategic formation and development.

- A strategy should be able to lead organizations to success throughout their life cycle, in an uncontrollable and unexpectedly changing environment.

- A good strategy is articulated in such a way that it will be able to correct itself and redirect itself in response to changing conditions.

THE CAPTAIN Strategy acronym: C+A+P+T

• T for Target

- Every strategy must be built around a clearly defined and strongly pursued vision: a target, purpose or goal, and be geared towards achieving them, above anything else.
- No matter what your targets or goals are, they must be: a. clearly defined, and b. modifiable in accordance with the ongoing strategic process.

THE CAPTAIN Strategy acronym: C+A+P+T+A

• A for Aspiration

- Hamel and Prahalad (1993), claims that ... "Competitiveness is born in the gap between a company's resources and its managers' goals".
- This paper claims, and rightfully so, that fewer resources will not stand in the way of greater aspirations.
- Ambitions create visions and visions drive growth. Aspirations are the crucial component your strategy will need if you want your organization to reach the "beyond" part of our definition of strategy. Aspirations separate the phenomenal from the crowds, the outstanding from the average.

THE CAPTAIN Strategy acronym : C+A+P+T+A+I

• I for Implementability

- Implementability is of vital importance. The less implementable a strategy is the less relevant and efficient it will be, and vice versa.
- The more implementable a strategy is, the better the results are going to be. Better implementation possibilities also means that strategists will have more time at hand to be creative and come up with novel ways to drive the organization forward and reach better and higher goals, since they will not be needing all their creativity for the sake of implementation itself.

THE CAPTAIN Strategy acronym:C+A+P+T+A+I+N

• N for Narrative

- A strategy is designed to produce a collective organizational orientation towards certain goals and certain ways of achieving them. It is an integrative organizational "to-do" list, reflecting on all of the organization – from the doorman to the CEO. Dressing strategy with a relevant and compelling narrative will not only improve the remembering capacities of the organization by enriching dull numbers and imperatives with meaning and logic, but will also help make sense of relationships between the multiple factors, contexts, correlations and parties involved, thus making implementation a much more achievable process.

The Captain Strategy Template

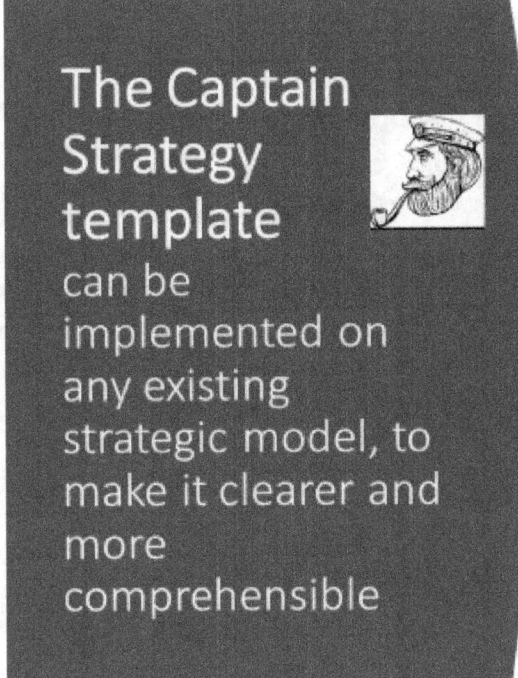

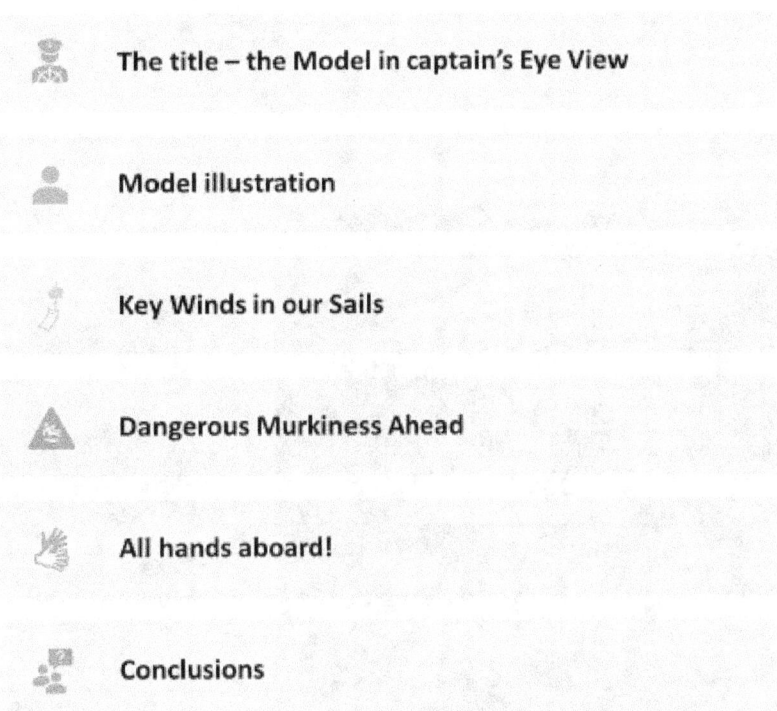

- The title – the Model in captain's Eye View
- Model illustration
- Key Winds in our Sails
- Dangerous Murkiness Ahead
- All hands aboard!
- Conclusions

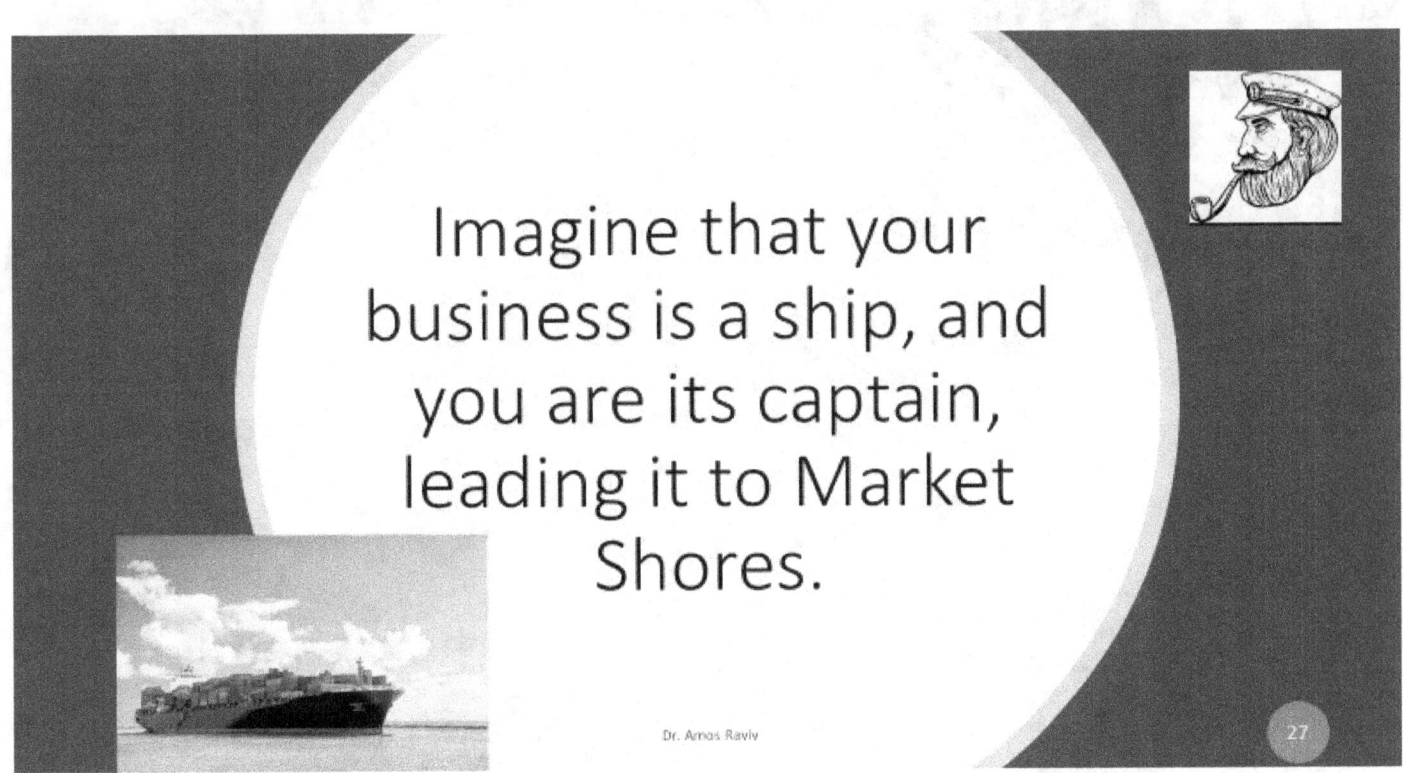

Imagine that your business is a ship, and you are its captain, leading it to Market Shores.

Dr. Amos Raviv

Summary

 In order to formulate a winning strategy which will be effective over time we will need advanced analyzing tools. These will be found in a wide array of strategic models which can be divided into three main groups:

 Methods of strategic planning through a one-way process of constructing a formal plan that uses descriptive strategic models.

 Methods of strategic planning with a market orientation, which deal with the analyses and mappings of a company's mix of products, services or brands, and an analysis of its portfolio.

 Methods of strategic planning which are based on dialogue focusing on possible scenarios.

 CAPTAIN STRATEGY provides innovative tools for advanced strategic analyses, with an environmental orientation based on the relationship between man and the vast seas

CHAPTER 4:
THE AMOSEA STRATEGIC BUSINESS MODEL FOR MARINAS

THE AMOSEA STRATEGIC BUSINESS MODEL FOR MARINAS

THESIS SUBMITTED IN PARTIAL FULFILLMENT OF THE
REQUEST FOR THE DEGREE OF "DOCTOR OF PHILOSOPHY"
Submitted to the Senate of Ben-Gurion University of the Negev, Beer Sheva

Abstract

This study includes documentation of a comprehensive and long-term investigation of the Israeli and international marina industry, encompassing both marina customers and managers. Although there has been little academic research in this field (and perhaps because of this), this study offers a road map for consideration, investigation, and planning in the marina industry.

The literature review in this study addresses management theories, such as strategic management, marketing theories, and service quality. It also proposes a unique classification system for research studies in the marina industry, which constitutes a foundation for describing the existing and lacking know-how in this growing tourist industry.

The literature review also proposes a system for classifying variables according to which marinas can be characterized. The uniqueness of the classification system is twofold: First, a classification system is proposed for the marina industry for the first time. This system allows marinas to be classified according to uniform criteria, so that marinas may be compared by quantitative methods as well as the qualitative descriptions (Raviv, 2001).

Second, these criteria are positioned in groups that marina managers consider to be interrelated, such that the structure of the classification process is similar to the marina managers' conceptual map. The groups are described in the chapter that outlines the results and discussion, and the full map appears in the chapter describing marina classification and service properties.

The literature review describes the results of the pioneer study that preceded this study. The pioneer study examined the reliability of service areas, as defined by Parasuraman (1988), and examined whether they are also given high reliability in the marina industry. It was found that the areas defined by Parasuraman (1988), for customers in the U.S. for other service areas are grouped into the same categories in the marina industry, and the categories also have high reliability for marina customers in Israel.

Before presenting the strategic influencing factors in the marina (the independent variables), which close the literature review, the development process of the occupancy index, which is the dependent variable in the research is described. As there is no scientific measure for marina occupancy in literature, the index may explain the marina's profitability or the attainment of its goals.

The author of this study proposes an occupancy index that expresses the occupancy rate as the ratio between the number of moored boats and the total mooring capacity in the marina.

The research assumptions chapter presents the strategic model for examination. This is the first model of its kind, which is customized for marina management. This model provides tools for strategic planning of an existing marina or for planning the establishment of a new marina and provides the marina manager with tools for ongoing management of the marina.

This model was developed by Professor Ehud Menipaz and Dr. Yaakov Weber of the School of Management at Ben-Gurion University of the Negev, based on the experience of the author of this study in his capacity as marina manager and secretary general of the International Council of Marine Industry Associations (ICOMIA).

The extensive research was performed in three stages: (1) In the first stage, a pilot study was conducted, in which 50 boat owners from three marinas in Israel were asked about their perception of and satisfaction with the marina. The conclusions drawn from the pilot were implemented and led to preparation of the second stage of the research, which is the pioneer study. (2) This stage examined how boat owners perceived marina services in Israel. Two hundred boat owners in seven marinas in Israel and one marina in Turkey were asked about their perception of and satisfaction with the marina. The research conclusions appear in Raviv (2001), and are described in the literature review. (3) In the third stage of the study, 130 marina managers (69% return of questionnaires) from 25 countries (60% in Europe) agreed to describe their perceptions of the marina under their management.

Prior to the statistical analysis of the data, the reliability of the factors was examined, as predicted by the details in the questionnaire. Cronbach's alpha for reliability of the dependent variable was 0.77, which indicates a sufficiently high correlation between the variables and this factor, as composed of the selected items, can be used for continued analysis in the study. Of the independent variables, six produced high validity: Marina location, local community in the marina, mooring services in the marina, environmental protection, and distance from competitors.

The next analysis will relate to these variables only. Other independent variables – government influence, security, proximity to customer, accessibility, and level of crowding – did not achieve a sufficient validity level, and were not further examined in this study.

The responses of marina managers around the world are described in the results chapter. According to the sampling data, the average berth for one boat in the marinas is 462 square feet. A boat is between 7 to 443 feet long, with an average length of 88 feet. The common size of small boats is 26 feet, and of large boats is 65 feet.

Presentation of the results according to marina ownership demonstrates that the private marinas have the highest profitability, reaching 58%. Non-profit public marinas constitute the second largest group, with 27% of all marinas.

The government marinas have the largest number of berths, with an average of 564 berths, while private marinas have the smallest number of berths, with an average of 340 berths.

The managers' perception also differ according to the marina under their management: According to their information, the facilities in the private marinas better meet the standards of the marina managers. They receive the highest marks in all the parameters that were examined. The managers of the private marinas estimate that investment in a marina is more feasible than other business investments, as the income ratio compared to the operational expenses is the highest, and the profitability of the marina is higher.

These managers estimate, in all parameters, that their marinas meet the standards that were set at a higher level than the government marina managers do: From a higher social and cultural atmosphere, image, security, landscape, environmental protection, and a higher level of usability and cleanliness.

The private marinas charge higher mooring fees, which reach an annual fee of over $11,000 per boat. In comparison, the government marinas charge an average of 20% less: Just over $9,000 per boat annually.

Examination of the results from the aspect of the type of customer that the marina caters to indicates that most marinas serve mainly local residents, with very few marinas focusing on tourists.

Marinas that cater to a balanced mix of local customers and tourists charge the highest price (an average annual fee of $11,500). This fee drops when catering to local residents only ($8,500) or tourists only ($7,200). The marina customers are an average of 16 miles from the marina, which is approximately of 47 minutes travel time; however, the difference is expressed mainly when examining marina ownership.

While the customer of a private marina has to travel 20 miles for 72 minutes to reach the marina, the customer of a government marina travels an average of 4 miles for 10 minutes only to reach the marina. In other words, government marinas are closer to customers than private marinas.

Examination of the research assumptions shows a positive correlation between the services provided at the marina and its occupancy, and between environmental protection at the marina and its occupancy. The proposed model could not be validated; however, it can be determined that there is a positive correlation between the status of the marina as perceived by the local residents and all landscape design details at the marina, and there is also a positive correlation between a higher security level, between the residents' love of the place, and between the view from the marina and landscape design at the marina.

Positive results of the consensus analysis of the responses (0.52) allowed examination and analysis of the ranking of importance of the different variables and the cognitive map of the marina managers. The results show that the marina managers regard value for money as the most important variable. This is followed by customer satisfaction, boating services (fuel, storage, repairs, etc.), and amenities offered to the customer (clubhouse, swimming pool, showers, etc.). The lowest importance is given to the level of government supervision over the marina. A cognitive map was produced to help understand the correlation between the variables (beyond their order of importance).

A multidimensional scaling (MDS) analysis presented a reasonable analysis level (0.11), thus the map is indeed a reliable reflection of the raw ranking data. This map shows that the managers relate to the accompanying services at the marina as the factor that is closest to customer satisfaction, followed by value for money.

The parameter analysis (correlations) shows that the accompanying services do indeed have a significant influence on occupancy/profit and it is reasonable to connect them to value for money. Another finding in the managers' cognitive map that correlates with the other findings is the distinction between view, travel distance, and mooring depth, which are related to the site location (and did not produce a significant correlation with profitability) and between environmental quality, which did indeed produce a significant correlation.

The research also discovered that managers perceive government intervention as almost unconnected to any other factor and has a very low influence on profitability of the marina. The closest connection to government intervention is in environmental quality. It appears that marina managers relate the need to ensure preservation of environmental quality with the need to comply with government enforcement more than with the need to meet the customer's requirements.

The support of this study for factors that were proven as having an impact on marina occupancy and profitability (accompanying services at the marina, environmental protection, and to a certain extent, the local community), is critical. Two of the factors are exogenic to the marina: The local community and preservation of environmental quality. The tendency of managers to express their opinion of these factors is low compared to internal factors in the marina, such as the accompanying services.

This study is a pioneer study of marina management. As such, questions that have not been asked previously are posed here, and it opens new avenues for consideration. The answers to these questions are a subject to a complex research journey, and it is fitting that other researchers will search for a way to anchor marinas to the business world through empirical validity.

Key words: Marina, strategic models, occupancy

INTRODUCTION

Literature Review

In this chapter we will review the relevant literature and researches in order to formulate the research questions. The review will begin by classifying studies on the tourism industry, and immediately afterwards, we will define the term "service," on the assumption that the core of marina activity is the provision of services (such as anchorage services).

An understanding of the process of marketing the service (including the formulation of the variety of services offered) and the choice of the quality of the service will form the business strategy that will lead the organization toward its goal. These subjects will be discussed in sequence immediately afterwards.

In the last section of the literature review, we will focus on the relevant strategic factors for the marina industry, factors that are likely to affect the formulation of the model being examined. This review will enable us to formulate the assumptions of the study and the possible dimensions of the strategic model on which the study is based, which will appear in the chapter following the literature review.

Flow chart of literature review

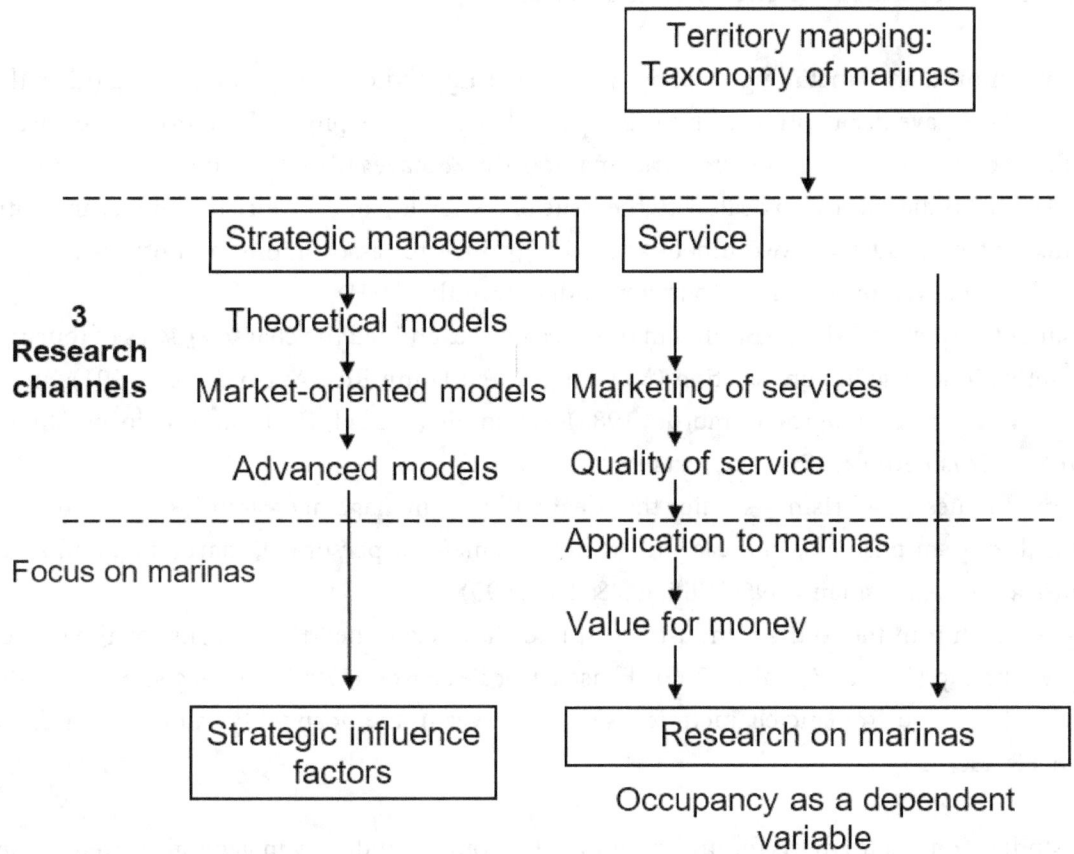

STUDIES ON THE TOURISM INDUSTRY

The academic studies on the tourism industry are varied, and they describe tourism from a variety of perspectives. We can describe two main approaches in tourism research:

1. Macro-level studies of the tourism industry –

a. The tourism industry, as an economic industry, contributes to the Gross National Product, paying attention to aspects of fluctuations between demand and supply, employment multipliers, exchange rates, and more. In this context, we can include topics such as tourism as a tool for developing peripheral and undeveloped areas, and as a means of creating sources of employment (such as Eadington & Smith 1992; Echtner, 1995).
b. Studies about the tourist environment, including geographical studies that combine aspects of the location of the attraction, influences on the physical environment, *et al.* (i.e., Smith, 1989).

2. Micro-level studies of the tourism industry –

a. The tourism product – including its planning, marketing, and consumption. Among other things, the researchers have dealt with the physical aspect of supply: The physical-environmental aspect of tourist attractions (such as Lundberg, Krishmamoorthy & Stavega, 1995; Gunn, 1994; Eadington & Smith, 1992). Studies have also dealt with the issue of ownership of the tourist business, and with the influence of factors such as government and ecology, investor associations, and others with vested interests in the development of the tourism product (Smith, 1994).

b. The tourist (the demand side) – Studies in this area have examined the characteristics of tourists and their motivation for going on vacation (McClung, 1993; Dunn Ross & Iso-Ahola, 1991); and have also dealt with anthropological (Grabrun, 1983), economic (Bakkal, 1991), and socio-psychological (Dunn Ross & Iso-Ahola, 1991) contexts.

c. Managerial issues in tourism – studies that deal with the management abilities required to run a successful tourism business, in areas such as management of personnel, marketing, and strategic administration (Athiyaman, 1995; Williams & Tse, 1995).

d. Entrepreneurship in the tourism industry – studies have examined the reasons for the success of entrepreneurship (Lerner & Haber, 2001; Fleischer & Felsenstein, 2000), management style (Tse & Ellwood, 1990), and strategic characteristics of initiatives in the hospitality industry (for example, Williams & Tse, 1995).

These studies constitute a basis for understanding the tourism industry in general, as well as specific issues in this industry. The tourism industry is a multi-sectoral industry that brings together a wide range of industries and businesses, including marinas – which are the subject of the present study.

An examination of one branch of the tourism industry lacks the overall vision of the interrelationship among the branches; however, this approach makes it possible to conduct a thorough study of relevant factors that influence the direction of the business strategy in the industry under discussion and to create tools for managerial decision-making, which is adapted to environments and consumers in the industry.

A study of a single branch enables researchers to examine aspects on the macro level (such as location and environmental influences) as well as the micro level (the influence of government factors, strategic management, and more), in order to shed light on the most significant processes and factors in the relevant branch. Before these factors are described, topics relevant to services in general and to marina services in particular are presented in the following subchapters.

What is Service?

Most companies in the Western world today have what is referred to as a service economy or a service society: The services sector is responsible for the increase in capital and for raising the rate of employment in society.

In their study, Fitzsimmons and Fitzsimmons (2000) present the dynamic nature of the services industry: In the early 20th century, less than one third of the manpower in the United States was employed in the service sector. In 1950, services accounted for about 50 percent of manpower, and toward the 21st century, this percentage reached 80 percent.

That being the case, what is service? Kotler and Armstrong (2004) define service as, "Any activity or benefit that one party can offer to another that is essentially intangible and does not result in the ownership of anything. Its production may or may not be tied to a physical product."

According to Grönroos (1990), service is, "An activity or series of activities of more or less intangible nature that normally, but not necessarily, takes place in interactions between the customer and service employees and/or systems of the service provider, which are provided as solutions to customer problems."

Research on the subject of marketing services began in the mid-sixties (Rathmell, 1966), and in the 1980s, it began to gain significant momentum with the study by Parasuraman, Zeithaml and Barry (1985) on the subject of quality of service.

The quality of products (goods) is traditionally related to technical details, and therefore, can be measured objectively. The quality of services, in contrast, is more abstract: In the processes of service, there is a problem separating their "production" and consumption.

The literature that deals with the marketing of services describes four principal attributes of service. According to Parasuraman, Zeithaml and Barry (1985), services are: (1) intangible, (2) inseparable in terms of production and consumption – tangible products are manufactured first, then sold, and finally consumed, whereas services are sold first, then produced and consumed simultaneously, a process that creates a connection between the consumer and the manufacturing process, (3) heterogeneity – the quality of the service can vary from one supplier to supplier, from consumer to consumer, or depending on the time of delivery, and (4) perishable – one cannot accumulate an inventory of services, a fact which undermines the ability of the company to adapt itself to variations in demand.

When a company sells a service, it is in effect selling a relationship. In every contact formed with a potential customer, it must ensure that the customer will be impressed by the sincerity, seriousness, and desire to listen and meet every demand it presents, as service is a subjective experience with the customer. Any sign of complications in this subjective contact will cause the customer "to walk away" and not to return in the future.

The problem is that many companies are not attentive to the needs of their customers, and thus, do not meet their expectations. Being attentive to customer needs and meeting their expectations is the foundation of the marketing approach, which enables an organization to present (by means of the marketing variables) a way of better providing for the needs of the customers, than do the competitors. The next chapter will present studies that deal with the marketing of services.

MARKETING SERVICES

Launching or managing new services involves great risk. Many goods and services have ended their lives early, while leaving behind failures and heavy debts for the company. The marketing process, which is composed of decisions related to marketing variables, has a direct impact on the organization's sales, and thus on its success and profitability.

As defined by Kotler and Armstrong (2004), marketing is "a social process by which individuals and groups obtain what they need and want through creating and exchanging products and value with others." The American Marketing Association, AMA, defines marketing as "the process of planning and executing the conception, pricing, promotion, and distribution of ideas, goods and services to create exchanges that satisfy individual and organizational objectives."

Firms that implement marketing plans for a new service, do so as cautiously and precisely as possible. They collect preliminary information about the needs, desires, and sensitivities of their customers, so that the company will be able to provide the most efficient and effective service possible to the potential customers.

From the moment that the service is launched into the market, the company has available means of influencing the process of the spread of the new service, by using decision variables of marketing planning: The company can choose to accelerate the dissemination of information about the services through advertising, increase the percentage of purchases by reducing the price and sales promotion, and reduce the uncertainty among potential customers by providing full warranty, obtaining the approval of relevant bodies, building up a brand name, etc.

Galai and Hillel (1989) admit that marketing planning is "the very heart of business strategy in general." They explain this using the modern business approach, which maintains that goods or services will be adapted to markets, rather than the opposite. They conclude that marketing planning is likely to be dominant, and to determine the course taken by the company. In addition, they emphasize the adaptation of the plan to the capabilities of the company, and the series of major decisions of the marketing plan, and the mutual dependence between them.

Bitner and Boom (1994), propose a combination of special marketing for services, which includes the traditional four Ps of a product marketing (product, price, place, and promotion) and three additional components: (1) Physical evidence, which includes the physical environment and all the tangible elements related to the service, (2) Participants, which includes all the people in the company, the consumers, and the other customers, and (3) Process, which includes the actual procedures, systems, and the level of service activities.

Grönroos (1984), also claims that the marketing of services according to the traditional marketing mix is not sufficient, and points out two additional components that should be included in the marketing of services: Internal marketing, and the marketing of mutual activities: (1) internal marketing – includes the activities of preparing workers who are involved in providing service, training and encouraging them to engage in teamwork, and to be client oriented, and (2) Relationship marketing – which means that the quality of the service as seen by the client depends on the interaction between the service provider and the recipient of the service.

These components are additional factors that are under the control of the directors of the service organizations, and that should be taken into account when planning and marketing of the services. After the general discussion on marketing services, attention will now be turned to how customers determine what quality of service means to them.

Quality of Service (QoS)

One of the strategies that has been proven to be related to the success of the organization is the provision of high-quality services. In the studies, a positive correlation was found between the quality of service and the performance of the organization and its place among competitors (Anderson, Fornell & Lehman, 1994).

Grönroos (1990), emphasizes the fact that companies in the service sector confront a continual problem of maintaining QoS, in order to create a competitive advantage. One of the reasons for the complexity of maintaining the QoS is the difference between goods and services:

The quality of goods is traditionally related to technical details, and therefore, can be measured objectively. In contrast, the quality of service is more abstract: In the process of providing service it is difficult to separate "production" from consumption – frequently, the consumer is an active partner in the process of "production."

The literature that deals with services is based on the following assumptions (Parasuraman et al., 1985):

a. It is more difficult for the client to assess the quality of a service than that of a product, because service is intangible. This is why it is hard to understand how the customer perceives the service and service quality.
b. The service is assessed through a comparison between the expectation of the customer and the actual performance.
c. The assessment of the service is dependent both on the final result and on the process of providing the service.

In their study, Wong et al. (1999), point out that when the QoS becomes a substantial part of the conduct of a business, it is important to measure and to investigate the effectiveness of the services provided. This information is particularly important for managers at the stage of resource allocation, because it enables them to focus on the services that will fulfill the expectations of the customer. This is especially critical as quality of service is a relative and not absolute concept.

Customers judge the quality of service they receive according to the quality of service they received at other places. If others improve the quality of service, it is expected that the others will as well. One of the common tools for measuring the quality of service is SERVQUAL. The tool was developed by Parasuraman et al., in 1985, updated in 1988 and 1991, and is comprised of 10 dimensions, by which clients assess the quality of service:

a. Responsiveness – the degree of contact with the service provider.
b. Competence – the degree of knowledge and skill that enables the provision of good and high-quality service.
c. Reliability – ability to perform promised service dependably and accurately over the long term.
d. Access – the degree to which one can make contact with the service provider.

e. Courtesy – the degree to which the service is provided politely, respectfully, and considerately; these qualities are expressed in the contacts between service providers and customers.
f. Communication – the degree to which the company communicates with its clients in the appropriate language and at the appropriate level to all the customers, or in a different manner with different types of clients.
g. Credibility – the degree to which the company behaves with integrity, out of a sincere concern for the good of its customers.
h. Security – the degree to which a customer of the company feels that his contact with the service provider does not restrict or endanger him.
i. Understanding the customer – the degree to which the company makes an effort to understand the genuine needs of the customer.
j. Tangibles – the degree to which the service can be subject to some type of tangible investigation.

In their study of the quality of service, Parasuraman, Zeithaml and Berry (1988), expand on how to test and achieve quality of service. Quality, as it is seen by the customers, is tested by the excellence and/or overall superiority of a company. The authors emphasize the differences between an objective definition of quality, and the perception of quality, and point out that the customers do not use the term "quality" in the same way as do researchers and marketers, who define quality conceptually. The conceptual meaning distinguishes between two types of quality: Mechanical quality and human quality.

In their study, Parasuraman *et al.* (1988), add that quality of service is determined by an overall assessment, similar to the assessment of attitude and/or approach, and that the customers use the same general criteria to assess the quality of different types of services. However, there is still a need to distinguish between "approach" and "satisfaction" when one comes to examine the subject of quality.

Approach is the effect on the customer, which represents in a relative way his/her attitude toward the product, store, or process. Satisfaction, in contrast, is an emotional reaction that follows an experience, and stems from a basic approach to a specific need (Oliver, 1981), just as boat owners assess the service provided in a marina by means of his expectations of specific items of service that they expect from the marina. These items are specific to the marina. For example, that "the sea entry to the marina is free of sand" or that there are maintenance/repair services for boats at the marina.

Parasuraman *et al.* (1988), believe that the quality of service, as perceived by customers, stems from a comparison between what they feel the service companies should offer, and how they perceive the performance.

Their study on the subject of quality of service enumerates 10 dimensions according to which customers assess the quality of service: Tangibles, credibility, responsiveness, communication, reliability, security, competence, courtesy, understanding the customer and his demands of the supplier, and accessibility.

These 10 dimensions can be narrowed down to five principal components: Tangibles, credibility, responsiveness, guarantee, empathy, and identification. After an examination of the relative importance of the five dimensions of quality, these researchers discovered that credibility is regularly the most critical and important dimension, reliability is the second most important, and tangibles is more important than responsiveness in certain industries (such as banking services), whereas empathy and identification are the least important dimensions.

A comparison among good retail chains (such as supermarkets, shopping chains, etc.), demonstrates that they sell many identical products, while the quality of service is the main means for comparing and distinguishing among them.

On the other hand, for retailers that sell a service only (such as communications companies and airlines), there is very little to offer their customers if their service is poor (Berry, 1986). Parasuraman *et al.* (1988), reinforce this opinion, and argue that a proper use and an understanding of quality of service will help the company identify the main, and most important, dimension of quality of service in the target market in which it operates.

With the help of these dimensions, the company will be able to compare itself with its competitor in terms of its strengths and weaknesses, and identify the desired order of priorities in terms of the quality of service required. Haim Schor (1998), presents three conclusions derived from the study of Parasuraman *et al.* (1988):

1. Consumers perceive the level of service by comparing their expectations before receiving the service with the service they actually receive.
2. The view of quality is also determined according to the process of service, and not only according to its results.
3. The quality of service is of two types: The quality of normal service, and the quality of service in handling "exceptions" or "problematic cases." In guaranteeing the quality of service, each of the two types should be handled separately.

Up to this point, marketing of services and general determination of quality by customers has been discussed. Now the specific services of the marina will be examined. What do customers want from a marina? How should marina services be marketed? What is the uniqueness of marina services relative to other businesses or services? These questions are addressed in the next chapter.

Marina Services

According to the marketing approach (Kotler and Armstrong 2004), it is important for the planning of the services to be provided by the marina (as well as by any other organization) – to begin with an understanding of the needs and desires of the target market. In this way, it will be possible to supply the needs of the target market in a manner that will satisfy it.

During the course of the preliminary study (Raviv, 2001), which examined customer satisfaction with the services of the marinas in Israel, owners of sailing vessels were asked about the mix of services provided at the marina. Using a factor analysis, we found six factors that explain 69 percent of the differences of all the items that comprised the questionnaire (see Appendix A for the detailed results of the factor analysis). The factors were:

Safety and professionalism, value of parking, value of member club, environmental protection and cleanliness, crowding, ease of access, and use of information.

The first factor, safety and professionalism, was comprised of the following items in the questionnaire: Professionalism of marina employees, knowledge of marina employees, courtesy shown by employees, safety of marina as a place to leave boats, safety of marina as a place of entertainment, and compliance with safety guidelines at marina.

The second factor is the value of parking. The factor includes the following items: Distance from marina, view from the marina, parking in the vicinity of the marina, and price of membership at marina.

The third factor is value of members club and it includes the following items: Use of cranes, social atmosphere at marina, gas station at marina, and members club.

The fourth factor is environmental protection and cleanliness of the marina. This factor includes the following items: Convenience of services provided at the marina, cleanliness of the water and the ports, cleanliness and use of showers, environmental protection at the marina, and environmental protection in the areas surrounding the marina.

The last factor included in the calculation of the findings is ease of access and use of information. This factor includes the following items: Ease of access for visitors, ease of access for use of marina facilities, and informational publications about the marina.

It is important to stress that the perception of marina services presented above reflects <u>customer</u> opinion, while the study itself relates to the perception of the <u>managers</u>.

The questionnaire information from the flow chart can be found in Appendix C.

The above indicates that there are several aspects that distinguish marina services from other leisure activities or other services. This uniqueness is not in any single item, but in the overall basket of services and the various points of emphasis provided by marina customers.

Like a golf course, the marina is perceived as a sports venue of the upper class. Therefore, the behaviors displayed at popular sporting events are not appropriate at marinas. Also like golf courses, marinas are perceived as a sports and leisure venue. Both of these areas emphasize nice and clean landscaping (views).

Unlike golf courses, most of the views at a marina are not close and are not cared for solely by club management. Another difference from golf is seen in the equipment and material required for sailing, which without proper care may pollute the view.

It is reasonable to assume that customers expect marina management to ensure that the view is clean, despite the equipment and material present there.

This poses a unique challenge to service provision at marinas. Another unique challenge (perhaps shared with motor sports in another way) is the need for security.

Club members place valuable equipment in the hands of the marina. Without proper security, it may be stolen or damaged. It can, therefore, be assumed that a marina member will expect there to be appropriate security and safety arrangements in place.

Another unique characteristic is that while other sports or leisure activities can be performed to satisfaction in one place, marina members may expect the marina to allow them to travel to other marinas, as is the case in the tourism industry. Consequently, it can be seen that marinas, when viewed as a sports/leisure activity have characteristics similar to other sports/leisure activities, given the overall characteristics and the unique points of emphasis, the marina is a venue for sports/leisure activity of a different type. It is a "whole other ball game."

Now, after having determined the uniqueness of the marina service and having provided the background to understand the marketing and quality of service, the next question that begs asking regards value for money for marina customers. This question will be addressed in the next chapter.

Value for Money at the Marina

In the tourism industry, providing value for money is an important factor in explaining the development of the industry (Weiermair & Fuchs, 1999). Value for money is the subjective assessment of the customer, who compares the cost and the usefulness of the service. The cost of the service is related to the price of the service, but is more comprehensive.

The overall cost includes other hidden "prices," such as the effort made by the customer to obtain the service (like the existence/absence of parking/public transportation near the place where the service is offered), a comparison to similar services/prices and more.

The usefulness of the service is a subjective assessment by the customer regarding profit from the service purchased. Profit here is not only in the economic sense, but a broader term that can include dimensions such as the status the customer gains by being among the recipients of the service, the pleasure derived from use of the service, and more. In his study, Raviv (2001), examined how marina customers perceived the concept of value for money and used five factors to describe it:[7]

Item/Question
54. Fairness of price considering the level of service.
55. Fairness of price considering the level of facilities.
56. The return you receive for you money.
57. The degree to which you feel that the marina services are a suitable return for the price of anchorage.
58. The value that the marina provides for the price it exacts.

The numbers of the items match the questionnaire in Appendix A.

The above table shows the result of Cronbach's alpha reliability analysis of the items comprising the value for money factor: The fairness of the price in view of the level of **service** (item no. 54 in Appendix A), the fairness of the price in view of the level of the **facilities** (item no. 55 in Appendix A), the return you receive for your money (item no. 56 in Appendix A), the degree to which you feel that the services of the marina are a suitable return for the price it exacts (item no. 58). The reliability analysis indicates that these items indeed show the factor as a single entity.

Frederick P. Reidzahler (in: Aviva Rosen, 1998), claims that creating value for the customer of the marina is a series of economic outcomes that begins with loyalty and is conducted in five stages:

1. The income and the market sector increase as the best customers are attracted to the marina and generate repeat sales for the marina and recommendations to additional customers. At this stage, the

---

[7] Reliability analysis of these items yielded a Cronbach's alpha of .95, which is high by all standards.

marina can be selective when choosing new customers, and can focus its investment in the customers who are most profitable and have the greatest potential for loyalty, and engender long-term growth.
2. The growth enables the marina to attract and keep the best employees. Providing high value to customers gives the employees pride and satisfaction with their work. As veteran employees, they are very familiar with their customers and know how to provide them with added value, and reinforce even further the contact with customers and their loyalty.
3. The faithful employees learn to limit costs and improve quality, and they increase the value of the marina and its output. The marina uses the surplus to improve compensation to its employees, provide training, and better tools for them, steps that further increase productivity and loyalty.
4. The combination of high productivity, high efficiency, and customer loyalty creates a cost advantage that the competitors find difficult to imitate. The stable growth and the cost advantage attracts investors and makes it easier for the company to choose the appropriate investors for itself.
5. Loyal investors behave like partners. They stabilize the system and lower the cost of capital, and guarantee cash flow back into the business, to pay for investments that will increase the potential for creating the value of the marina.

Quality of Service in Marinas

In order to examine the theory that one can predict overall satisfaction of marina customers with the service being offered them, Raviv (2001), examined general service factors previously mentioned by Parasuraman et al (1985), (as well as in articles from 1988 and 1991), factors specific to marina services, and the customer's perception of value for money. Below is a breakdown of a regression analysis in which the dependent variable is overall satisfaction. We introduced 12 items – independent variables – into the prediction formula:

1. Five overall satisfaction factors, which emerged from studies of overall satisfaction in the United States (Parasuraman *et al.*, 1985): Tangibles, Reliability, Responsiveness, Assurance, and Empathy.
2. Six satisfaction factors specific to marinas, which emerged from a factor analysis reported previously: Safety and professionalism, the value of parking, the value of the members' club, environmental quality and cleanliness, density, and ease of access.
3. The factor of value for money.

In the preliminary study conducted by Raviv (2001), a stepwise square regression analysis[8] was conducted to examine which items predict satisfaction from the service among marina customers. It can be seen that despite the representation of each of the areas in prediction of satisfaction, not all of the areas predict satisfaction significantly. The results of the regression indicate that four of the independent variables do indeed significantly predict general satisfaction ($P<0.05$) – responsiveness, safety and professionalism, crowding, and value for money.

---

8 The method was selected as the research was to examine the construction of a model and not examination of the model.

Ranking of the influence according to the Beta scores[9] indicates that satisfaction with the service can actually be predicted according to the following factors (in order of influence):

- Value for money
- Responsiveness
- Crowding
- Safety and professionalism

In another section of the same study (questionnaire), <u>the participants were asked to rank 11 service items in order of importance to them</u>. The following is the results of the ranking:

Ranking of importance of service items

Item

Staff professionalism

Value for money

Facilities

Ease of access to shore

Credibility of staff

Staff responsiveness

Faith in staff

Concern

Environmental protection

Leisure & entertainment options

Status marina offers

As can be seen in the table, the most important service item is staff professionalism (average ranking = 4.02). The second most important item is value for money (average ranking = 4.11), and the third most important item is the marina facilities (average ranking = 4.71).

In contrast, it can be seen that the least important item is the status the marina offers (average ranking = 8.17), and the third least important item is environmental protection (average ranking = 6.62).

Although a Multidimensional Scaling (MDS) analysis can indicate the location of the items on the map as well as the number of dimensions required to map the items, like a factor analysis, it cannot indicate or conceptualize the dimension. In both factor analysis and mapping, the conceptualization

---

9   Beta was standardized using the following standard formula: Beta = B regression coefficient multiplied by the ratio: standard deviation of the independent variable divided the standard deviation of the dependent variable.

of the factor/dimension remains in the hands of the researcher.

In the map, the two dimensions are named as the researcher saw fit:

The horizontal dimension indicates the dimension of the importance of the factor as perceived by the participant. The three most important items according to the ranking in the previous table: Professionalism, value for money, and facilities, appear at the left end of the map, and indicate the most important items in the opinion of the customers.

The three least important items, according to the participants: Status granted by the marina, entertainment opportunities, and environmental preservation, appear between the extreme right and the center of the map, and indicate the items of least importance to the customers. If the items are read in order from left to right, the list is similar to the ranking of importance reported above.

Apparently the first (horizontal) dimension, around which the items of service in the opinion of the participants are organized, is the dimension of the importance of the areas: They are arranged from left to right – from the most to the least important.

The vertical dimension is more difficult to conceptualize. We can see that whereas value for money, facilities, and caring on the part of the staff of the marina are at the bottom of the map, ease of access and the professionalism of the marina staff are located on the upper part of the map. One way of conceptualizing this dimension is from "open" items that are easy to identify (value for money, facilities, caring on the part of the staff) to "hidden" items, which are difficult to identify at first glance (ease of access and professionalism of staff).

Another interesting finding is that value for money is seen as most closely related to facilities (tangibles). Apparently, to the participants in the study, the facilities (easy to identify – open) have the greatest influence on their opinion of value for money, because these items are mapped in close physical proximity to value for money.

Quality of service, which was discussed in this chapter, is a result of the total of the administrative decisions and operation of the organization, which guides its activity and the direction of its progress in the environment in which it operates. This definition suits the definition of Michael Peri (1991), of the term "strategic management," which is discussed in the next chapter.

STRATEGIC MANAGEMENT AND STRATEGIC MODELS

What is strategy? In the literature, there is no uniformity of opinion regarding the meaning of the term "strategy." Knowledgeable people who have tried to describe the process of strategic thinking and planning have defined it in various ways, which basically include similar values: Michael Peri (1991), defined the term strategy (which means "general" in Greek) as "a series of decisions, actions, and allocation of resources, which determines the organization's place and the direction of its progress of the in the environment in which it operates."

In contrast, Yair Aharoni (1997), in his examination of the components of strategy, emphasized the element of "balance among: (1) the opportunities and risks in the environment, (2) the resources and abilities in the firm, and (3) personal values and ambitions" as a major stage in the formulation of strategy, which precedes the implementation stage.

According to Porter (1991), strategy is a direction of activity, or long-term planning, which is designed to fulfill the goals of the organization. Hamel (1991), on the other hand, maintains that it is important to distinguish between the concepts of planning and strategizing. According to him, the concept of planning relates to thinking from the present forward, thinking that outlines ways of reaching the anticipated future, whereas the concept of strategizing relates to thinking from the future backward.

Based these definitions, the concept of strategic planning contains an internal contradiction. According to Hamel, strategic planning means that an organization must define where it wants to be at the end of a target period, and to plan its steps to reach this future.

As Van Der Heijden (1996), puts it, what is necessary is the ability to conduct "strategic conversations" – thinking about possible scenarios, and the flexibility to change means of operation to reflect the changing business environment, and to adapt the chosen strategy to these changes.

All these scholars agree that a process of formulating strategy is the only process likely to lead the company toward its goal.

The concept of **strategic planning** originated in the 1950s, and became popular in large companies until the mid-1970s. During this period, there was an increasing belief that strategic planning could solve any problem. In the 1980s, the spotlight was diverted from strategic planning as a result of the emergence of additional planning theories, which did not provide better results.

Since the 1990s, strategic planning has once again become popular, and is being used increasingly in various areas in most companies.

Business strategy is designed to achieve the company's target and goals (maximum profit for the shareholders, maximum survival, good reputation, etc.), and it generally does so by putting the company in the strongest competitive position possible in its environment. The business environments change throughout the entire life cycle of the product, so the business strategy is also supposed to be in a dynamic process of trial and adaptation.

Kotler & Armstrong (1993) define the term business strategy as, "a process to develop and maintain the strategic alignment between an organization's targets and its changing marketing opportunities. It is based on determining a clear task for the company, setting appropriate targets, designing a well-structured business portfolio, and development of adjusted functional strategies."

Strategic management was defined in the book by Fred (1986), as a process that includes three stages: (1) Strategy formulation – developing a vision; characterizing the external environments (with a focus on opportunities and threats), and the internal environments (locating the strengths and weaknesses); formulating goals; locating, identifying, and evaluating alternative strategies; and selecting a specific strategy, (2) Strategy implementation, and (3) Strategy evaluation.

The changes that take place in the business strategy over time directly influence the **functional strategies**, among them the marketing, operations, and human resources management strategies.

The planning of business strategy begins with the **gathering of information and the analysis of the business environment**. In light of the company's resources and its administrative values, the goals of the company and the horizon of its activity are posited, as well as the goals of introducing the new product.

According to Dan Galai and Lior Hillel (1989), the company should gather information about: (1) the needs of potential customers, (2) the market potential, (3) the characteristics of the customers, (4) the competitors and the competitive environment, (5) the technological environment, (6) the funding environment, and (7) the broader environment (i.e., economic, political).

According to Eisenhardt & Sull (2001), the strategy should be specific and simple, and the critical aspect is the implementation – the best strategy is of no value if it is not properly implemented. Proper implementation depends on the ability of the management to introduce the strategy to its employees, and the simplicity of the strategy helps the management do so.

According to Gadish and Gilbert (2001), the way to implement strategy in the field is based on formulating a strategic principle, and a correct strategic principle is simple. Simplicity and brevity are the basic requirements for a scientific explanation.

According to the principle of Occam's Razor, if there are two explanations for a phenomenon – the simpler one is the valid one (Wilson, 1998). In other words, a model should be very simple, and should include a minimal number of rules and assumptions. In addition, a strategic model should be clear and measurable.

There are various approaches to strategy, from which it is possible to derive the following conditions, as conditions for effective strategy:

a. Efficiency – the way in which resources are used in order to produce value for the product or service.
b. Uniqueness – a focus of attraction for customers, although it is not necessarily the competitive advantage.
c. Fitness – the components of the strategy must suit one another, and not cause opposing or clashing feelings.
d. Profit accelerators – a strategy must contain within it a system that increases the company's growth rate. There are four types of profit accelerators:

1. High yields (through the network effect, positive feedback, or learning).
2. Blocking competitors (getting ahead of competitors, creating areas of marketing leadership or attracting customers).

3. Strategic savings (through size, focus, or scope).
4. Strategic flexibility (ability to innovate and flexibility in operation).

For the purpose of building the strategic model in this study, we examined the possibility of presenting the model visually, in order to make it simpler for marina managers who are not skilled in analyzing strategic models to understand what they must implement during the analysis and the strategic planning. For that purpose, the following models were examined:

1. Methods of strategic planning through a one-way process of constructing a formal plan, using descriptive strategic models.
2. Methods of strategic planning with a market orientation, which deal with the analysis and mapping a mix of company products, or a mix of its services, and an analysis of the portfolio.
3. Methods of strategic planning based mainly on dialogue about possible scenarios.

Descriptive Models

Descriptive models are methods of strategic planning by means of a one-way process of constructing a formal program. A strategic model, according to Hamel (1991), includes four bases:

1. Contact with customers – the point of contact between the organization and its customers. The points of contact are the means of distribution of the product or the service, and the place where the prices are presented to the customer and the policy of customer contacts is implemented.
2. The core strategy – the main elements around which the business is built. Every business must define its vision and the areas in which it is involved. The competitive advantage is the area in which we are better than others, the differentiation that enables us to distinguish our company from the competitors. The basket of products supports the mission, the vision, and the advantage. The link between the core strategy and the interface with the customer must be useful to the customer. This usefulness should be maximized completely and systematically.
3. Strategic resources are resources with which it is possible to conduct the core strategy, resources such as the core competencies, strategic assets (both tangible and intangible), processes, and human capital in the organization. The link between the core strategy and the strategic resources determines the configuration of the company, which is the way in which it operates in order to achieve its goal.
4. The value chain – the external factors with which the organization comes into contact in order to expand its boundaries. Partnerships and alliances can, for example, add knowledge to the organization and reduce costs, as well as expand the boundaries of the company. The link between the strategic resources and the value chain determines the boundaries of the company.

A strategic model that makes it possible to position the organization relative to the competitors and the environment is the SWOT model: According to this model, an organization must identify its internal strengths and weaknesses, as well as the threats and opportunities of the external environment. In order to analyze the threats and opportunities, the organization must analyze both its distant and immediate external environment.

To analyze strengths and weaknesses, the organization must analyze its internal environment, in other words, the company profile. A strategy according to the SWOT model must take advantage of opportunities, neutralize threats, base itself on internal strength, and reduce the effect of its weaknesses.

One of the strategic models for analyzing the external environment is the PEST model (Porter, 1980). According to this model, the external environment should be analyzed according to several factors: The political, economic, social, and technological environments. Similarly, the environment of the organization can be presented as comprising 10 sectors (Samuel, 1996), the four principal ones being: Technological, economic, human resources, and political. A change in one of them affects the balance of the organization, and obligates it to adjust its strategy.

Porter's Five Forces Model (Porter, 1980), is a strategic model for analyzing the industry in which the organization operates, and it assumes the existence of five main forces that affect the degree of competitiveness in the industry: Barriers to entry and exit, bargaining power of buyers, supplier power, threat of substitutes, and existing competitive rivalry between suppliers in the industry.

A famous strategic model for analyzing the internal environment of an organization, i.e., the company profile, is the value chain model (Porter, 1980). According to this model, one does an in-depth analysis of both the main and the supporting activities in the organization; each activity should affect the value of the product/service provided by the organization.

Models with a Market Orientation

Models with a market orientation are tools for analyzing and mapping a mix of company products or a mix of its services in a portfolio analysis. The results produced by the analysis and the mapping serve as a strategic decision-making process in accordance with the situation.

The BCG matrix was developed by the Boston Consulting Group in the 1960s. It evaluates the products or services of the company along two dimensions: The company's relative market share and the market growth rate of the industry.

A product with low growth and high market share is a cash cow, i.e., a product from which the company generates cash, which it invests in other products. A product with a high growth and high market share is a star. Stars use large amounts of cash, but also generate large amounts of cash. A product with a low market share and a high industry growth rate is a question mark – it may succeed in attaining a market share and become a star, but it may fail. A product with low growth and low market share is what is known as a dog, which constitutes a cash trap because of a problematic competitive position and a problematic market.

Another model is the McKinsey Matrix (Grant, 2001), which classifies the strategic business units in a specific company according to the attractiveness of the industry and their competitive position in the company. In addition, the model presents the size of the business units in the company through a frontal presentation of circles of various sizes, which indicates the size of the product's market share.

A similar model, the GE Matrix, presents the business units three-dimensionally, and makes it possible to see where the center of gravity is located, and what strategy is required for each business unit. The model presents the business units on two dimensions: The competitive strength of the business unit and the market attractiveness over the long term. On the dimensions, the market share of the various business units is illustrated by circles of various size, and in addition, the market share of the company is displayed as a section of the circle, with the angle of the section reflecting the trend in the company.

Another model that examines a company's basket of products or services is the "core and environmental" model, which classifies the company products into two main groups: Core products and environmental products (Grant, 2001).

A core product is one from which the company generates revenue. It is the main product from which the company has to make a profit. An environmental product is a by-product of the core product, which helps it to survive, or strengthens it. Since there is no "black and white," the classification of the products is done sequentially (0-1). The closer the product is to 1 (core product), the greater the expectation that its profit rate will be high.

A complementary product, on the other hand, can also cause losses since it supports the sale of the core products. In the final analysis, the model makes it possible to draw a line of anticipated profitability from any product along the sequence, and to examine which products "fall" below this line, which require improvement or removal from the basket.

Another model classifies the products in the basket in to three groups: Anchor, differentiation, variety (Grant, 2001). The assumption in the model is that every company must examine its product basket and try to have products of at least two types out of the three.

A similar model is "the seven departments" model (Grant, 2001). The model divides the product basket into five groups, so if a product does not belong to one of them, it belongs to the sixth group, that of products that need to be removed from the basket: The seven departments are: Anchors, anti-anchors (products that are a response to the products of competitors), "me too" products, innovative products, profitability centers, complementary products, and supporting products.

Some of the strategies are suitable for a group of companies, and not for a single company. In every market or industry, each competitor can be classified with the strategic group to which it belongs according to two main parameters: The competitor's variety of goals (the target sectors it addresses) and the competitor's strategic strength (Peri, 1999).

Focus Models

Kaplan & Norton (2001), present strategic models as a dialogue about specific scenarios in the organization, and recommend implementing a system of monitoring and evaluation of the chosen strategy in the organization under study, and adapting it to the changing business environment.

Menipaz (1999), presents a paradigm for leaders of strategy. This is a graduated process of constructing the strategy according to a formula focused on the specific company, providing precise instructions as to the tasks the leaders of strategy must perform at each stage.

According to the researcher, there are three levels of tasks: Constructing a strategic infrastructure, developing the strategy, and implementing it.

In summary, we can see that there are various methods for building strategic models, which can be roughly divided in to three groups:

1. Methods of strategic planning through a one-way process of constructing a formal plan that uses descriptive strategic models.
2. Methods of strategic planning with a market orientation, which deal with the analysis and mapping of a mix of company products, or a mix of its services, and an analysis of the portfolio.
3. Methods of strategic planning are based on dialogue about possible scenarios.

All the aforementioned strategic models and approaches were designed to help the organization to achieve its goals. As noted, we assume that there are strategic factors that affect the dependent variable, which serves as a measure for achieving the goal of the organization, or a measure for assessing its operations.

The next chapter describes studies on the subject of marinas, and immediately following it is a discussion of the index of use (which is the dependent variable in the study) and strategic factors that are likely to affect the capacity index. These two chapters will enable us to offer research theories and a strategic model for examination.

Studies on the Subject of Marina Management

There is a substantial body of literature concerning strategic business models, but very little that deals with models for managing marinas. It should be noted that no strategic business model exists in the field.

In effect, the paucity of material reflects the situation on the ground, and the absence of a model for marinas leaves marinas managers without guidelines relevant to their specific industry. A summary of the research literature was presented at the economic conference in Arles, France (Raviv, 1999), and included four practical studies on the subject:

1. A socioeconomic study (Talheim, 1993).
2. A study on the subject of segmentation (Perales, 1998).
3. An economic study that examines government expenditure (Stynes, 1999).
4. A study on the subject of supply and demand, which examines capacity rate (Talheim et al., 1998).

At this conference, it was proposed to formulate a strategic business model for marinas as a pioneering study on the subject.

Talheim *et al.* (1998), described the situation of marinas in Michigan (U.S.), during the last two decades of the 20th century. They report on stable capacity during the 1980s, which led to the construction of additional marinas. The demand seemed to increase with the supply, "When new marinas were built, customers readily appeared" (Talheim *et al.*, 1998).

At the end of the decade, occupancy began to decline, and the authors tried to understand the changes in use, through a study of the market segmentation of marina users. The prevailing philosophy was "Build it and they will come," but over time, the waiting list for anchorage places turned in to a list of vacant anchorage slips.

At this stage, market analysis became an important component in the development of marinas and the renewal of the existing ones. The study demonstrated that the proper products (services and facilities) should be built in the right places, at the right time, and at a reasonable price. Because of the differences between users of the marinas, the overall need for anchorage slips is no guarantee that one marina or another will have good occupancy.

The authors point out that despite the changing conditions (more marinas, preferable location, in this case a general move northward, the fact that the fishermen had left the marinas), there are marinas that "have got it," and the question is, how can "it" be described. It was clear that users choose a marina first and foremost according to the services it provides.

Marketing philosophy maintains that market segmentation is one of the ways to transmit information to producers, but the problem in the marina industry is that there is no classification of the products and the market segments.

Yacht owners do not want only a storage place for their yacht. The marina is a reflection of socio-economic status, the yacht owner's stage in life, and his lifestyle. The marina affects the leisure time activity, the social ties, and perhaps even the business connections of its users. From that point of view, i.e., an economic and social analysis, the authors recommend examining the marinas based on the services they provide, and adapting them to potential consumers.

A study done for the marine routes division of the U.S. Army Corps of Engineers (Perales, 1998), examined the economic effects of those using the water lanes on the projects of the U.S. Army Corps of Engineers.

The researcher examined two market segments according to the type of permits issued – an anchorage permit in the project and anchorage in the marina. The model used was an engineering model of input/output, and it was designed to serve as a tool to guide policy regarding expansion, reduction, or change in the demand for the activity on the site. The study attempted to examine the changes in the use of the site by visitors, as a means of learning about economic changes in the region.

A Taxonomy of Marina Strategic Models

Study	Overall approach	Unit examined	Independent variables	Dependent variables	Analytic approach
Talheim 1993	Socioeconomic input/output	Profile of visitors	Population: age, income. Value of assets. Self-report on quality of life. Allocation of public funding. Patterns of movement flow.	Socioeconomic effect	Weighing and sampling of variables
Perales 1998	Market segmentation	Visitors segment	Profile of expenditures, renting: sailing and anchoring, fees for storage, and insurance.	Economic effect	Market segmentation
Stynes 1999	Economic output/input	Visitor profile	Sailing: point of origin, number of people, expenditures.	Government expenditures	Market segmentation
Talheim *et al.*, 1998	Supply and demand	Services at location	Services: maintenance and repairs, winter storage, fueling, anchorage capacity, bathrooms, and parking lots.	Percentage of occupancy	Market segmentation

In summary, in a world in which there are various approaches to strategy in general, and criticism of the need/ability of strategic planning in particular, we prefer to focus on a particular strategy: A strategy that will focus the marina as it is in today's reality – a leisure time business – with the resulting need for a business strategy.

Without a strategic framework, the study of the subject would have lacked direction, and the administrative aspects of marina managers would have remained open to intuitive preferences of a local director. A review of the literature reveals several attempts at models for managing marinas, but none of them is empirically based or inclusive, like the model that should be developed and validated.

OCCUPANCY AT THE MARINA AS A DEPENDENT VARIABLE

The dependent variable of the study is the index of occupancy at the marina. This variable is a proxy variable for profitability, which will not be examined in the context of this study. Most of the marinas in the world are privately owned: They are not required to publish their business results, and marinas managers are not interested in reporting on them publicly.

A proper business model should be based on the variable of the goal of the organization – profit as an index of the effectiveness of the marina (which is run for profit). Since this index is unavailable, and since there are marinas that were not built essentially for profit, the researcher decided to use the index of occupancy.

Occupancy is directly related to profit, as a substantial percentage of a marina's income stems from the fees for use of the marina paid by all the boat owners who anchor in it. Given the fact that the literature does not contain a scientific index for marina occupancy, the researcher has developed an occupancy index that expresses the rate of occupancy as the ratio between the number of boats anchored and the anchorage capacity at the marina.

The use of the occupancy index is common in hotels as well, with the index expressed as the ratio between the number of rooms occupied and the total number of rooms in the hotel. There are hotels that use a serial model to calculate the occupancy index, which includes a reference to prices, to the length of the customer's stay, and to the capacity of the hotel. The occupancy index in hotels must also take into consideration the demands of the business environment of the hotel.

To enable an effective measurement of the managerial efficiency, a distinction must be made between the increase in occupancy stemming from operative changes and that resulting from an increase in environmental demands. The goal of the marina managers, like that of managers of hotels, parking lots, etc., is to reach an occupancy index as close as possible to 1 (100 percent), since the higher the index, the higher the income.

As is the case in every industry, reaching a high occupancy index, demands alignment between supply and demand. The same is true in a marina: There must be alignment between demand (the number and type of boats that want to anchor) and supply ("the anchorage basket"). Marina managers can control the supply by planning the marina.

Planning the Capacity of the Marina

Planning the marina includes planning the number of slips, as well as the "anchorage basket," in other words, the size of the slips and the number of slips of each type. This planning, in effect, determines the marina's capacity for boats.

Drawing 1 illustrates the plan of the anchorage basket of the Herzliya marina, which includes 800 places for boats between 23 and 131 feet in length.

Work Plan – Herzliya Marina

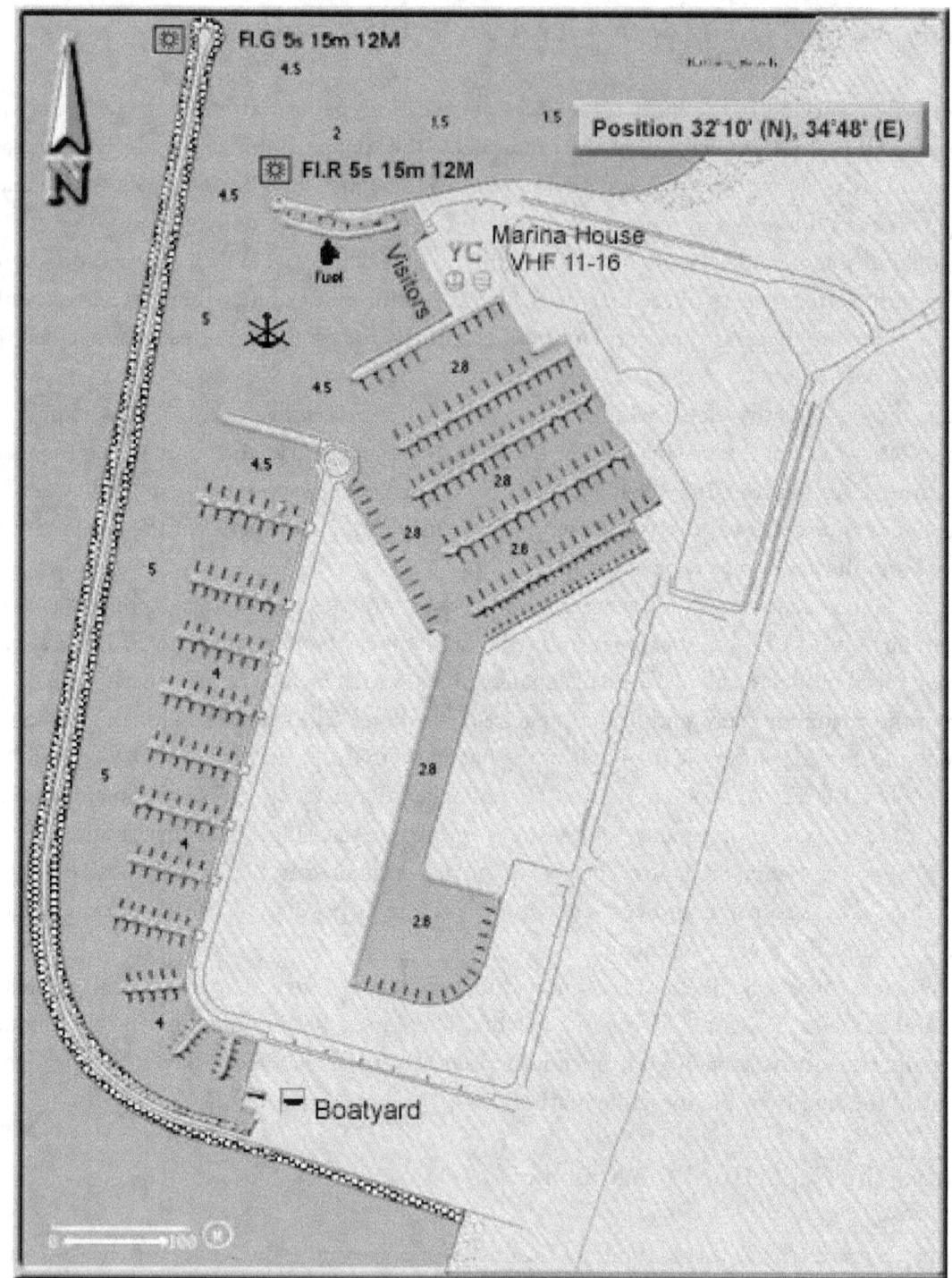

In planning a marina, capacity should be planned based on a forecast of demand by the various market sectors in the target audience. The number and types of boats that will anchor should be estimate, and the capacity of the marina and the "anchorage basket" should be planned accordingly.

To this end, an orderly list of past data should be compiled and external studies and databases (such as collecting information about those with boating licenses in the country, the expected number of those completing courses to obtain boating licenses, the marine education industry and its market potential, the number of vessels manufactured or imported, and the waiting list for anchorage slips in existing marinas) should be used.

A similar forecast according to segments began in the airline industry when the airlines offered different products to different customers. These products, such as a flight in a Concorde for target audiences who wanted to fly from London to New York in four hours, were usually limited to narrow the choices of a specific market segment and to prevent the leakage of customers from one segment to another.

In an analogy to marinas, there is the anchorage basket for "mega yachts", over 82 feet long, or marinas for small boats, no larger than 65 feet.

In planning capacity, the operational manager in the organization must ascertain that the available resources (area, people, infrastructure, work hours, etc.) can provide the required capacity in the required time (Jarvis, 2002). Management of capacity, in other words, implementing change in capacity, depends on the degree of flexibility. If a change in capacity can be made only over the long term, capacity planning is a strategic step (similar to warehouses, hospitals, and factories).

If a change in capacity can be made in the middle range, there is a need for periodical management, which involves future forecasts and adjusting capacity to the forecast. If there is maximum flexibility (a change can be implemented in the short range), there is a need for ongoing management, with the capacity manager adjusting current demand to current supply.

Planning of capacity in service organizations differs from such planning in organizations that manufacture durable goods (Smith, 1989). Whereas in manufacturing organizations, inventory can be produced and saved for future high demand, in service organizations there is no possibility of meeting future demand. Therefore, in service organizations, capacity must be planned to meet extreme situations (peak condition) in which they want to meet demand, and for that purpose, suitable infrastructure must be constructed.

A 70 percent use of maximum capacity in service organizations is generally considered optimal (Smith, 1989). This rate enables a reasonable use of resources, as well as high quality service to the customers. However, the optimal rate of use depends on the service. If the level of uncertainty and the maximum capacity are high, the rate of use (or occupancy) will be low.

For example, hospitals must plan for a low occupancy rate in the intensive care units, because of the great uncertainty and the nature of the activity. In contrast, organizations in which the level of certainty is high, such as train services or mail services, can plan for 100 percent occupancy.

It is important to note that the assumed relationship between occupancy and profit is not a direct one, but instead an asymptotic relationship with a "hump" facing the positive side of profit/occupancy (negatively skewed). This is because, on the one hand, full occupancy is perceived by customers as overcrowding, with no room to maneuver. On the other hand, full occupancy does not leave marina management with the room for maneuvering required to allow visitors' or tourists' boats to anchor, even if they are not members of the marina. Visitors and tourists may pay a higher price and provide better profit per service than a marina member.

In short, we believe that the occupancy rate is likely to be a very good reflection of the profitability goal of the marina. Consequently, this study will examine the impact of the strategic influence factors (which are discussed in the next chapter) on the occupancy index.

Strategic Influence Factors: The Independent Variables

This study assumes that a number of strategic factors affect marina occupancy and, in turn, its profitability. These factors were chosen after the exploratory study, which is explained in detail in the section on research methods.

The View at the Marina

It can be assumed that the view is important in deciding where to live, selecting a vacation site, and choosing an anchorage place. People's attraction to beauty and to a good view creates the great demand for residential and office buildings with a view, and raises the price of the apartments or the offices on the upper floors. For the same reason, there is a greater demand in hotels for rooms with a view, and this accounts for the additional cost of a room with a view of the sea.

In studies of the landscape in parking lot areas, it was found that if possible, parking areas should be isolated by bushes and shade trees, which can reduce the amount of heat rising from the asphalt (Dale, 1994). If we treat the marina as a parking lot for sailing vessels, vessels that anchor for most of the year in a covered area are better preserved, their color does not fade and the equipment on them lasts for years.

There has recently been a trend toward designing and landscaping parking lots to make them less obtrusive in residential areas, and to create a friendlier environment (Dale, 1994).

There has also been development in the design and planning of forests. Instead of considering landscape a natural factor that cannot be changed, it turns out that the landscape of forests can be designed mechanically. For example, in many areas where the landscape is a natural forest, it is possible, after a long period and using various means (by replanting trees, paving roads, and the like) to create an area that is convenient and accessible for tourists and hikers (such as the work done by the Jewish National Fund in Israel over the past decade).

The purpose of landscape planning is to create a balance between human needs and nature. Although many factors affect the environment (including a construction master plan, size of the population, and future growth rate, rate of land use, animals, ecological systems, the horizon, highways and roads, and more), the landscape and environment can be changed. This is a long and multi-stage process; however, through redesigning, the existing landscape can be fully exploited and improved. Of course, the various parts that comprise the landscape should not be seen in isolation. We should examine how they combine with one another, while creating a balance between man and nature.

The strategic model in this study assumes that the more beautiful the view from the marina and to the marina, the higher the occupancy index.

The view that can be seen from the marina and toward it, as well as the design of the marina, play an important role in creating the beauty and aesthetics of the marina, and constitute a source of attraction for potential customers.

Government Intervention and Regulations Affecting the Marina

It can be assumed that the method of operation of every organization and its profitability rate are affected by the local rules and regulations (Zeghal *et al.*, 1999). The marina, as a business organization in every sense, is also subject to rules and regulations.

An examination of this subject indicates three main influence groups for rules and regulations concerning marinas (Weiss, 2001):

1. The effect of municipal, national, and international rules and regulations on the business results of the marina.
2. The effect of rules and regulations (anchored or not anchored in law) that relate to the relationship between the marina and its employees on the marina's business results.
3. The effect of the contracts between the marina and its customers on the marina's business results.

The Influence of Rules and Regulations

The first influence group includes rules that the marina must follow as part of the amendments to national and international laws in various areas, such as environmental quality. In this context, the marina is obligated to provide containers for the collection of oils, systems for the clearing of dirty water, and bathrooms and showers for visitors, in accordance with the Ports Authority laws (Ports Authority, 2002).

This influence group also includes international conventions signed by various countries (such as the MARPOL 73/78 Convention for the prevention of marine pollution), as well as various municipal bylaws, such as property tax laws, a business permit fee, a sign fee, and a radio fee. An overall look at this influence group shows that marina managers have very little ability to control the level of expenditures that they must pay as a result of these rules and regulations.

A study on the effect of regulations of this type on the shift of users from one marina to another indicates that for 85 percent of the respondents, this issue had no effect on the decision (Raviv, 2003).

Laws Affecting the Relationship Between the Marina and its Employees

This influence group includes a number of subgroups:

a. The first subgroup includes rules and regulations imposed on the marina by employer-employee laws in every country (for example, in Israel, National Insurance laws, compensation for in-service courses, employer liability, etc.). In this subgroup, too, the influence of the marina manager is limited, as s/he cannot ignore or violate these laws. The study mentioned in the previous section (Raviv, 2003), also demonstrates that the quality of the service provided at the marina is not a function of salary, but of various other types of compensation, and therefore, this subgroup has no significant influence on marina results.

b. The second subgroup includes the various procedures and regulations that the marina implements for the purpose of its own administration. This group changes from marina to marina. However, it can be argued that this item does not constitute a significant economic burden on the marina either, because these rules are made by it, and are taken into account at the stage of its financial planning.
c. The third subgroup includes regulations imposed by the marina on its employees, in an attempt to improve the level of service that they provide the customer. These regulations are also internal regulations, and they include service workshops, trips, lectures, *et al.*, but as opposed to the second subgroup, these regulations constitute a certain burden on the marina's budget. However, a link was found between improving the level of service at the marina and a rise in its level of income.

The effect of the second group of regulations (internal procedures) on the profitability of the marina demonstrates that the only situation in which this group has an influence is when the procedures are designed to improve the marina's level of service. In that case, the customers react positively, and there is an increase in occupancy at the marina, which leads to an increase in its profitability as well.

Contracts Between the Marina and its Customers

The third influence group includes the nature of the relationships and contracts between the marina and its customers. The anchorage agreements between the users and the marina can be included in this group. A study (Raviv, 2003) conducted in this field found no connection between the anchorage contract and its degree of "friendliness", and the marina's income level. It should also be noted that there is a great similarity between the various anchorage agreements in marinas the world over, and that most of the agreements are based on identical principles.

External rules and regulations imposed on the marina by the laws of the country and by international conventions influence the income level, and therefore, the level of profitability. In light of this, it can be assumed that the greater the number of regulations, the lower the profitability of the marina, as a result of the costs involved in complying with the regulations.

Crowding at the Marina

In a limited area there are two forces at work – a desire to maximize use of the area and a desire to avoid undermining the level of service and the required safety level.

In parking lots in the United States, there is currently a trend to reduce the parking area per car, given the increasing trend of replacing large cars with compacts (Dale, 1994). There are still parking lots that are built according to old standards, but the result of not updating the present standard is additional areas that are not used for parking. In some parking lots, places are marked for compact cars, and when a large vehicle has to park, a double parking area has to be vacated for it, and space is wasted. In other parking lots, the preference is not to mark parking places, but then a safety problem is created, since they are not strict about the necessary passages and space.

At marinas, in contrast, the trend is toward an increase in the dimensions of the sailing vessels: The length of the average boat that anchors in Israeli marinas has changed over the years, and if in the past the average length was 39 feet, today it is 49 feet (Raviv, 2001).

The assumption in the model developed in this paper is that crowding has a negative effect on customer satisfaction, and therefore, reduces the number of boats that anchor. In other words, assuming that the index of occupancy = the number of boats anchored relative to the total number of slip areas, crowding reduces the index. On the other hand, however, increasing the crowding of the slips leads to a more efficient use of the water area in the marina. Therefore, if we define:

The occupancy index = the water area in which the boats anchor (the number of boats x the size of the average boat [length x width]) relative to the water area, then we will expect that the more crowded the marina, the higher the index.

It is possible that this index is related to profit not directly, but as a curve. On the one hand, the more boats that occupy the anchorage area, the higher the income of the marina. And on another hand, crowding beyond a certain point can (unless there are adequate planning solutions) become a nuisance for sailors and causes dissatisfaction with the service, and result in a decline in the number of customers who turn to the marina and/or the level of prices the marina can demand.

The Level of Associated Services at the Marina

According to Miller (1991), services that are associated with a product or a main service help promote sales and create customer loyalty. Business managers who know their customers can identify their special needs and improve the level of services offered them, and in turn, expand their business. Providing services that exceed customer expectations creates long-term customer loyalty.

The importance of the level of associated services is gaining currency at the level of local services and that of international services (Wong & Perry, 1999). Today, in the global business world, businesses have difficulty finding a competitive advantage that will enable them to confront competing firms in the industry. An organization must differentiate itself, provide a unique service or product, and be the best in the world for that product/service ("Best in World Capabilities") (Quinn *et al.*, 1997).

One of the strategies that has been proven to be related to the success of differentiation is the provision of high-quality services. In studies, a positive correlation has been found between the quality of service and the organization's performance, on the one hand, and its position among competitors, on the other (Anderson *et al.*, 1994).

When quality of services become a substantial part of the business operation, the ability to measure and examine the effectiveness of the services offered is important. This information is particularly important for managers during the allocation of resources, because it enables them to focus on services that lived up to the customer's expectations (Wong *et al.*, 1999).

The research in this study relates to technical quality, and examines the associated services that are offered to the customer at various marinas, and their level. In the model developed in the current study, the assumption is that the level of associated services has a positive effect on the main results (by way of the occupancy index). The assumption is that the wider the entire array of services offered, the higher the level of the services.

Transportation Access to the Marina

The location and structure of transportation infrastructure is of critical importance: It is vital to plan a structure that will provide convenient access to the users. According to Raviv (2001), customers ranked accessibility as the factor that is second in importance – immediately after value for money. The roads themselves can be an important component in the process of economic development, but before building the roads, the policy of using space must be understood.

Over the past decade, a scientific engineering field dealing with planning traffic and measuring its effects has developed (Dale, 1994). This field, called TIS (Traffic Impact Studies) is designed to solve local problems resulting from projects related to traffic in a certain area. The broader the development, the more important the need for a thorough analysis of traffic in the region. TIS studies have to answer the question: Does the traffic caused by the development have a negative effect on the level of service or safety? If there is a negative effect, the TIS study has to assess how traffic and access can be improved; capacity and the flow of traffic depend on the planning and design of the structure.

Marinas constitute an intersection of marine and land transportation. Since a marina is a tourist attraction focused on boats, but with shopping centers, places of entertainment, and restaurants surrounding it, as a land junction the marina requires proper administrative attention. A study that examined the number and location of access points found that a large number of access points in a commercial area are liable to create traffic problems (Dale, 1994). As a result, many places have imposed regulations to limit access to transportation and reduce the points of passage from the sidewalks to the road. If the number of access points are limited, there is more control, and it is possible to provide a place in the parking area that will enable cars to exit without blocking traffic and without being blocked. Any business model that is developed for a marina must, therefore, include the variable of accessibility.

The model presented in this study assumes a positive correlation between accessibility to the marina and its facilities – including access to the boat – and the occupancy index. The assumption is that easy and convenient access raises both the level of convenience and the safety level.

Safety and Security at the Marina

Since the second half of the 20th century, there has been increasing awareness of safety in places of work and entertainment. Both employees and customers have begun to pay attention to the level of safety of the organization or the site where they are located, and to judge the attitude of the organization or the site toward visitors, according to criteria of safety maintenance. The basic assumption is that safety is an inherent element of management, and if we want to promote safety, the correct and efficient way to do so is through management.

The Hebrew Even-Shoshan dictionary defines safety as: "The awareness of guarding against the danger of being hurt or the danger of damage (especially due to accidents)." This definition includes the aspect central to the concept of safety: "The awareness of guarding against…"

Modern organizations and sites are aware of the need to maintain a high level of safety, because this is directly related to the level of employee or customer satisfaction. In order to survive and thrive, every organization is required to provide goods and/or services that meet the demands and expectations of its customers, and at the same time to take in to account two additional factors:

1. Safety and employment hygiene.
1. Environmental protection.

As is reflected in the work done by occupational standards institutes in the Western world (including Israel), behind the creation of the standard for safety management, is the principle that safety is not merely a means of protection. Safety also involves policy and management, which are reflected in the involvement of the management and in the creation of norms that compare safe behavior and improper behavior, which is not accepted in the organization (Minter, 2000).

The relationship between the level of employee or visitor satisfaction and the safety level, becomes even more important in light of the fact that today, the formulators of safety rules in organizations are responsible for their operational significance. Although the purpose of the safety rules is to prevent accidents, they are also designed to prevent exposure to lawsuits. Organizations must ensure the existence of safety rules they formulate for themselves, and to be aware of their significance, otherwise they are liable to be exposed to lawsuits related to negligence, and to customer dissatisfaction.

Safety at a marina involves safety rules as they are determined by government regulations and by the regulations of the marina itself, and safety and security efforts that are meant to enforce these regulations. The assumption in this study is that the stricter the marina is about safety rules, the higher its occupancy index.

Awareness of security is also on the rise. Security is required for guarding both people and equipment. It is important to everyone to guard valuable equipment that they own, which is the reason why it is important to provide security services.

In the case of public facilities, security is required to prevent damage, dirt, destruction and the like to public facilities at the site. In a large percentage of public facilities (like parks), people stay to sleep, or alternatively, they leave their personal belongings, as is the norm at camping parks in Israel around the Sea of Galilee.

A study conducted among 2,000 hikers in one of the parks in the United States, revealed that the knowledge that the park is guarded and covered by security personnel led to a high level of perceived personal security – 93 percent.

In another study conducted in the United States, a direct relationship was found between the level of security services and the number of hikers in the park. A larger number of hikers increases income for all the groups that benefit from the hikers: Inns, hotels, restaurants, gas stations, etc. In contrast, the moment there is a decline in the sense of personal security among hikers, their numbers in the park will decline, as many will prefer to stay away (Pendleton, 2001).

The level of safety and security awareness varies among countries. It is natural, for example, that in a country where theft is common, there will be awareness of a greater need to guard equipment. Similarly, in countries exposed to terror, the awareness of the need for guarding people is higher.

In a survey conducted at marinas in the United States (Marina Survey, 1998), 57.3 percent of those asked said that their marina had been a victim of vandalism or robbery, or of crimes against individuals. They all reported having added independent means of protection in response.

In marinas, many people tend to leave their boats for a long period of time, and there are tourists who come with their boat and live on it. Therefore, personal safety and security for the boats are of great importance.

The model assumes a positive correlation between the level of safety and security and the occupancy index. The assumption is that customers will prefer to anchor in a place that provides protection for their property and their personal items and takes care of their personal welfare, and in addition, is strict about safety rules that reduce the potential for accidents.

Environmental Protection at the Marina

Environmental protection is a consequence of the interrelationship between human beings, flora and fauna and minerals, and natural and man-made environment.

Protecting the environment is part of an overall culture that also includes economic interests (Alper, 1993). For years, environmentalists and businesspeople stood on opposite sides of the barricades.

Environmentalists proposed regulations for preserving natural resources, based on capitalistic principles as well. Company managers expressed a willingness to accept monitoring of pollution and preservation of natural resources. Both sides discovered that they have a common interest that served as a basis for working together.

The increasing awareness of environmental protection is reflected in many ways: an increase in the number of organizations working to protect the environment, an increase in the number of conservation laws legislated in various countries around the world, an increase in the environmental protection regulations, and the number of companies with such regulations, an increase in public awareness of recycling, and more.

In the marine area, environmental protection is of great importance, and in this regard the marinas arouse much debate. Marinas harm the environment, and their location should be considered carefully. The damage caused by a marina is direct, such as the leakage of oils and other material from the yachts that anchor at the marina, and indirectly, including the destruction of beaches (Klein, 1996).

There is a direct correlation between marinas and the destruction of beaches (Mintz, 1996). Marinas prevent the shifting of sands and damaging beaches near them, which causes erosion mainly on the northern side of the marinas in Israel.

Additional evidence of this can be found in Spain, which suffers from the disappearance of sand on its beaches as a consequence of the project to construct ports and marinas. Fischelson (1998), describes the marina as a "wart" that spreads over its entire surroundings, not only on a coastal strip of 1-2 miles, but in the area near the sea as well. The structures at the marina prevent rainwater, that collects, from flowing out to sea. This rainwater, which carries with it part of the city materials that contain hazardous substances, is absorbed into the ground near the marina instead of being dumped into the sea. In this way, all the toxic materials are absorbed in the ground and pollute it.

In terms of health, Fischelson (1998), claims that a marina causes the destruction of the ecological system of flora and fauna, because every marina is a center of mechanical activity. The yachts leak fuel, oils, and poisonous gases. Most of the toxic materials are absorbed in the ground, by the animals, and in the food chain. The poisoned water in the marina destroys the surrounding environment of flora and fauna.

In light of the great awareness of the subject of environmentalism and the desire of customers to be part of an environment that is not polluted or polluting, the assumption made in the strategic model presented in this study is that the more the marina engages in environmental protection, the higher the occupancy index. The assumption is that the degree of influence of this factor on the occupancy index will steadily increase as awareness of the importance of environmental protection increases.

Distance from Competitors

Monitoring the entry of competition into markets for sustainable good reveals that competition forces players to improve the level of the products or services they provide based on market demand, in order to meet the changing demands of the customer.

In their study, Anderson *et al.* (1994), present a situation in which the presence of a number of competitors in geographical proximity are likely to increase the sales of each competitor. The very fact that several competitors are concentrated in one place leads to an increase in the level of interest of potential customers, because of their expectation of a higher level of service due to the existence of competition.

Proximity to the Customer

The distance in miles between the marina and the nearest major city.

The Local Community

The attitude of the local community toward the marina, as influenced by the activity of the marina: environmental protection, landscape, activities of marine culture and education, activities for the general population, boating competitions, and more.

In summary, this chapter has presented the 10 strategic factors believed likely to affect occupancy at the marina.

In the next chapter, these influence factors are placed in a strategic model, which will be designed as a tool to help marina managers make decisions.

RESEARCH HYPOTHESES

Methodology

This chapter presents the methodology used to research the hypotheses presented in the previous chapter. This chapter reviews the populations that participated in the study and the method for data collection and analysis. This chapter also presents the steps taken to protect study participants and adherence to ethical guidelines.

The Research Population

Marina managers from all over the world participated in the study. A "manager" is defined as someone who actively manages the marina, makes operational and strategic decisions, and is responsible for the quality of service and the profits.

Managers were approached personally, and were told that their participation was a contribution to a university research study on the subject of marinas. The response was voluntary. Time needed to fill in the questionnaire – about 20 minutes.

Deciding on the Size of the Sample

Power Analysis (Kraemer & Thiemann, 1987), is the scientific method of determining the minimal size of the sample desirable for a study. The analysis is guided by the type of statistical analysis required by the hypotheses of the study.

The most complex statistical analysis in the study will be Structural Equations Modeling, as will be described below, and will direct the analysis of the required size of the sample according to what is required for structural equations.

The other statistical analysis will, in any case, require a smaller sample, so that determining the size of the sample according to the demands of the analysis of structural equations will determine a minimum threshold, which will suit all the rest of the statistical analyses of this study.

The use of structural equations is relatively new on the landscape of statistical tools in the social sciences (the first practical algorithms began to appear in the 1970s, as compared to other tools such as the Pearson Correlation, which was developed about 80 years earlier).

In the scientific literature, there is no clear decision regarding the preferred method of determining the size of the sample. There is a lively discussion in the literature concerning the desirable size of the sample for examining models through the use of structural equations. A substantial portion of the literature is not based on actual research outcomes (since there is still very few validated studies based on the method), but rather on Monte Carlo Simulations.

According to Bentler (1989), the size of the sample should be determined according to two ratios – the ratio between the number of variables in the model and the number of those participating in the study, and the ratio between the number of parameters for assessment in the model or in the comparison of models, and the number of participants (Tanaka, 1990).

The first distinction necessary for determining the size of the sample is the distribution of the data. Data that is distributed normally requires a smaller sample than data that is not distributed normally, and that requires non-parametrical methods of estimation. On the basis of the existing material regarding the implementation of the items of generic satisfaction (Parasuraman, 1985), it seems that normal data distribution can be assumed. In any case, researchers suggest 100 participants as the minimal number for testing models.

The approach that assesses the size of the required sample according to the ratio of variables/parameters to participants (Tanaka, 1987; Bentler, 1989), determines that the size of the sample should be assessed by the multiple of at least five participants by the number of free parameters and the factors being assessed.

In the model being tested, there are 8 factors (distance, community, location, intervention, density, environment, facilities, and occupancy) and 27 free parameters (any directional connection that points to a factor is a parameter. The first of the parameters must be fixed – not free).

Such a model produces a total of 36 parameters to be assessed. By multiplying 36 by 5, we get 180 participants, which according to Tanaka and Bentler is the minimal number of participants necessary to assess the model using structural equations.

Another approach for assessing the size of the sample is based on the fact that the index for adapting the model to the data is χ^2 (Hoelter, 1983; Bollen et al., 1988; Bentler, 1989). According to this approach, the size of the sample will be determined according to chi squared. This division comes from the level of probability that is determined for a first type error, α and the degrees of freedom – the result of the comparison between the two models, and the effect size that the research considers significant. The formula will look like this: $N = [\chi^2(\alpha, \textit{fl}\ ) \div (sizeeffect)]$.

The required size of the sample was estimated using the Ex-Sample program (Scolari, 2000), and the estimate showed that the required size of the sample is at least 77 participants (for alpha = .05. And the desired effect size = 0.5, half a point on a scale of replies from 1-5, which appears on the research questionnaire).

Researchers have also suggested a connection between the size of the sample and the "daring" of the researchers' conclusions based on the results of the analysis. In cases of small samples, the recommendation is to be very cautious about the conclusions that can be reached from the statistical analysis.

Apparently, a sample that numbers 100-180 participants is big enough to test the model. After weighing all the approaches proposed above, it was decided that the questionnaire would be sent to 200 participants.

The Sampling

To ensure proper representation for the marina managers worldwide, marinas from various regions in the world were sampled. The marinas were located over the internet, in books, and in pamphlets. Of about 15,000 marinas around the world (Raviv, 1999), questionnaires were sent to 200 managers at various marinas on five continents, in order to receive a representative sample.

The questionnaires were distributed for the most part via e-mail (where an address was available), some by fax, and additional questionnaires were distributed at the international ICOMIA conference for marina managers, held in Sydney, Australia.

Research Tools

The research tool is a questionnaire (see Appendix B) that includes:

1. An opening page. A description of the goals of the questionnaire and the sender, instructions for completing the questionnaire, an address for questions and comments, and an address for returning the questionnaire after completing it.
2. Questions to the manager. The manager is asked to assess various factors related to the marina itself (such as profitability, occupancy, crowding), and to its surroundings (such as the attitude of the local residents, the number of rules and regulations relating to the marina). The answers are placed on a Likert Scale, each question based on its content.
3. A description of the marina. The manager is asked to give numerical data (such as distance from competitors, distance from the city, number of anchorage slips). In this section, the questions are open questions, without any delineation of range of values.
4. A ranking of fulfillment of expectations. Managers are asked to rank various topics at the marina according to the degree to which their expectations were fulfilled (for example, safety and environmental protection). The ranking is on a scale of 1-5, with 1 describing a failure to fulfill expectations, and 5 describing a situation that exceeds expectations.
5. A ranking of marina infrastructure. Marina managers are asked to rank the operation of the existing infrastructures at the marina (such as fueling, maintenance and repair services) as compared to their standards (1-5). A grade of 1 expresses the inefficiency of service and infrastructure, a grade of 5 expresses a high degree of efficiency.
6. Factors influencing the profitability of the marina. Marina managers are asked to rank 15 different issues based on an estimate of their effect on the profitability of the marina. A grade of 1 means that the manager sees the factor as the most important for profitability, a grade of 15 expresses a low relationship to profitability. According to the instructions, no two factors should receive the same grade.
7. General data and remarks. Marina managers were asked to provide data about location and description of the marina (such as the name of the marina, the maximum boat length), and to feel free to add comments.

Collecting the Questionnaires

The questionnaires were returned to the researcher in the same way that they were sent. Participants who did not return the questionnaires received a reminder and another request to complete it. Some of them replied after the reminder, and some did not return the questionnaire.

Classification of the Questions According to the Variables Examined in the Study

Variable	Item No.	Content/Comments
Location of site/view	25, 26, 27	The view from the marina to the sea, from the sea to the marina, and the beauty of the design, as seen by the marina manager.
Government intervention	5, 28, 35	The number of restrictions and rules at the marina as seen by the manager.
Crowding	4, 32, 17, 19	The anchorage crowding at the marina, both as seen by the manager (4, 32) and by an estimate and assessment of the crowding index in each marina.
Associated services in the marina	38, 39, 40, 41	The quality of services provided at the marina, in addition to the anchorage itself, as seen by the manager.
Accessibility Safety and security	33, 36 2, 23, 24	The degree of access of those anchored to the marina and its facilities, the ease of entry of guests to the marina. The degree of observing safety rules and the level of guarding at the marina.

Environmental protection	3, 29, 30, 31, 34	The degree of environmental protection practiced at the marina – cleanliness of facilities, sewage and garbage services, development of the internal and external surroundings.
Distance from competitors	14, 15	Number of competing marinas in geographical proximity to the marina under study (a distance under 38 miles).
Proximity to customer	12, 13	Proximity to major city (distance in miles and traveling time).
Local community	1, 7, 21, 22	Status of marina and attitude toward it in the eyes of the nearby local residents.
Occupancy dimension (the dependent variable)	8, 9, 37, 17/18, 19/20	The occupancy rate at the marina, both according to the data of the manager and by means of estimating the occupancy dimension at each marina. In order to estimate the dependent variable, i.e., the occupancy dimension, we divided Question 18 (average number of boats anchoring at the marina) by Question 17 (the number of anchorage slips in the marina).

The dependent variable – the variable of occupancy, combines the questions of profitability (questions 8, 9, 37) with the objective questions regarding occupancy (17-20). The use of the objective questions regarding occupancy was implemented by finding the occupancy rate:

a. The ratio of the number of occupied places at the marina (question 18) to the total number of anchorage slips in the marina (question 17); and
b. The ratio of the occupied anchorage area (question 20) to the total anchorage area in the marina (question 19).

Method of Analysis of the Strategic Model

The type of statistical analysis that suits the testing of the model is a structural equations analysis, which is known in literature as Covariance Structure Modeling and (SEM) Structural Equations Modeling (Martin, 1987; Tanaka *et al.*, 1990).

Structural Equations Analysis

A structural equations analysis is currently the accepted statistical method for testing multivariable models. The method has a clear advantage over running a number of regressions (whose running increases the chances of finding a clear regression) and is preferable to Path Analysis, because it enables consideration of hidden factors in which the researcher sees structures that explain the numerical results, but are not directly predictable.

In general, an analysis of structural equations is a highly robust tool. It is safe from certain deviations arising from assumptions about the distribution of the data and from outliers, and is considered preferable for testing theoretical models to other methods of statistical analysis, such as Exploratory Analysis, Path Analysis, and Multivariable Regression Analysis. Structural Equations Analysis has a number of advantages for testing models:

1. We can separate the difference between that which stems from the contexts assumed by the theoretical model and that which stems from the methods of measuring and errors in measuring, and receive more precise assessments of the suitability of the model to the data (Bagozzi & Phillips, 1982; Huba & Harlow, 1986).
2. We can examine the explained difference with a complete model instead of focusing only on certain relationships (Huba & Harlow, 1986).
3. We can introduce changes and test them with changes in the explained difference (Bagozzi & Phillips, 1982).
4. When the data does not justify circumstantial "validation" for the model, we can compare various theoretical models and provide information about the advantage of the suitability of one model or another to the data (Huba & Harlow, 1987).

An SEM analysis is a method of estimating the gap between two series of statistical data: The first series is the measurement model, and the second is the structural model. The measurement model describes the ratio between a number of manifest variables and latent variables. Manifest variables are the scores that will be derived from the research questionnaires. In contrast, a latent variable is an assumed factor that explains the difference in the observed variables.

In an SEM analysis, two main groups of numerical results are produced. One group includes goodness-of-fit indices, which estimates the degree of coordination between the theoretical model fed into the analysis and the numerical data that was entered into the assessment. High coordination indices indicate coordination between the data observed on the ground and the theoretical model.

However, it is possible that a number of different theoretical models will fit the same data. In such a case, some of the goodness of fit indices enable the testing of the most suitable. In effect, proper use of the method requires a comparison of various models, and one should be particularly careful regarding the implications of suiting the theoretical model to the data. Suitability does not yet require a situation in which the "reality" does behave as the model determines. The validity of the model must be determined experimentally, rather than according to a statistical analysis.

The second group of numerical results describes the intensity and direction of the relationship of the variables. These numbers are identical in significance with the factor loadings in factor analysis, and to regression coefficients in a regression analysis. These numbers are meaningful only in a situation in which the model fits the data.

Method of Analysis of Cognitive Mappings

In order to understand the viewpoint of the marina managers, the profit factors were mapped as they were reported, on a cognitive map. In Hypothesis 11, we proposed four sub-hypotheses regarding the proximity among latent variables, in accordance with the viewpoint of the marina managers. (For example, because in many cases they are strict about maintaining environmental protection in accordance with government regulations, we would expect to find these two factors – environmental protection and government intervention – near each other.)

To test this theory, we did an MDS (Multidimensional Scaling) analysis (Kruskal & Wish, 1978), on the participants' ranking the importance of the areas of service, as it appeared after question 41 in the questionnaire.

In the MDS analysis, we estimate and map the "distance" between various items, by an analysis of the average distances between the items on a square matrix of the correlations between them.

According to the method, the participants in the study perceive the items that are near one another in the mapping as close to one another (cognitive proximity). The logic that guides the method is that cognitive proximity "equals" an indication of correlation. The more positive and the higher the correlation between two items, the closer they are seen on the cognitive level, and are mapped closer on MDS.

The data included in the estimate can be indications of similarity, a result of presenting paired comparisons to the participants, other indications of correlation (such as triads), or as in the present case, indications of rank order. One of the advantages of the method is that the map enables parallel mapping of all the existing connections among the different variables, and creates a graphic map of these connections. The method also produces a number of indices in a manner required for the best mapping of these connections.

The MDS method includes an index of the degree of correlation between the mapping and the raw data in the original matrix. The index is called Stress (the name comes from the degree to which there was a need to "stretch" the data in order to map them).

Usually, a Stress score of less than 0.15 is considered a good score, in other words, the map does in fact properly represent the relationship among the items entered into the matrix. The Stress score also serves to test whether there is a need for additional dimensions in order to map the relationship among the items (it is possible to carry out multidimensional mappings – but they are difficult to understand).

The MDS analysis[10] produced a two-dimensional map with a Stress level = 0.11, which is considered reasonable, and indicates that the two-dimensional map describes the matrix of raw data that comprised it with reasonable accuracy, and that there is no need for additional dimensions in order to describe the participants' responses. The raw data entered into the analysis are the forced ranking that participants completed for the question on page 4 of the questionnaire. On that page, we mentioned 15 possible profit factors, and the participants were asked to rank them in order of their contribution to the profitability of the marina.

A map produced by MDS is read like a geographical map – items that are relatively near one another are also close in the view of the participants (a correlative relationship is possible), whereas items that are relatively distant from one another are seen by the participants as unrelated to one another. The map is also organized around dimensions, which are interpreted by the researcher in the first stage. There is a method of confirming the dimensions statistically, but it requires distributing an additional (different) questionnaire to the sample of participants.

Adherence to Ethical Guidelines – Protecting the Participants in the Study

The questionnaire contains no personal questions, it relates only to the personal opinions of the participant, and requests general demographic information about the marina. In order to ensure that the questionnaire remains anonymous, the following steps were taken:

1. The forms were collected personally by the author of the study and remain in his possession.
2. Each completed questionnaire (that was delivered personally) was placed in a sealed box, accessible only to the researcher.
3. The questionnaire was sent only after the agreement of the marina manager was received.
4. The data analyzed will be published as a collection, without identifying any specific marina.

---

10 The MDS method includes an index of the alignment between the mapping and the raw data in the matrix. The index is referred to as Stress (the name comes from the extent to which the data have to be "stretched" in order to map them). A stress score lower than 0.15 is generally considered good, meaning that the map properly reflects the relationships between the items entered into the matrix. The stress score is also used to examine whether additional indices are required to map the relationships between the items (multidimensional mapping can be done, although they are difficult to understand.

FINDINGS

The chapter will present the findings of the sample and the data, and will examine the reliability and the hypotheses of the research tool.

Description of the Sampling and the Data

In this subchapter, we will describe the characteristics of the respondents and of the marinas they manage. Most of the respondents are managers of marinas in Europe, as presented in the table and the chart.

Country of origin	N	Percentage
Italy	20	14.49
France	19	13.77
Spain	13	9.42
Turkey	12	8.70
The Bahamas	11	7.97
England	8	5.80
Finland	7	5.07
Israel	6	4.35
Australia	6	4.35
United States	6	4.35
Canada	4	2.90
Sweden	4	2.90
Norway	3	2.17
United States	3	2.17
Estonia	2	1.45
Denmark	2	1.45
Holland	2	1.45
Belgium	1	0.72
New Zealand	1	0.72

Thailand	1	0.72
Portugal	1	0.72
Singapore	1	0.72
South Africa	1	0.72
Saint Lucia	1	0.72
United States	1	0.72
Missing datum	2	1.45
Total 100.00		138

Continent and Country of Origin of the Respondents

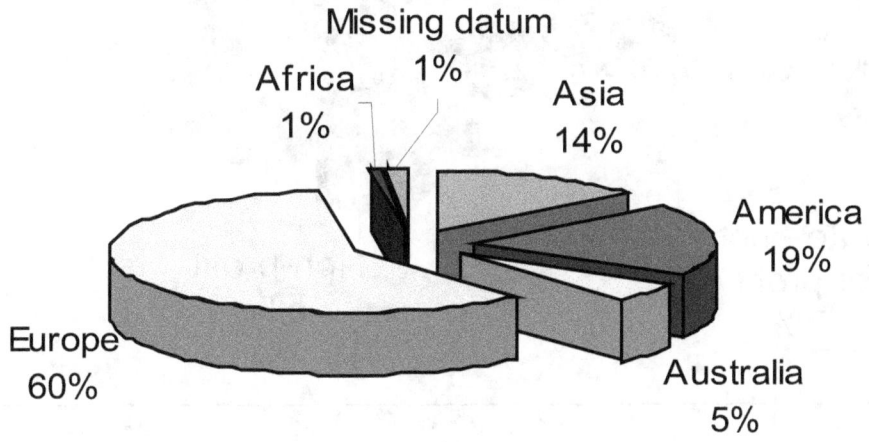

The data indicate that Europe, Asia, and America are well represented in the sample. On the other hand, fewer questionnaires were received from Africa and Australia. The respondents came from 25 different countries in all, according to the table on the right.

The following data will be described according to marina ownership (private or government), and according to the type of customers to which the marina caters (local residents or tourists).

Classifying the Types of Marina Ownership and Their Characteristics

Classifying tourist businesses according to ownership demonstrates that entrepreneurship in the tourism industry exists in three sectors: The private sector, the public sector, and the voluntary sector (not for profit). Each of these sectors have different motives for establishing and developing the tourist attraction.

While the motive of the private sector is profitability and economic growth, the motive in the public and voluntary sectors is to provide service to the community (entertainment, places of employment, economic activity, preservation of sites, and education). The public and voluntary sectors operate on the basis of a defined budget, and their economic goal is to enlarge the budget and to remain within it (Swarbrooke, 1995).

In the following table, the marinas are divided in to four groups, according to their business goals and the type of ownership of the marina:

Classification of Marina Ownership and its Profit Goals

Figure: Two-dimensional classification of marinas

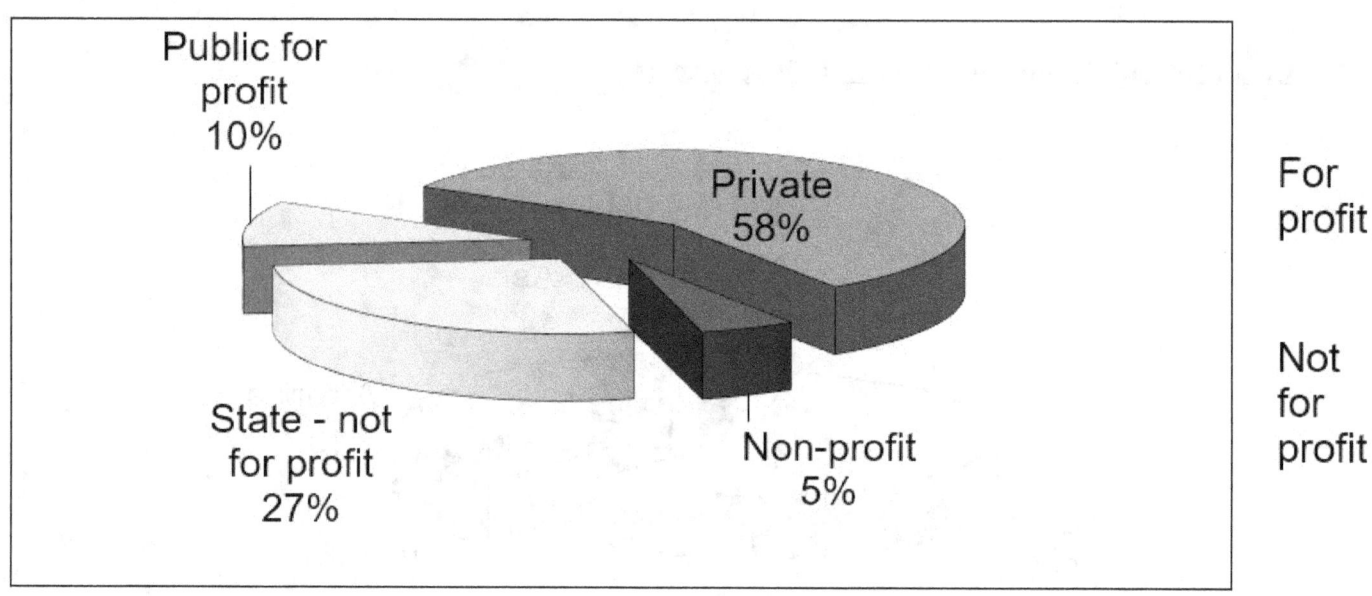

The percentage of private marinas is the highest, at 58 percent. Not-for-profit government marinas constitute the second largest group, with 27 percent.

According to the data, marina customers live an average of about 17 miles from the marina, which is about a 47 minute drive. These distances are reflected when we examine the customers of the private marinas as opposed to the government ones, in the following manner: Whereas the customer of the private marina travels 20 miles for 72 minutes to the marina, the customer of the government marina travels only an average of 5 miles, for only about 10 minutes, to the marina. In other words, the government marinas are closer to the customers than the private marinas.

Anchorage Slips and Areas in the Marina, According to Ownership

According to the sample data, the average anchorage area per boat in the marinas is 462 square feet. The range of length of the boats is from 7 feet to 443 feet, and the average length is 88 feet. The most common size of the small boats is 26 feet, and the most common size of large boats is 65 feet.

The following chart describes the differences among the average number of anchorage slips in a marina, according to ownership.

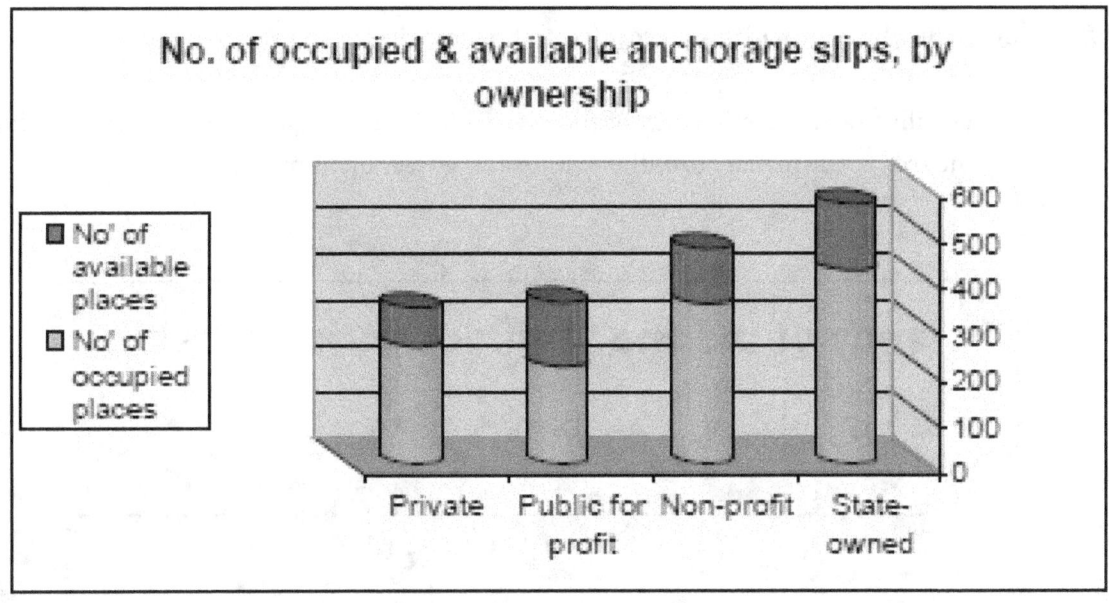

We can see that the state-owned marinas have the largest number of anchorage slips, about 564 on the average, whereas the private ones contain the smallest number, about 340. On the average, the rate of occupancy according to ownership is 74.3 percent – 75.4 percent, excluding the for-profit state-owned marinas, where the occupancy rate is 60 percent on average.

The average size of the marina is displayed below, according to ownership

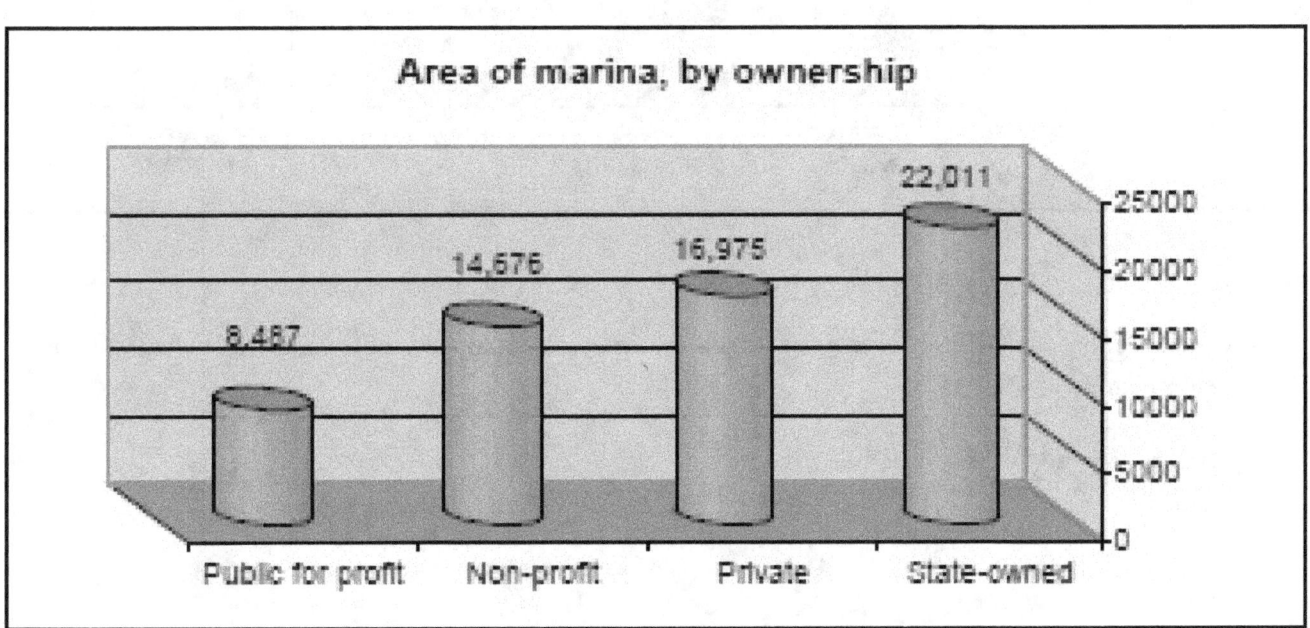

It can be seen that the state-owned marinas have the largest area, about 72,000 square feet, whereas the for-profit public marinas are the smallest, only about 28,000 square feet.

The Efficiency of the Marina Facilities, According to Ownership

The following chart illustrates the efficiency of the marina facilities, according to the way in which they meet the standards of the managers of the private and government marinas:

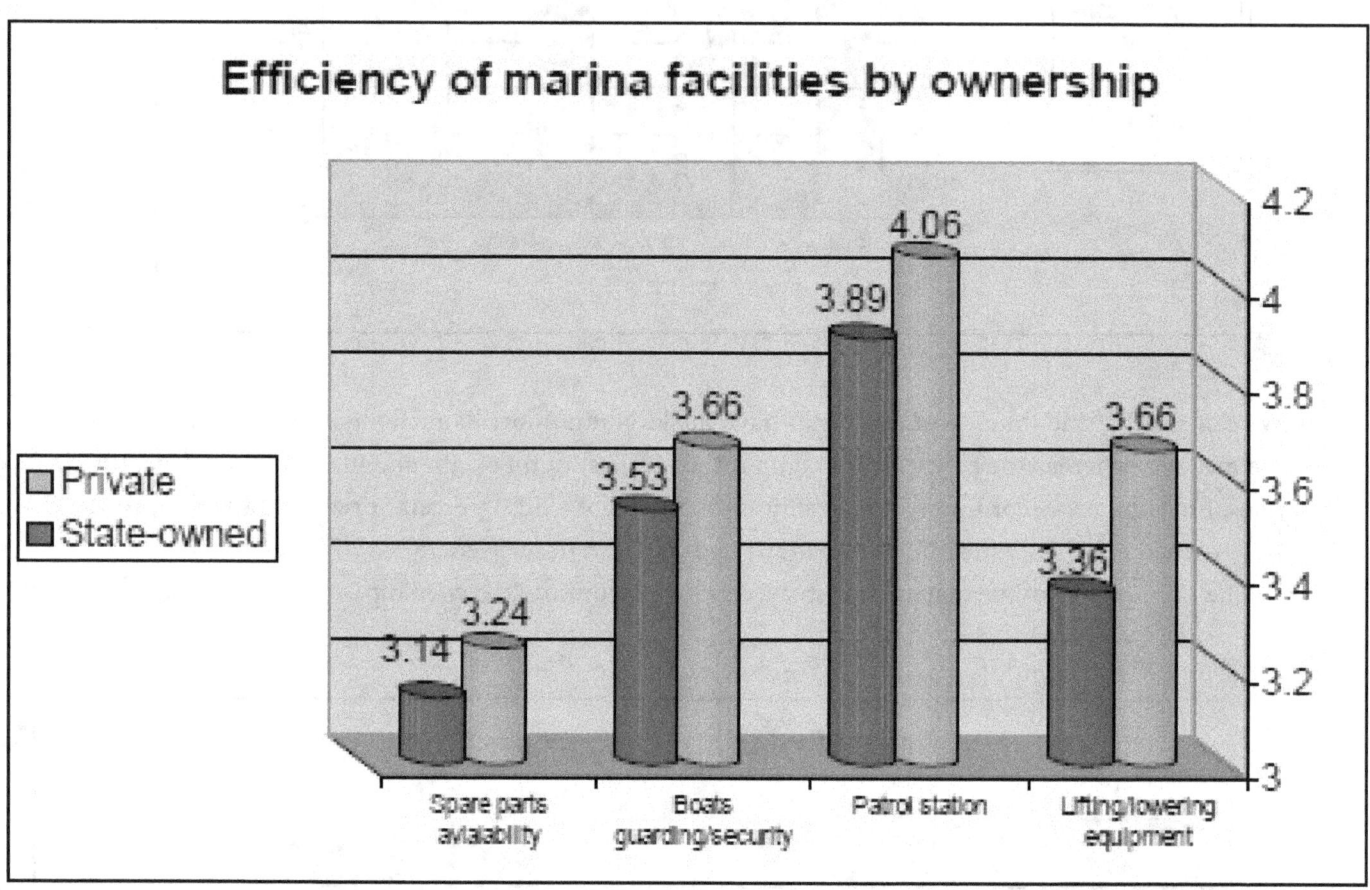

We can see that the facilities in the private marinas meet the standards of the marina managers to a greater degree.

Business Assessment of the Marina, According to Ownership

The following chart illustrates the average assessment by marina managers with respect to the financial activity of the marina.

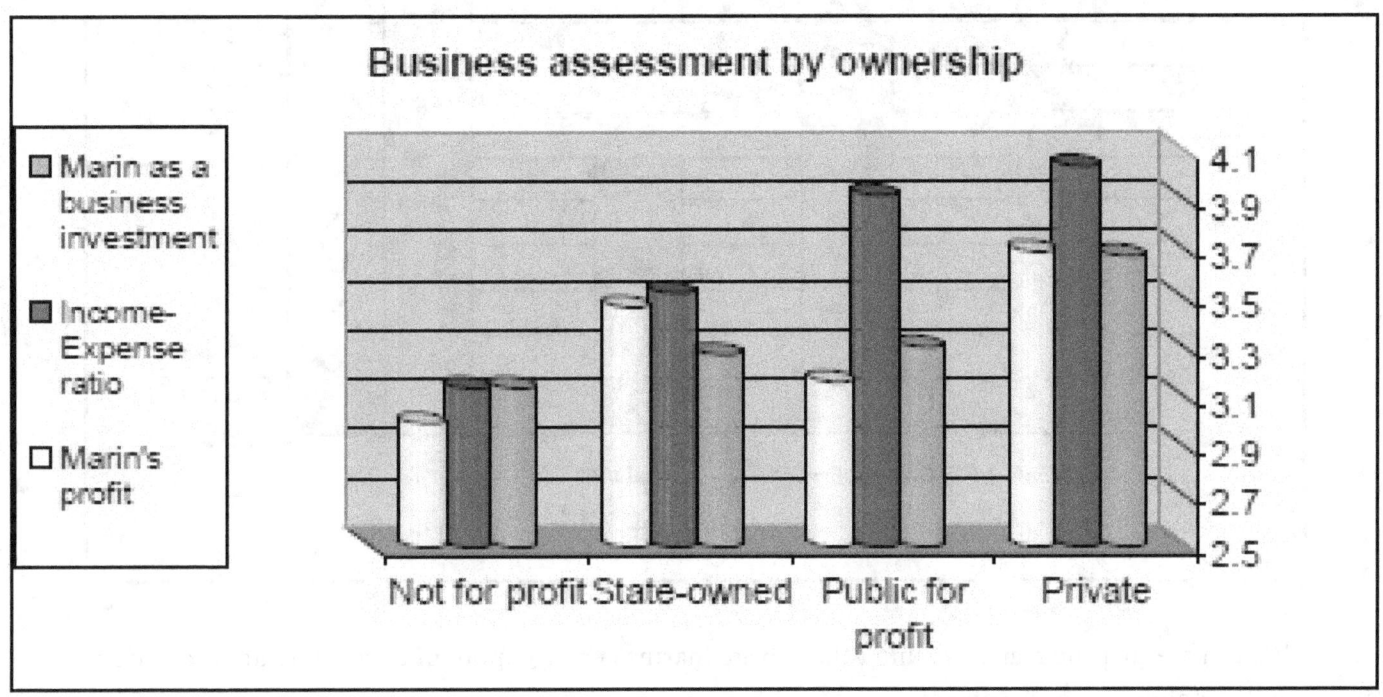

We can see that the private marinas receive the highest scores on all the indices examined: More than the others, managers of the private marinas feel that a marina is a worthwhile business investment, because the ratio of income to operating expenses is the highest, and because the marina is more profitable.

Perception of Environmental Protection, According to Ownership

The following two charts present the level of services related to maintenance of cleanliness and environmental protection, according to ownership of the marina.

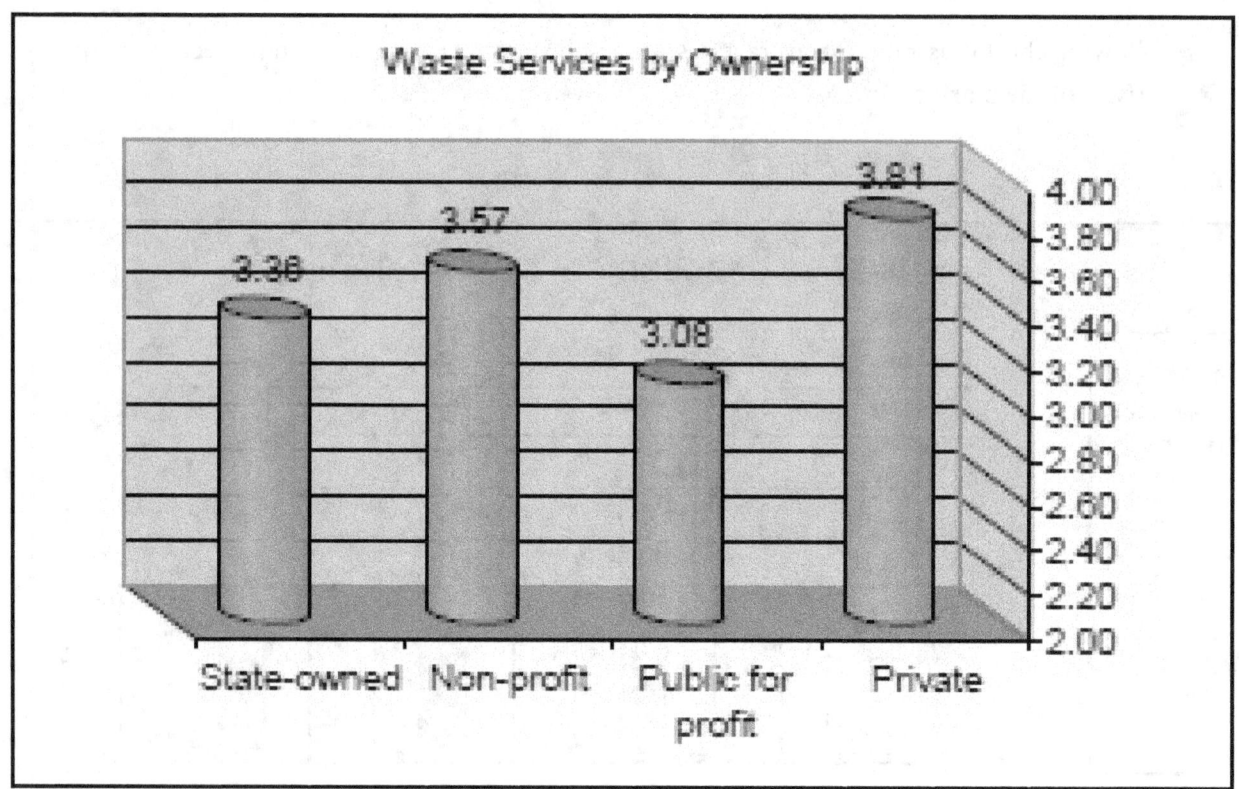

We can see that the managers think the private marinas engage more in environmental protection and cleanliness than the others.

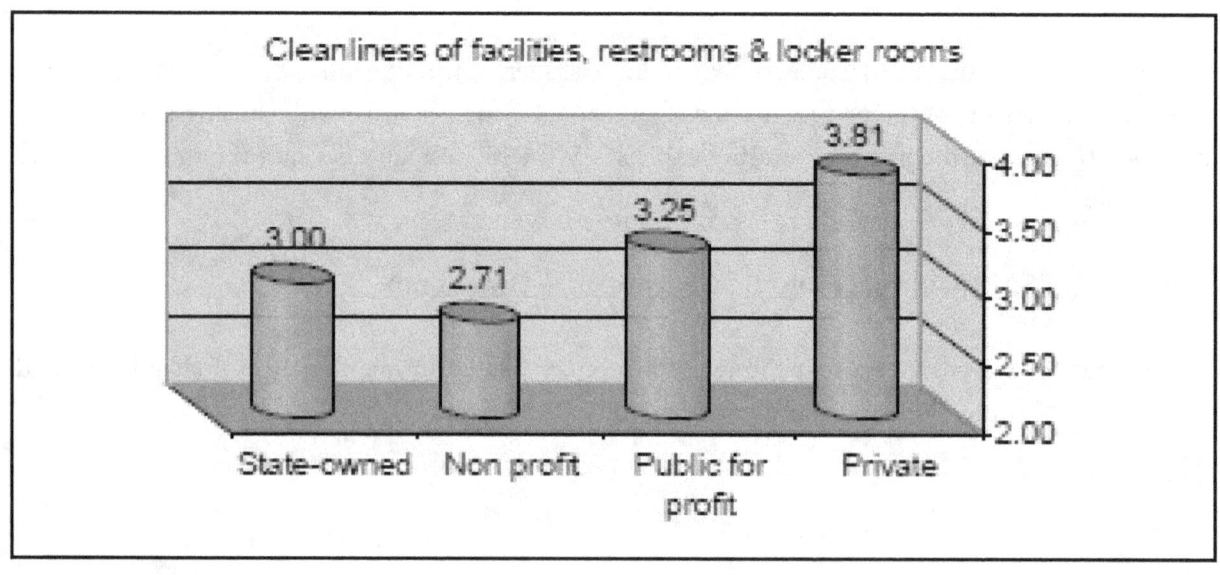

Ranking of Fulfillment of Expectations, According to Ownership

The following chart illustrates the views of the managers as to whether the marina meets the standards/expectations of the manager.

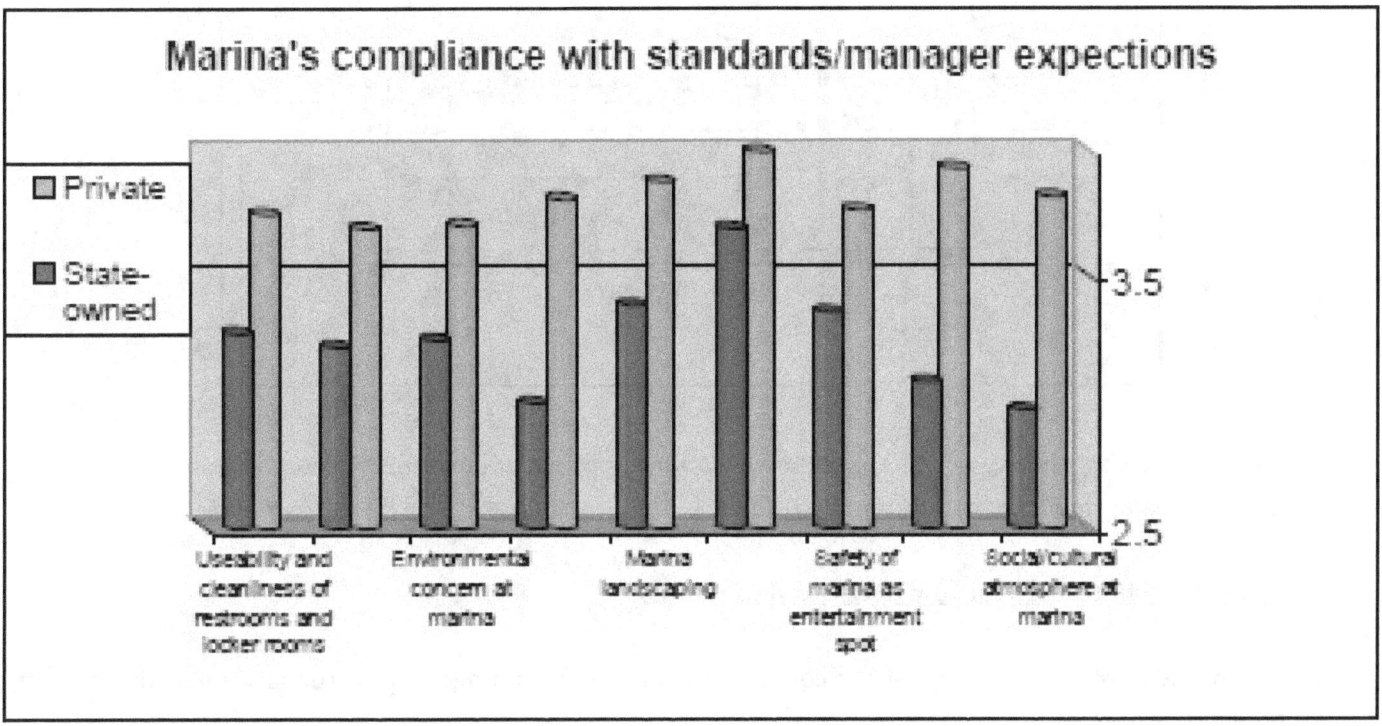

As illustrated above, managers of the private marinas have a higher assessment, in all the parameters, as to whether the marina meets the standards that were set, as compared to the managers of the state-owned marinas: These include a better social and cultural atmosphere, as well as image, safety (as an entertainment site and protection of boats), view, cleanliness of restrooms, greater environmental protection (in and outside the marina), greater usability, and cleanliness.

Perception of the Flexibility of Government Regulations, According to Ownership

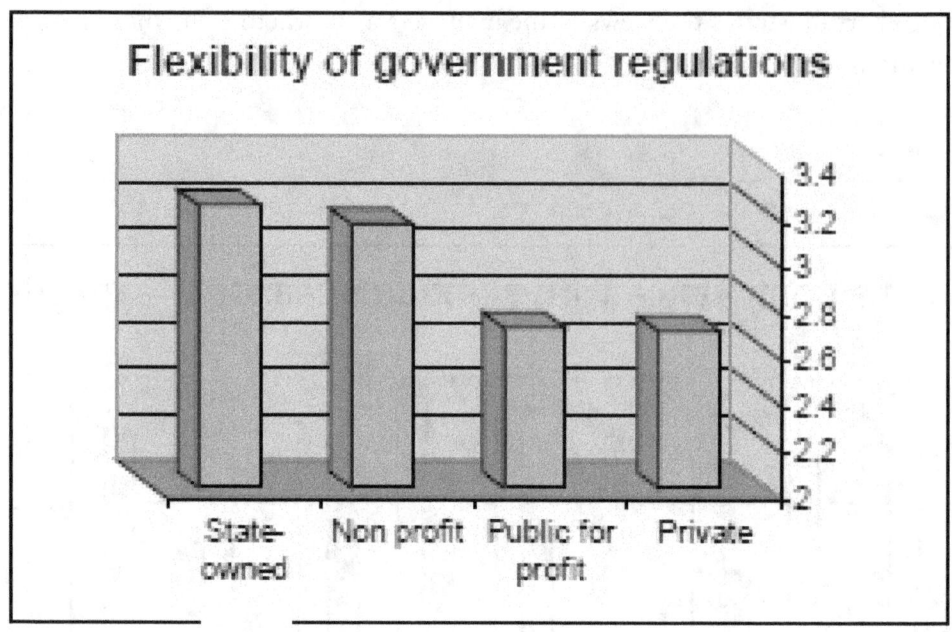

We can see that the managers of the state-owned marinas consider government intervention stricter than do managers of the private marinas.

Price of Anchorage, According to Ownership

One of the most interesting questions concerns the price of anchorage, depending on ownership of the marina:

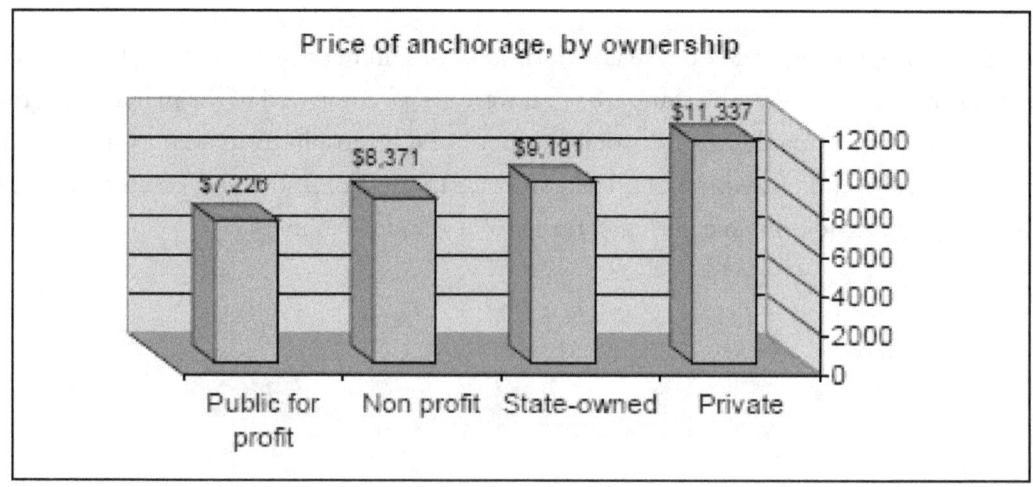

It can be seen that the private marinas charge the highest prices for anchorage, over $11,000 a year for a 40-foot boat. The state-owned marinas charge an average of 20 percent less: slightly over $9,000 for the same boat. The high standard deviation of the results is in line with expectations, as marinas in different places around the world adjust their price scales to local costs and consumption habits.

Customer mix at Marinas

The following two charts illustrate the customer mix in the private and government marinas:

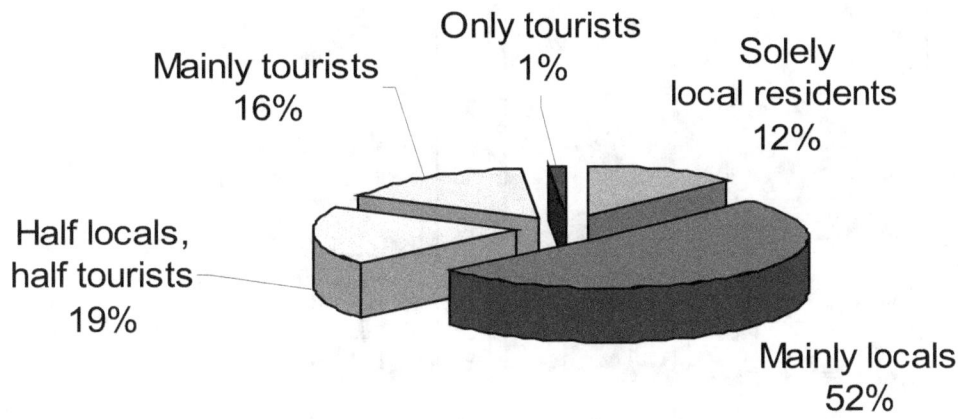

Customers of the Private and State-owned Marinas

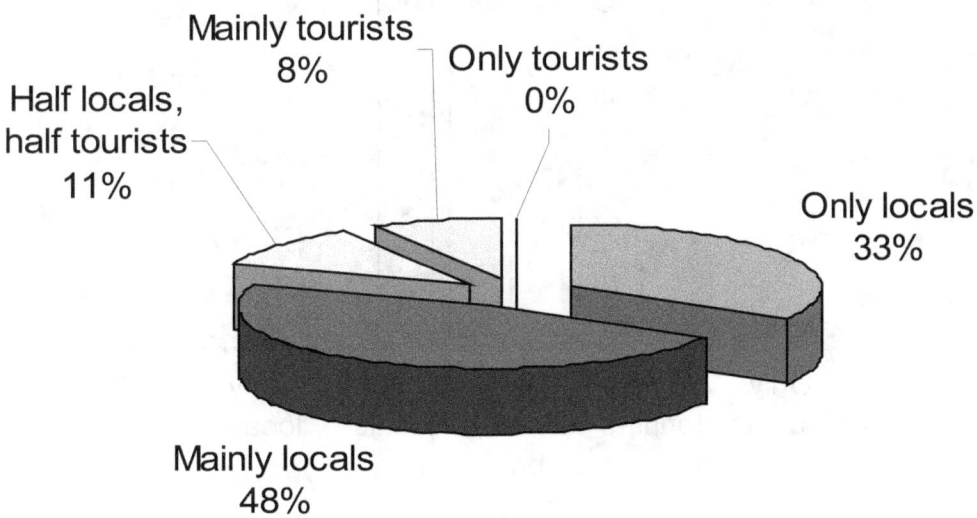

As can be seen, 81 percent of the state-owned marinas serve only, or mainly, local residents, whereas only 64 percent of the private marinas serve this community.

Marina Customers

The following chart illustrates the number of marinas that presented their mix of customers:

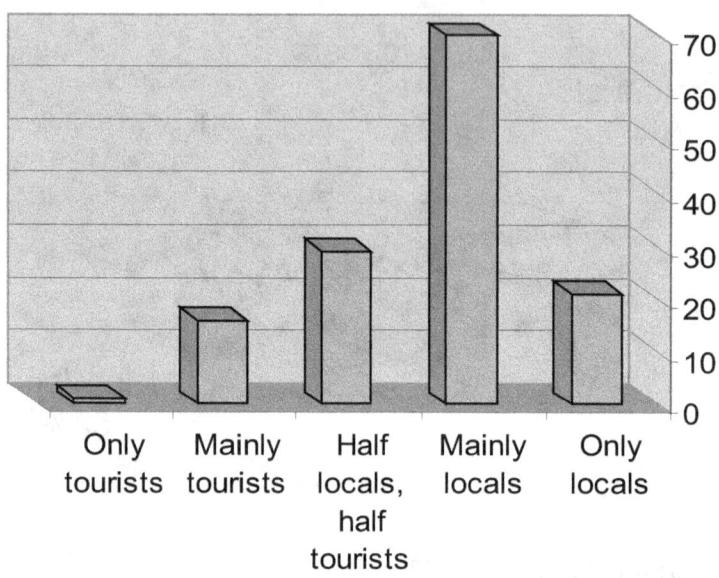

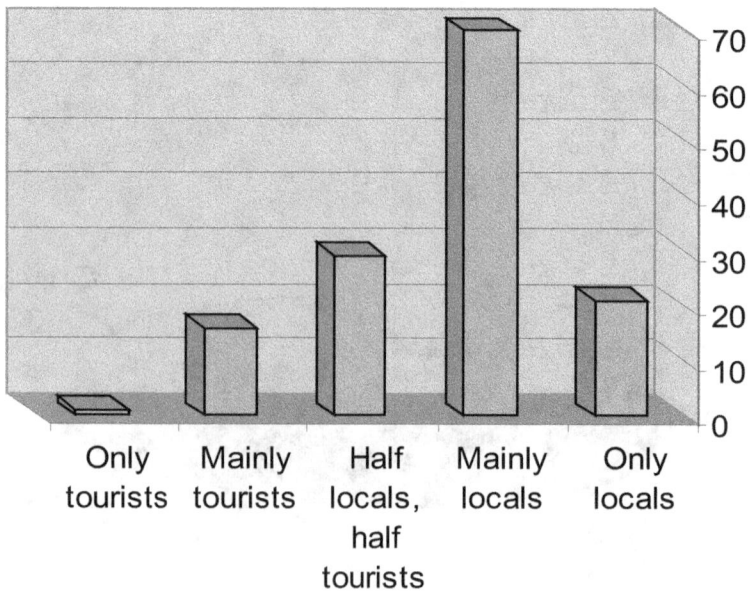

As can be seen, most of the marinas serve mainly local residents, and very few marinas focus on tourists.

Price of Anchorage by Customer Type

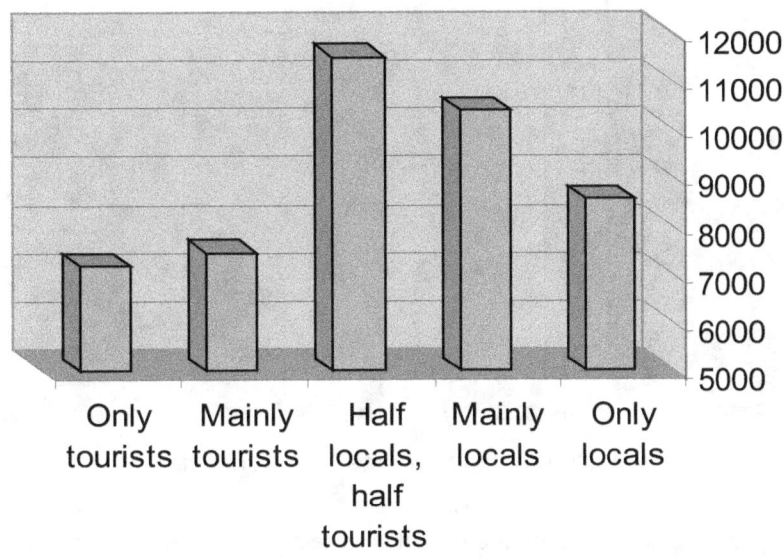

Annual cost of anchorage for 40-foot boat

Marina customers	Mean	N	Standard deviation
Local residents only	8571.05	19	5054.022
Mainly local residents	10409.60	67	9584.539
Half locals, half tourists	11533.48	23	10215.054
Mainly tourists	7461.67	12	5838.930
Only tourists	7200.00	1	
Total	10018.88	122	8805.831

As can be seen, the highest price is demanded by marinas that cater to a balanced mix of local customers and tourists (about $11,500 annually), and it decreases as the marina caters to local residents only ($8,500), or tourists only ($7,200).

The Local Community

About 53 percent of the managers replied that the local community views the marina as detrimental to the community, or considers it a nuisance. Only 14 percent of the managers believe that the marina is useful or essential to the community, as presented in the following chart:

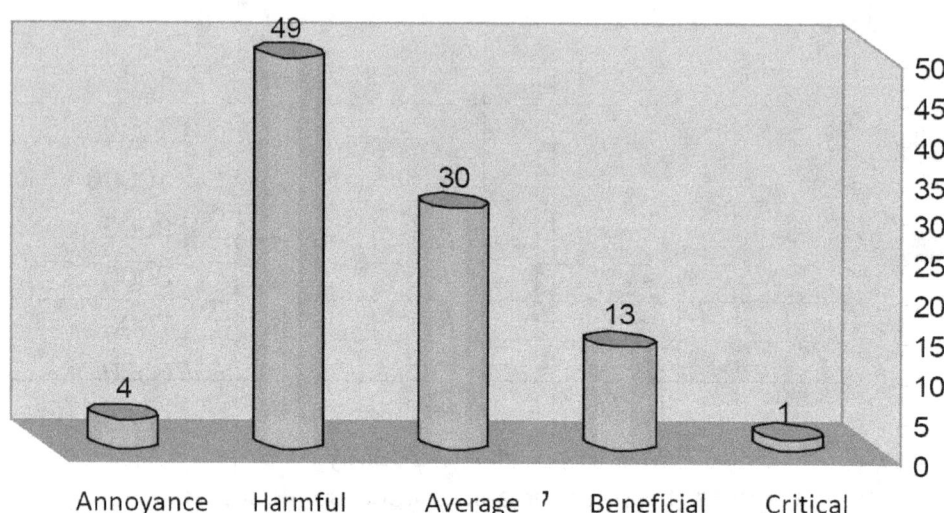

At the same time, when managers were asked whether the marina meets their expectations and standards, about 55 percent replied that the image of the marina in the eyes of the residents is beyond, or far beyond, their expectations, as emphasized in the following chart:

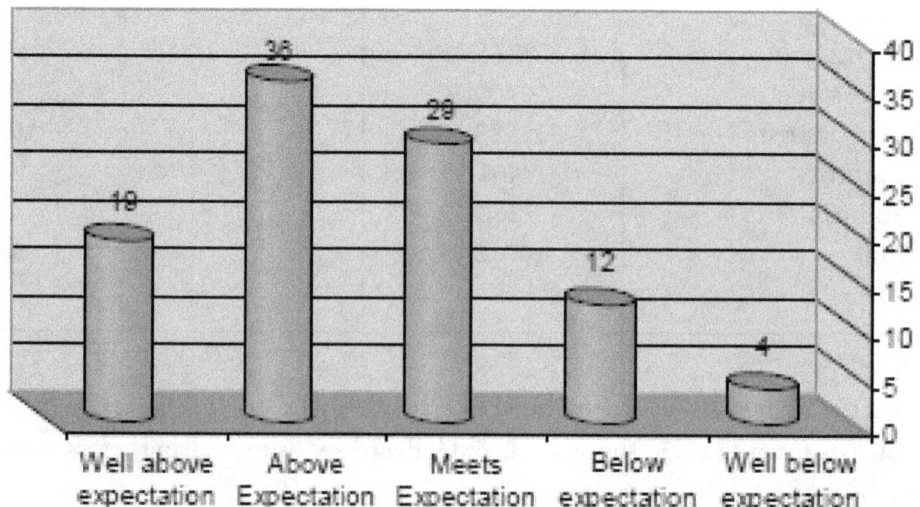

When it comes to the attitude of the local community regarding the marina, in a ranking that begins with "they (the local residents) don't like it at all" and ends with "they like it very much," about 68 percent of the managers believe that the local residents like the marina, or like it very much, and only about 6 percent estimated that the local residents do not like the marina, as described below:

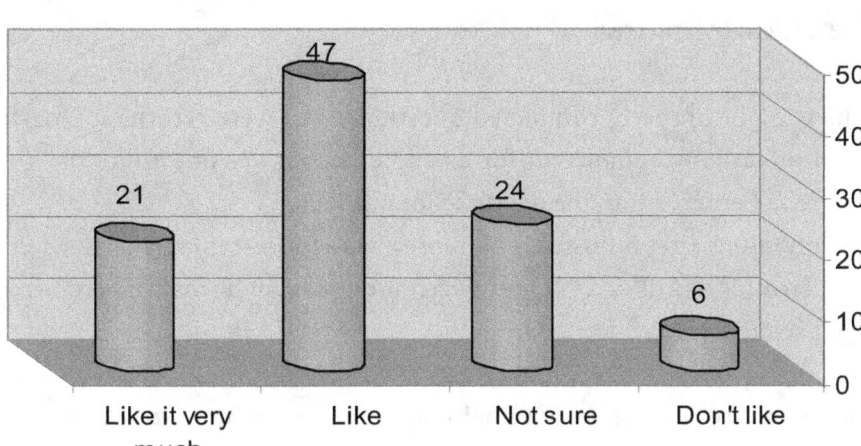

Local residents like the marina (percentage)

The following table presents the relationship between the landscaping and the attitudes of the local community.

The Relationship Between Landscaping and the Local Community

Correlations

		The view from the marine	The view of the marine from the sea	The design of the marine's view	Local residences liking of the marine	Status of the marine in the eyes of local residences
The view from the marine	Pearson correlation Sig. (2-tailed) N	1 . 138	.798** .000 137	.430** .000 138	.221** .010 135	.362** .000 137
The view of the marine from the sea	Pearson correlation Sig. (2-tailed) N	.798** .000 137	1 . 137	.390** .000 137	.189* .029 134	.396* .000 136
The design of the marine's view	Pearson correlation Sig. (2-tailed) N	.430** .000 138	.390** .000 137	1 . 138	.327** .000 135	.389* .000 137
Local residences liking the marine	Pearson correlation Sig. (2-tailed) N	.221** .010 135	.189* .029 134	.327** .000 135	1 . 135	.468** .000 135
Status of the marine in the eyes of local residences	Pearson correlation Sig. (2-tailed) N	.362** .000 137	.396** .000 136	.389** .000 137	.468** .000 135	1 . 137

**. Correlation is significant at the 0.01 level (2-tailed)
*. Correlation is significant at the 0.05 level (2-tailed)

A significant relationship was established between all the variables: Design of the view from the marina, view for those entering from the sea, landscape design at the marina, extent to which local residents like the marina, and the status of the marina as perceived by local residents. It can be claimed that the more attractive the landscaping of the marina (as viewed from the marina and by those entering the marina), the more the local residents will like it.

Returning the Questionnaires

One hundred thirty-eight properly completed questionnaires were returned. Questionnaires that were partially and/or casually completed (for example, an answer of 5 to all the questions in the questionnaire) were not entered into the database for analysis.

The number of questionnaires returned, 138, represents a 69 percent response, a percentage that is considered particularly high (Miller, 1991) for questionnaires sent by mail. There are several reasons for the high response rate:

a. Participants who did not return the questionnaire were sent a reminder to return it two weeks later. Anyone who did not respond to the first reminder received another reminder.
b. The questionnaire is relevant to the participants, and an analysis of the results interested the marina managers.
c. The researcher personally visited almost 50 marinas, and collected the questionnaires himself.

Examining the Reliability of the Measuring Tools

Prior to the statistical analysis of the data, the reliability of the factors was examined, as they are predicted by the items in the questionnaire.

Below are the results of the reliability analysis of the factors:

Examination of Reliability of Each Variable in the Questionnaire:

Variable in model	Composed of items	Cronbach's *a*
Location of site (Nof)	25. View from marina 26. View for those coming from direction of sea 27. Design of marina	.77
Government intervention (Memshala)	5. Degree of restriction of local/government regulations 28. Level of government supervision of marina 35. Quality of local/government supervision of marina	n.s.
Crowding (Tzfifut)	4. Degree of crowding at marina 32. Average crowding of boats at marina	n.s.
Anchorage and equipment services (Sherutim)	38. Crane/lifting/unloading equipment of boats 39. Gas station at marina 40. Maintenance and repair of boats 41. Shop for boating equipment	.73
Access (Negishut)	33. Ease of bringing guests to marina 36. Accessibility of marina facilities to customers	n.s.
Safety (Bitachon)	2. Marina meets safety rules and regulations 23. Security in marina as place of entertainment 24. Security in marina for leaving equipment/boats	n.s.

Environmental protection (Aichustv)	3. Dealing with garbage at marina 29. Cleanliness of restrooms at marina 30. Care of environment inside marina 31. Care of environment around the marina 34. Cleanliness and efficiency of restrooms	.83
Distance from competitors	14. Average traveling time to competing marina 15. Average traveling distance to competing marina	.72
Proximity to customer	12. Average traveling time to marina 13. Average traveling distance to marina (L_Distcu)	n.s.
Local community (Kehila)	1. Local residents like/don't like the marina 7. Local community considers the marina useful/a nuisance 21. Social/cultural atmosphere at marina 22. Status of marina among local residents	.75
Variable of occupancy and profitability (profitability index) (ATFUSA)	<u>Questions about profitability:</u> 9. Income as compared to monetary expenditures 37. profitability of marina	.77
	<u>Questions about occupancy:</u> 8. Vacant as opposed to occupied spots in marina 17-18. Percentage of occupied slips 17. Number of anchorage slips in marina 18. Number of occupied anchorage slips 19-20. Percentage of anchorage area occupied 19. Anchorage area in marina 20. Size of occupied anchorage area	

The dependent variable received a Cronbach's alpha of 0.77, which testified to a sufficiently high correlation among the variables. This means that this factor can be used as is, as it is comprised of the items that appear in the table, for a continuation of the analysis in the present study.

From among the independent variables, six produced high reliability: Location of the site, local community, anchorage services, environmental protection, and distance from competitors. All demonstrated sufficiently high reliability, and the analysis will relate to these variables later on.

The independent variables: Government intervention, safety, proximity to customer, access, and crowding, do not achieve a sufficient level of reliability.

Testing the Hypotheses

Because the dependent variable and the independent variables are continuous variables, the most suitable method of analysis is the Pearson Correlation, whose results are presented in the following table:

Correlations between the independent variables and the occupancy index

Hypothesis tested	Variable	Significance
Hypothesis 1	Landscape/Location	P=0.71
Hypothesis 2	Gov't intervention	P<0.001
Hypothesis 3	Crowding	P=0.004
Hypothesis 4	Services	057. P=0
Hypothesis 5	Accessibility	P=0.666
Hypothesis 6	Level of security/safety	P=0.558
Hypothesis 7	Environmental protection	P=0.309.
Hypothesis 8	Distance from competitors	P=0.297
Hypothesis 9	Proximity to customer/city	P=0.051
Hypothesis 10	Local community	P=0.846

The table above shows the results of the Pearson correlation between occupancy and other variables.

As is indicated, the correlations between crowding and government intervention and crowding – are significant. The correlation between government intervention and occupancy is a negative correlation, meaning that the greater government intervention, the lower occupancy. The correlation between crowding and occupancy is a positive correlation, meaning that the higher occupancy is the greater the crowding.

The remaining correlations are not significant. This shows that it is not possible to claim a relationship between the occupancy index and the other variables examined: View, services, level of security/safety, environmental protection, distance from competitors, proximity to customer/city, and local community.

As the above table shows, Hypothesis 2, which claims that there is a correlation between occupancy and government intervention, cannot be rejected.

To better understand the government intervention factor, the three items that comprise it in the questionnaire were examined:

Item 5 – The degree of restriction by local/government regulations: There is no correlation between occupancy and the marina manager's view of the restrictions stemming from government intervention.

Item 28 – The degree of government supervision of the marina: There is a significant ($p = 0.002$) negative correlation (-0.282) between the occupancy and the marina manager's view of the scope of the government rules and regulations that apply to the marina. The fewer the number of actual rules and regulations as compared to the manager's expectations, the higher the occupancy.

Item 35 – The quality of the local/government supervision of the marina: There is a significant ($p = 0.001$) negative correlation (-0.290) between occupancy and the marina manager's view of the government supervision of the marina.

In addition, as the above table shows, we cannot reject Hypothesis 3, which claims that there is a correlation between occupancy and crowding. The two items that comprise the factor were found to be significant.

Item 4 – degree of crowding at the marina (0.241 p =0.007).

Item 32 – average density of boats in the marina (0.222 p =0.014(.

The two assumptions that were rejected received very borderline results: Hypothesis 9 – proximity to customer (0.178, p=0.051) and Hypothesis 4 – associated services (0.173, p=0.057). The customary cut-off point for significance is 50. Therefore, this result is not significant. However, based on the distribution of the data, it can be assumed that a larger sample would have produced a significant result – had the sample behaved like the respondents who answered the questionnaire.

Two other factors were found to be significantly related to occupancy, and were not included in the assumptions of the study: the anchorage area in the marina (0.298, p=0.002) and the number of anchorage slips in the marina (0.256, p=0.004).

Linear Regression

In order to examine which of the variables can predict occupancy, a linear regression was conducted. To approach a normal spread, we used an arcsine transformation on the occupancy variable (a more detailed explanation of the occupancy variable and its different variations in the questionnaire can be found in Appendices I and J). Following are the results:

Variables Entered/Removed^a

Model	Variables Entered	Variables Removed	Method
1	MEMSHALA	.	Stepwise (Criteria: Probability-of-F-to-enter <= .050, Probability-of-F-to-remove >= .100).

a. Dependent Variable: ATFUSA

Model Summary

Model	R	R Square	Adjusted R Square	Std. Error of the Estimate
1	.356a	.127	.119	.24766

a. Predictors: (Constant), MEMSHALA

ANOVA^b

Model		Sum of Squares	df	Mean Square	F	Sig.
1	Regression	1.018	1	1.018	16.590	.000a
	Residual	6.992	114	.061		
	Total	8.010	115			

a. Predictors: (Constant), MEMSHALA

b. Dependent Variable: ATFUSA

Coefficients[a]

Model		Unstandardized Coefficients		Standardized Coefficients	t	Sig.
		B	Std. Error	Beta		
1	(Constant)	1.553	.121		12.882	.000
	MEMSHALA	-.170	.042	-.356	-4.073	.000

a. Dependent Variable: ATFUSA

Model		Beta In	t	Sig.	Partial Correlation	Collinearity Statistics
						Tolerance
1	NOF	-.088[a]	-.996	.321	-.093	.979
	TZFIFUT	.168[a]	1.892	.061	.175	.953
	SHERUTIM	.164[a]	1.893	.061	.175	.995
	NEGISHUT	-.083[a]	-.916	.362	-.086	.942
	BITACHON	.022[a]	.245	.807	.023	.993
	AICHUTSV	.032[a]	.355	.723	.033	.941
	TRAVEL TIME IN MINUTES	-.010[a]	-.118	.906	-.011	.998
	TRAVEL TIME IN KILOMETERS	.034[a]	.384	.701	.036	.983
	AVERAGE TRAVEL TIME	.127[a]	1.435	.154	.134	.963
	LDIST_CU	.139[a]	1.597	.113	.149	.999
	KEHILA	-.081[a]	-.912	.364	-.085	.975

a. Predictors in the Model: (Constant), MEMSHALA

b. Dependent Variable: ATFUSA

As can be seen, the factor of government intervention, in inverse ratio, can predict the occupancy rate in the marina. The second factor that was found to have a significant relationship to occupancy, crowding, does not any significant explanation to the occupancy factor.

Operating the Model

None of the examinations of the model produced sufficient convergence of the data to confirm any model. There can be attributed to various reasons, whether based on the model itself, or on methodological reasons.

The most immediate reason is that the participants do not think in the terms presented by the model. This may stem from the fact that the participants do not have such a model in their awareness at all: The participants do not have an explicit or intuitive tacit model according to which they completed the questionnaire, or alternatively, they have an alternative model, something which was not mentioned in all the literature reviewed.

Additional reasons may be methodological, such as the wording of the questions, the manner of data collection, etc. In any case, the reason cannot be found from an analysis of the structural equations, and this subject requires a thorough qualitative examination, which is beyond the scope of this study.

Ranking the Importance of the Variables

In order to discover whether there is a consensus among the participants regarding the ranking of the variables, the consensus analysis was examined, with the following results:

Analysis of consensus among the respondents regarding the ranking of importance of the variables:

SD	Average knowledge	Ratio	Pseudo reliability
24.	52.	2.5	98.

This analysis is an essential stage before analyzing the cognitive map of the participants, because it constitutes a type of validity check to ensure that the map does, in fact, describe the perception of most of the participants in the study.

Results indicating that average knowledge is lower than .050 and/or a ratio lower than 1 would indicate a lack of consensus among the respondents. Since the subject belongs to the field of social sciences, it is rare to find consensus data above 70. The results of this analysis show that there is agreement among the participants, making it possible to move on to analysis of the cognitive map and analysis of the importance ranking.

Variables in Order of Importance

Variable	Average ranking[11]
Value for money	3.17
Customer satisfaction	4.29
Associated services	5.73
Facilities and equipment	6.37

---

11 In the ranking directions, the respondents were asked to mark the most important factor with the number 1. Therefore, the lower the average, the more important the factor was ranked.

Anchorage cost	6.64
Safety and security	8.18
Occupancy	8.25
Anchorage depth	8.76
Density	8.82
Distance/Driving time	8.85
Accessibility	8.94
Environmental protection	9.38
Location of site/view	9.44
Distance to competitors	10.22
Government intervention	12.47

The above ranking indicates that the marina managers consider value for money the most important variable. After it, in decreasing order of importance: Customer satisfaction, services the marina provides for the boats (fuel, storage, repairs, etc.), and services the marina provides its customers (club, swimming pool, showers, etc.). Last, in importance, is the variable of government intervention. It is important to note that all of the variables were ranked as important by the marina managers; otherwise they would not appear in the questionnaire. Importance was ranked for these relevant factors.

In order to understand the relationship among the various variables, we produced a cognitive map (in marketing, such maps are also called consensus maps), by using an MDS (multidimensional scaling) analysis. The stress level of a two-dimensional mapping presented below is 0.11, and this is definitely a reasonable level for this analysis (Less than 0.15 is considered reasonable stress), so that we can state that the map does in fact reliably reflect the raw data of the ranking.

Cognitive Mapping of the Variables, According to the Marina Managers

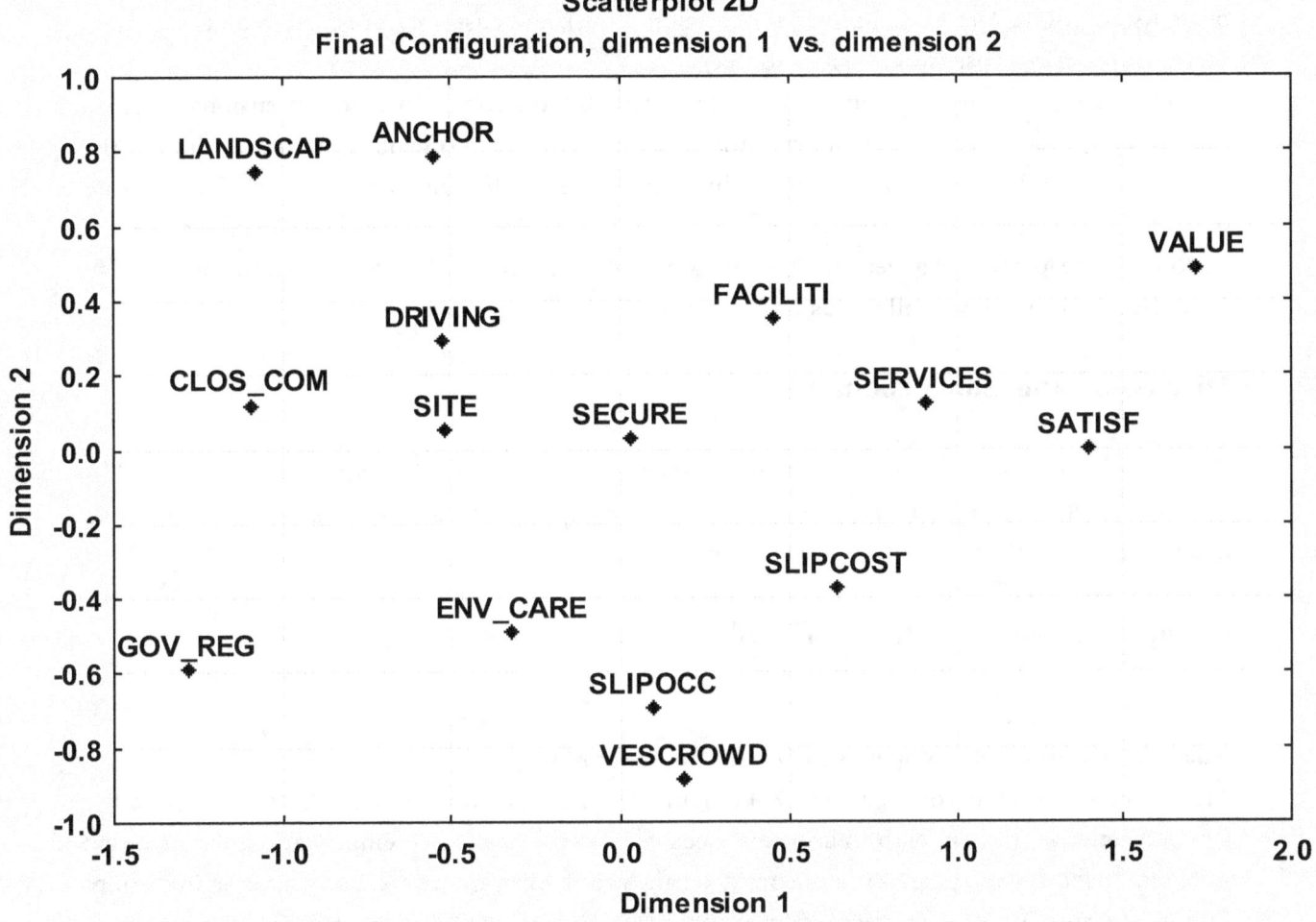

Maps of this kind are read like a "geographical" map. The proximity of the variables to one another means that these factors are seen by the respondents as being strongly related to one another (and there may be a cause-and-effect connection as well – but examining this connection demands a stage of qualitative validation, which is beyond the scope of this study).

An example of proximate factors is the depth of anchorage and the landscape (on the upper left side of the map). The distance of factors from one another means that the participants believe that they are unrelated. An example of distant factors are value for money (center right) and government intervention (bottom left).

Combining the order of importance with the map shows that Dimension 1 is the dimension of importance of the variable, the variables on the right are the most important, and those on the left are less important. The spread of Dimension 2 is subject to the interpretation of the researcher, and requires a qualitative examination – this issue will be covered in the discussion chapter.

We can see that occupancy does appear in the center of the map, on the horizontal axis, slightly toward the lower side of the horizontal axis, a dimension that we are not yet familiar with. Occupancy and crowding do appear in close proximity. Environmental protection and government intervention also appear in proximity, as we assumed. As far as value for money – it turns out that all the factors we assumed would appear in proximity to one another did, in fact, do so, with the anchorage cost the most distant (of the factors mentioned in the assumption), and customer satisfaction and associated services appearing closer to value for money.

The ranking and the mapping enable us to discuss the question of which dimensions organize the mapping of factors above? In other words, what are the rules of organization in the minds of the marina managers? If we are aware of these dimensions, we will be able to understand why the sense of value for money for the customers and accompanying services were placed on the upper right, as opposed to the location of government regulations and environmental protection on the bottom left.

In the next chapter, we will discuss the results presented in this chapter.

Discussion and Conclusions

This chapter discusses the findings and conclusions that can be drawn in light of the findings. Additionally, the chapter presents the examination of the complete model and presents a cognitive map of a marina manager as produced from the study data.

Occupancy as a Proxy for Profitability

Analysis of Validity of Occupancy in Questionnaire to Managers

The high correlation (Cronbach's $a = .77$) obtained in the reliability analysis, between profitability (the subjective assessment of the marina manager) and occupancy, grants empirical validity to the assessment that occupancy can serve as a proxy for the profitability of the marina. This is an important finding, because it creates an opening for using the occupancy dimension as a variable in empirical studies, whose absence in the field is felt, as mentioned already in the literature review.

The basis for use of occupancy as a proxy index arose from a previous study the researcher conducted on occupancy and profitability in Israel, which is described below.

Occupancy Index and its Applicability to Examining Profitability of Marinas: Examination of the Marinas in Israel

The first marina was built in Tel Aviv and opened in 1973. Since that time, the sector has experienced growth, and marinas are now not only a place to anchor boats, but have become a leisure area that attracts the local population.

The marina is a business, and it must, therefore, be studied using business tools. The occupancy index presented in this study will be used here to examine the profitability of marinas, compared to known financial data.

Before the actual test, let's repeat several of the definitions essential for understanding the index and its implementation:

Anchorage: The marina's protected water area.

Actual occupancy index: The area of the boats actually anchored at the marina.

Maximum occupancy index: The maximum area of boats the marina can hold.

Equilibrium occupancy index: Percentage of water surface for which revenues equal operating expenses.

Profit in maximum occupancy index: The profitability according to current anchorage fees in maximum occupancy, less current expenses.

Use of Indices

Occupancy Indices as a Function of Marina Area

The indices listed above, all the planned designation of the subject marina to be studied. A large **Maximum Occupancy Index** indicates that the marina was built for the use of small boats and does not use large areas for maneuvering circles and waterways (for example, Atarim Marina and Acre Marina).

In contrast, a marina designed for large boats ("mega yachts"), the **Maximum Occupancy Index** will be small (for example, the marina in Ashdod).

These indices can also be used to show the operational status of each marina separately.

Occupancy Versus Profit

A tool used to present specific and comparable profitability of marinas, both at real points in time and at equilibrium, and it presents potential maximum profit as a function of the occupied area at a specific marina. The data in Table 1 compares the marinas in Israel. The data is accurate as of May 2001.

	Ashkelon	Ashdod	Atarim	Herzliya	Kishon	Acre**
Anchorage area (sq. m.)	90,000	240,000	35,000	137,000	46,000	4,500
Anchorage slips	600	550	300	800	340	70
Max occupancy area (sq. m.)	24,000	24,200	11,000	46,000	14,000	2,100
Actual occupancy rate (sq. m.)	6,000	3,000	11,000	19,000	9,000	2,100
Maximum profit (loss) (NIS)	(300,000)	(660,000)	740,000	3.4 million	(190,000)	(65,000)
Maximum profit (loss) (NIS)	4 million	1.73 million	740,000	10.2 million	(65,000)	(65,000)
AOI*	6.4%	1.25%	33%	14%	15.6%	46%
MOI*	28%	10.1%	33%	33.5%	23.9%	46%
MOI profit (NIS)	3 million	1.73 million	740,000	10.2 million	(36,500)	(64,000)
OIE*	8.6%	3.6%	23.6%	4.3%	25.8%	59.8%

*AOI = Actual Occupancy Index
MOI = Maximum Occupancy Index
OIE = Occupancy Index at Equilibrium

**Loss is not precise, and is solely for Marina Acre and Marina Kishon. The factors taken into consideration by the licensee include the exclusivity and savings in anchorage fees for their commercial vessels. The licensee is the party that provides security and maintenance services at no additional cost.

Possible Reasons why Occupancy is not a Proxy for Profit for Managers

In methodological terms, it should also be noted that five factors from the questionnaire were found to be sufficiently reliable for analysis (distance from competitors, local community, location of the site, associated services/services provided, and environmental protection), whereas five additional factors (government intervention, crowding, proximity to the customer, accessibility, and the level of security/safety) did not achieve a sufficient level of reliability.

These five factors also join the variables through which we can expand the empirical research in the field. Since the factors were taken (in an exploratory manner) from the academic and professional literature about marina management, the fact that almost half of the factors turned out to be unreliable demonstrates that the field primarily nourished by practical experience rather than academic/rigorous research.

The reason why five additional factors were found to be insufficiently reliable for a statistical analysis in the reliability analysis of the questionnaire may be attributable to the wording of the items in the questionnaire – a methodological problem. It may be that these factors, as assumed by the researcher, do not exist in the awareness of the marina managers, although they are part of the non-research literature that deals with the subject, and part of the discourse of investors in marinas and of customers.

Another possible reason for this is the conceptual "blindness" of the marina managers, attributable to a lack of understanding of the viewpoint of investors in the marina. The investors in marinas are occasionally aware of the problems/advantages/disadvantages of government intervention and proximity to a major city, but they prefer to handle that via unofficial channels, and far from the public eye. In addition, in these matters, they do not make proper contact with the acting marina managers, which results in the lack of awareness of the managers.

It may be that the marina managers are not sufficiently aware of the customer perspective, and do not know what will cause them satisfaction with the marina's services. Therefore, although the customers greatly value accessibility, lack of crowding in the marina, and a high level of security and safety (see a previous study by the researcher regarding satisfaction), the marina managers are unaware of that.

Some of these factors are important to the marina's customers, and are subject to manipulation (if only partial) by the marina manager.

The difference between use of the occupancy index in this study and the perceptions of managers will be discussed later, as part of the discussion on government intervention. In any event, this study has provided findings, which are important to explore in depth in order to understand the reason for the lack of reliability of the factors.

Location of the Site/landscape

The examination showed that this factor does not have a significant impact on the occupancy index, a result that is surprising if we recall that marinas are a leisure-time business, in which landscape is of great significance in the choice of the place of recreation. Furthermore, the factor of location/landscape was ranked toward the end of the list of the most important factors for marina profitability (in 13th place of out a possible 15, in which 1 signifies the most important factor).

In the hypotheses of the study, this factor was classified as a permanent/variable factor, because the landscape, in terms of environment, is not subject to change by the manager. It may be that the location of the site affects mainly occasional customers of the marina (tourists), and not the local customers, who are apparently the majority of the marina customers. This hypothesis requires an additional empirical test.

Another hypothesis that should be tested in this regard is the importance of the (partial or full) tax-free status in areas the administration want to develop. It may be that this aspect does impact significantly on the profitability of the marina that was built with this consideration in mind, but the present manager of the marina does not treat it as a factor that affects the profitability of the marina, but rather as a permanent background factor, which was relevant when the marina was built, but is no longer relevant. This hypothesis also requires an empirical test.

At the same time, the findings show a significant relationship between the factors of landscape and local community, and the items in the questionnaire that comprise them. This finding is important for marina managers whose marketing goals relate to improving the status and positive perception of the marina in the minds of local residents.

Government Intervention

Interesting findings were obtained with respect to government intervention: According to the analysis of the correlations, perceptions of the marina managers regarding government intervention are inversely and significantly related to occupancy. In other words, the smaller the number of actual rules and regulations compared to the expectations of the manager, the higher the occupancy.

According to a regressive analysis, government intervention is the main factor that may be required to explain the difference in the level of occupancy at the marina. Despite this, when they had to rank the most important factors for marina profitability, the marina managers ranked government intervention as the least important factor. There may be several explanations for this conflicting finding. One explanation may be the slight difference in the wording of the questions.

In the ranking, the managers were asked to rank their level of satisfaction with each of the factors in terms of marina profitability. In the regression analysis, the intent was to find the factor (or factors) that explain the largest amount of explained difference for the occupancy factor. As claimed earlier in the study, occupancy can indeed be a proxy for profitability, but this may not be the case from the perspective of the managers. Another possible explanation is that when ranking the factors that impact on profitability, the managers did so thinking only of the short term, while government intervention is a factor that has a long-term impact on the actual decision of whether building the marina is financially feasible. A third explanation may be that when ranking the factors, managers related primarily to factors under their control and related less to factors that they cannot control. These explanations do not conflict with each other and do not fully explain the phenomenon. In any event, all of the explanations require additional empirical study.

The results indicate that there is no correlation between the occupancy and the marina manager's perception regarding the restrictions attributable to government intervention (Item 5 – the degree of restriction by local/government regulations). We assume that because, for the most part, managers are part of the administration or civil servants, they do not expect the degree of restriction caused by the local regulations to affect occupancy.

This is in contrast to their view regarding the quality of supervision (Item 35), i.e., enforcement of supervision of the boat owners, which is seen as having a significant influence on occupancy.

The bureaucracy and the paperwork involved in entering a country like Turkey, which requires the entrants to complete a list of crew and to purchase a journal that has to be stamped in every marina – make mobility difficult, and convey to the boat owners that they are entering a "police state." In these places, therefore, occupancy is lower than in places where there is no requirement that the boat owner report after entry into the country, such as the Caribbean islands.

The results of Item 28 (which deals with the level of government supervision over the marina), indicate that there is a significant ($p = 0.002$) negative relationship (-0.282) between occupancy and the marina manager's perception of the scope of government rules and regulations that apply to the marina. In other words, the smaller the number of actual rules and regulations as compared to the expectations of the manager, the higher the occupancy.

Assuming the sailing world is one of freedom and leisure, restrictions in the form of rules and regulations are liable to be interpreted as having an effect on the occupancy of the marina. It may be that the marina manager believes that boat owners will fill the marina if they know that no government restrictions and rules apply to them. In terms of the quality of the local/government supervision of the marina (Item 35), it was found that there is a significant ($p = 0.001$) negative relationship (-0.290) between occupancy and the marina manager's perception of government supervision of the marina.

It is assumed that the marina manager believes that the stronger the supervision (enforcement), the fewer customers will be interested in anchoring at the marina. In the opinion of the managers, reducing the quality of the supervision will lead to higher occupancy. The researcher, however, believes these findings underscore the need to structure government supervision for marina managers clearly and systematically, before they begin their activity. Because if, in fact, the expectations do not suit the situation on the ground, a preliminary "expectations adjustment" regarding the rules and regulations included in government supervision is likely to create more profitable marinas.

Crowding

The crowding factor was found to be significantly related to the occupancy index. Although this result was anticipated, as a marina with higher occupancy is more crowded, the other phenomena that was examined, such as the effect of overcrowding on occupancy, did not lead to unequivocal findings.

As mentioned, the two items that comprise the crowding factor (Items 14-32) were found to have a significant relationship. At the same time, it is important to note that the crowding at the marina is likely to be seen by the administration as a safety problem – the more boats there are, the less turning diameter per boat, and the result is more crashes.

In the United States, for example, no sailing license is required, and since not every boat owner is an experienced sailor, there may be more problems of maneuvering in crowded marinas, and that has an effect on occupancy. The marina manager estimates that when customers can choose between a crowded and uncrowded marina, they prefer to anchor at a less crowded one, both for reasons of sailing safety, to protect their boats, which are expensive vehicles and are exposed to less traffic at the marina, and to make it easier for them to leave and enter the overcrowded marina, which prevents them from engaging in his hobby freely.

Services Associated With Anchorage Services

The basket of associated services at the marina includes two types of services: Those provided to the yacht owners (storage, laundry, etc.) and those provided for the yacht itself (repairs, fueling, and supplies).

Although the factor of associated services was ranked third in importance for marina profitability by the marina managers, and the marina facilities were ranked in fourth place (out of 15 possible places, immediately after value for money and satisfaction), it was found that associated services do not have a significant effect on the occupancy index at the marina ($p = 0.57$, $r = 0.173$). However, these scores are very borderline, and changes in the sampling method, for example, could possibly yield significant results.

An examination of the correlation between the associated services factor and the occupancy index, including the transformation (a transformation designed to approach a normal distribution, in the appendix), yielded a significant correlation between the associated services and the new occupancy index ($p = .049$, $r = 0.179$). These findings indicate the need for managers to invest at several levels:

- Ensuring that the associated services are in good repair and up-to-date;
- Conducting customer surveys on satisfaction with existing services;
- Conducting customer surveys on services that provide them with more value for their money, and offering these services;
- A creative search for additional services that yacht owners will consider additional value for their money (the most important factor in ranking in order of importance).

This finding positions the marinas as a leisure-time business similar to the hotel industry, in which the basket of associated services in addition to room and board is an important factor in the profitability of the hotel.

Environmental Protection

The activity of the marina has a great effect on the environment. First, construction of the marina requires a drastic change of the landscape and involves extensive engineering construction. Afterwards, operating the marina involves activity that pollutes the surroundings, mainly because of the leakage of oils and fuels from the yachts in to the sea.

The present study found that there is no relationship between environmental preservation and marina profitability. This weakens the claim of Chan & Mauborgne (2000), that one of the "levers of the customer needs" is the requirement that the service/product to be environmentally friendly.

Today, there are technologies and methods that can help marina managers interested in protecting the environment. They can reduce the level of pollution in the marina and its surroundings, and the manager can influence their use.

The present trend is to use holding tanks to collect the water from the bathrooms and showers; these tanks function as an integral part of the structure of the boats. The tanks require the installation of a special pumping system in the marina, which pumps directly from the boats. Facilities of this kind are already in operation at marinas in Turkey and in the United States, and their installation requires special regulations.

Awareness of the importance of environmental protection is steadily increasing, and the consequences are evident in many areas of life. Investment must be made at several levels:

- Establishing pollution-preventing infrastructure in the marina, and improving the existing infrastructure.
- Maintaining the cleanliness of the marina.
- Planning the marina activity with the goal of minimizing ecological damage. This activity should be carried out with the guidance of environmental experts.

When it comes to environmental protection, the marina manager has a great deal of influence – starting with awareness and concluding with the activity itself, which takes place in the short term.

Distance from Competitors

This factor, apparently, has no significant impact on the occupancy and profitability of the marina.

There are marketing models that claim two competing businesses located in geographical proximity increases the profits of both businesses, because the choice between competing businesses attracts more buyers than does one business alone, with no competitor in the vicinity.

There are shopping malls based on this principal; using a variety of balance formulas, the malls try to find the best balance to attract the largest number of customers to the mall itself (and as a result, to the business located in it). These models are applicable not only to retail businesses, but to leisure-time businesses as well. See, for example, the trend in movie theaters to open several such theaters in the same building/mall.

The finding of the study, which indicates no connection between the distance from competitors and profitability, demonstrates that marinas are different, and do not behave like other retail businesses, or even like other leisure-time businesses. A marina is apparently a leisure-time business with unique characteristics.

Examining the Model as a Whole

A statistical SEM run of the model as a whole did not converge. There may be methodological, conceptual, and theoretical reasons for that. Given that the three factors were found to be significantly related to occupancy, it is important to discuss these reasons, and even more important to develop a model that will be open to empirical examination, and will converge.

The methodological reasons may be attributable to the wording of the questionnaire and from the fact that it was sent to a global sample. Although the questionnaire was translated in to English, and was back-translated to test the reliability of the translation, it is possible that the marina managers from all over the world, who come from various cultures, have a different understanding of the same English term (note that all the managers completed the questionnaire in English, although English is not the mother tongue of all the participants in the study, although their job requires a certain mastery of the language).

Support for the idea that the non-convergence of the model may have been the result of differences in understanding the items that comprised it, among other things, can be found in the fact that the items that comprised five of the factors formulated in this study did not achieve a sufficient Cronbach's a level (government intervention, crowding, accessibility, proximity to a major city, and level of security/safety).

Additional support for the claim that the reason is methodological can be found in the fact that the items that comprised some of these factors (crowding, security/safety, accessibility) were taken from a survey conducted as preparation for this study, which was tested among marina customers in Israel, and yielded a sufficient level of significance.

The conceptual reasons were already mentioned in the analysis of the unreliable factors; it may be that marina managers are insufficiently aware of the needs of the investors in the marina and of their customers.

The theoretical reason may be that an insufficient number of factors were chosen related to the occupancy/profitability of the marina. This reason is particularly logical, given that the present study is a pioneering empirical study in the field, and all the factors assumed were taken from intuitive practical literature only, without an objective test, or from the discourse of people in the industry, which is also based on intuitive experience that is not backed by empirical data.

That is why this study is important. It points to two additional directions for academic research. One, to test the methodological tools for examining phenomena in a global sample – it may be that back translation is insufficient, and that qualitative testing of the comprehension of the questionnaires is required. The second, is the need to continue developing a theoretical approach based on empirical data.

The Cognitive map of the Marina Manager

Analyzing the cognitive map produced from the data and cross-checking it with additional findings in this study gave rise to a number of interesting points regarding the perception of marina managers. The complexity of their perception in certain places supports the previous findings discussed in this study, and in other places, it complements and expands previous findings.

Separating Occupancy From Value for Money

First, marina managers believe that the value for the customer's money (value for money, in the center of the right side of the map) is the most important factor for the profitability of the marina. Apparently, when weighing the contribution of various factors to the marina's profitability, marina managers give more weight to value for money than to occupancy.

In the scope of this study, it was not possible to examine what really contributes more to the profitability of the marina, and under what conditions. This distinction requires additional study.

The conceptual map may reveal more about the managerial ethos of the service-providing business today, i.e., what is politically correct, than about what really contributes to the profitability of the business, or is important to the customers. That said, it may be that value for money is more important than occupancy, or that under certain circumstances, the weight of each factor will change.

This cognitive map demonstrates the capability of paradoxical thinking among marina managers: On the one hand, they understand that they must provide value to the customer, and on the other, they realize they must ensure as high an occupancy as possible, even if that clashes with the needs of the customer (higher occupancy will cause a sense of greater crowding [see the cognitive map in the center below]).

Many researchers have pointed out the importance of paradoxical (dual) thinking for management (Denison & Hoojiberg, 1995; Evans, Pucik & Barsoux, 2002). This subject merits an in-depth empirical study.

Findings That are in Keeping With Previous Analysis

Managers link value for money as the factor closest to customer satisfaction. This is in keeping with the current managerial ethos in service industries, as well as with other studies in the field (including that of researcher, as preparation for the present study) (Raviv, 2001).

The managers also link associated services as the factor closest to customer satisfaction, and in second place to value for money. The parametric analysis (correlations) demonstrated that associated services have a significant influence on occupancy/profit, and it is reasonable to link them to value for money.

Another finding in the managers' cognitive map that is in keeping with the other findings is the separation between landscape, traveling time, and depth of anchorage, which are related to the location of the site (which, as previously mentioned, did not yield a significant connection to profitability), and environmental quality, (which did yield a significant connection). In fact, managers understand correctly that the location of the site differs from environmental protection. Another finding that is in line with the previous analysis is that managers link environmental protection to occupancy.

The following table compares the conceptual maps of the marina managers (the present study) and marina customers (Raviv, 2002), based on the order of importance determined by the respondents.

Customer Map

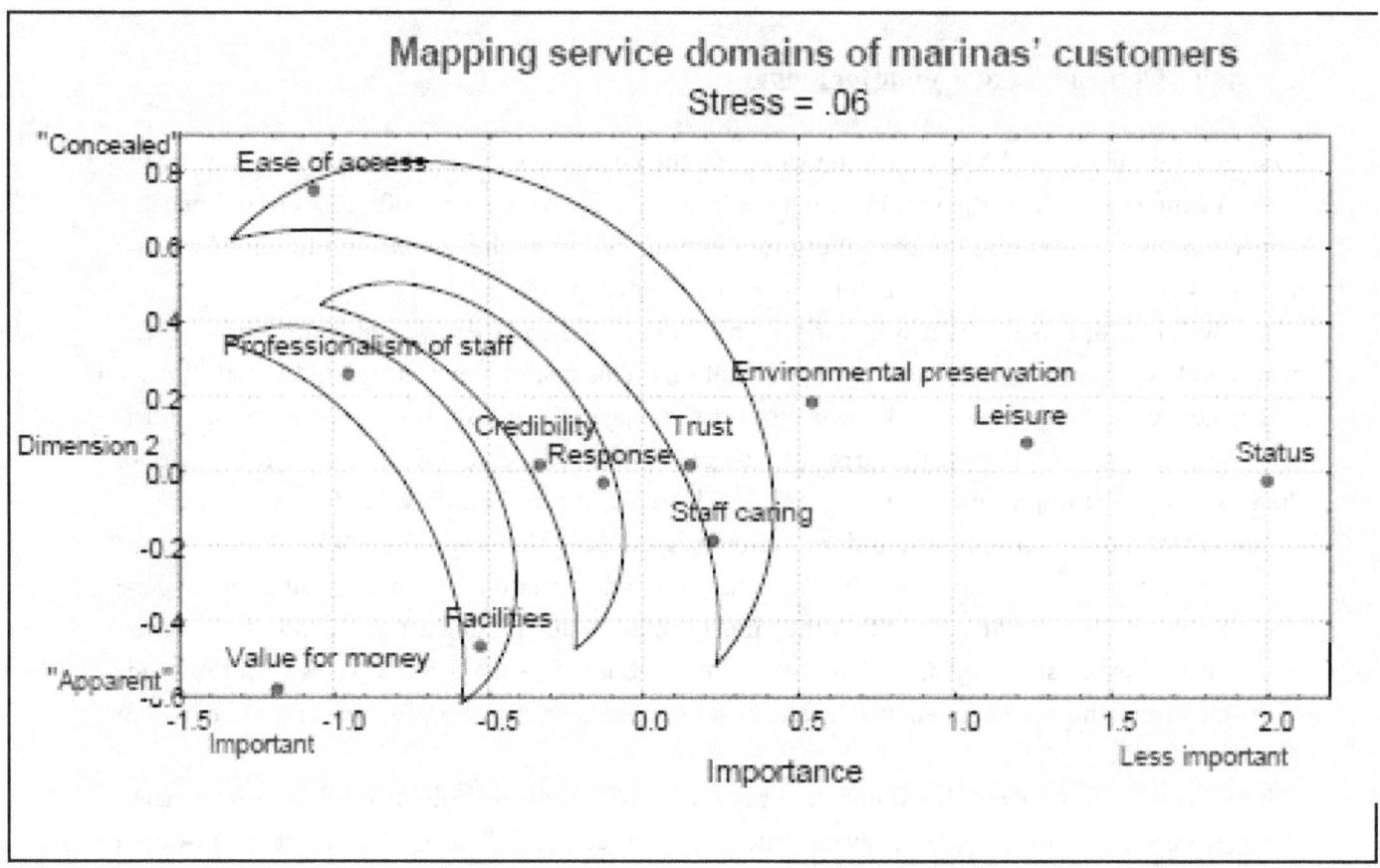

Manager Map

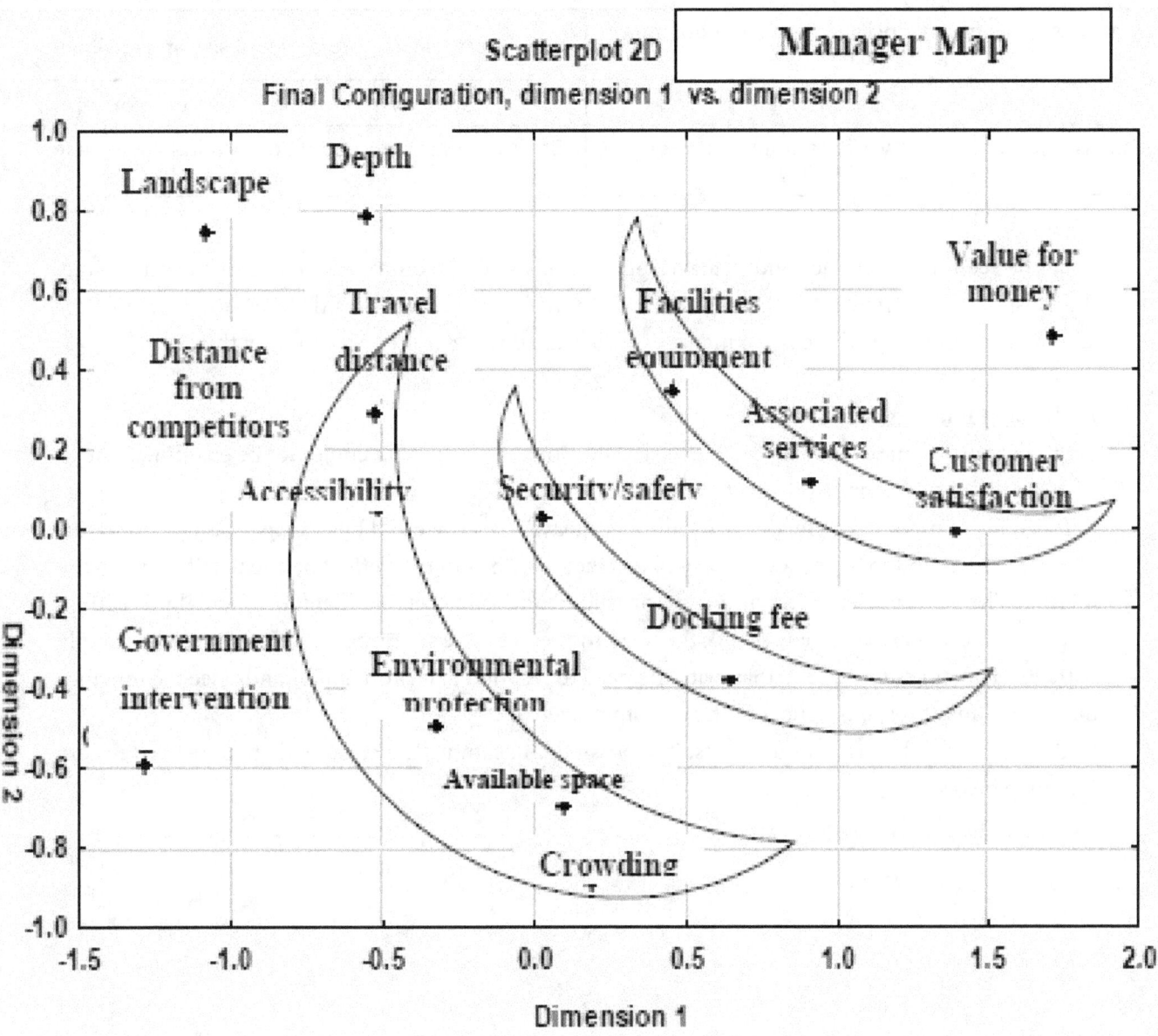

Table Comparing Customer and Manager Maps

Managers See manager map above	Customers See customer map above
Value for money	Value for money
Customer satisfaction, associated services, equipment, and facilities	Accessibility, professionalism, and facilities
Anchorage fee, security/safety	Credibility, responsiveness, trust, concern
Travel distance, accessibility, environmental protection, occupancy, crowding	Environmental protection, entertainment, and leisure, status

It can be seen that customer and manager perceptions share a common ground. At the same time, the most obvious difference is that the customers ranked ease of access as the most important factor after value for money, whereas the manager only ranked the factor of accessibility third.

Additional Findings

On the cognitive map it is also possible to see additional findings that could not be examined due to lack of reliability of some of the factors.

It can be seen, for example, that government intervention is viewed by managers as lacking virtually any connection to any other factor, and as a factor with very little effect on the profitability of the marina. The government intervention factor is linked most closely with environmental protection. Apparently, the marina managers link the need to protect the environment with the need to comply with government enforcement, than with the need to respond to customer demands (see the previous discussion about responsiveness to the customer needs).

By presenting the map in quadrants, it is possible to examine the clusters that characterize them (see map below):

Clusters on Cognitive Map

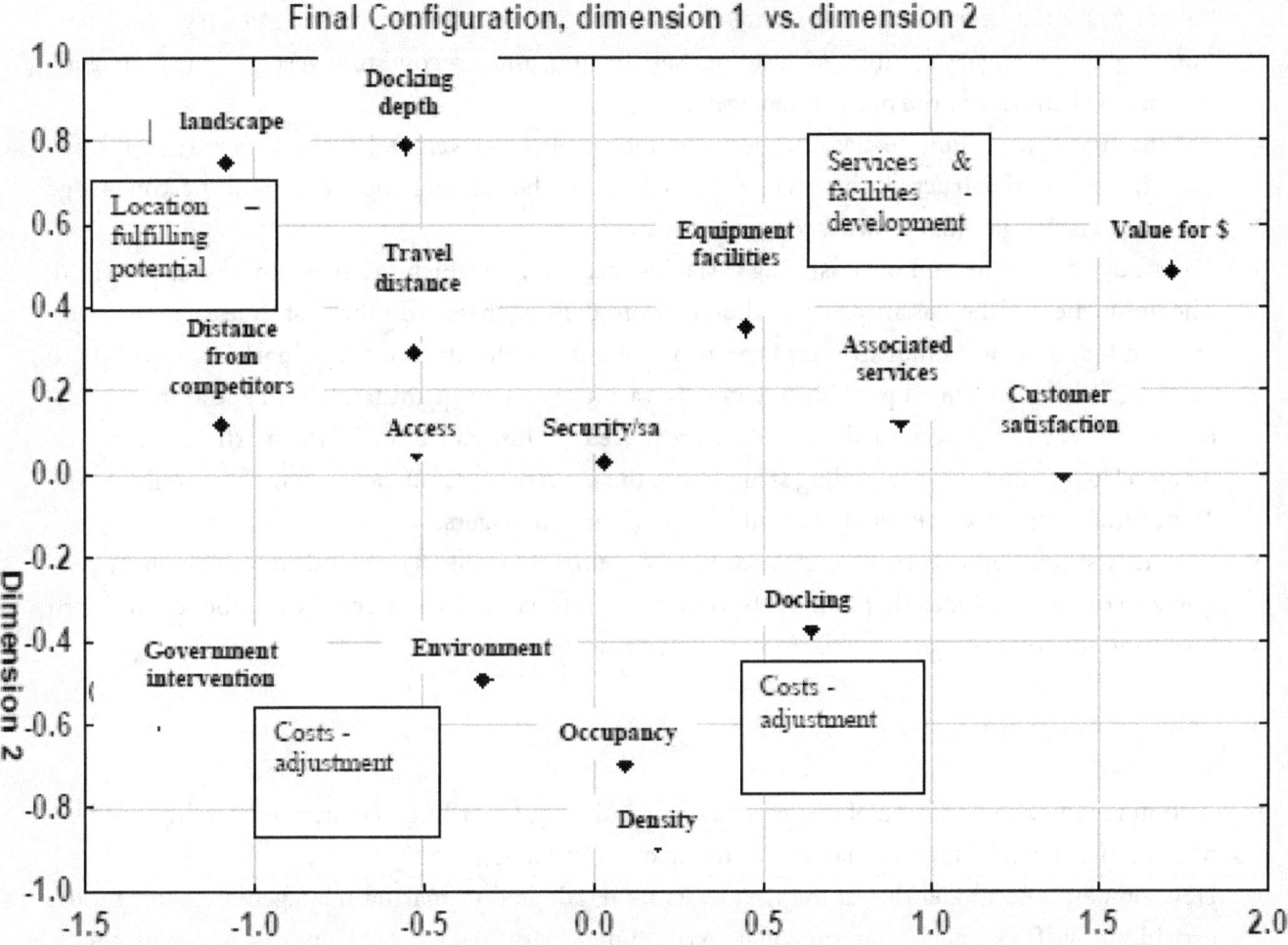

The first quadrant (top right, and afterwards clockwise) is the quadrant containing value for money (the most important factor), the services, and facilities provided to the customer. It is important for the marina manager to open and adapt these services to the changing needs of the customers.

Below it (lower right), at a lower level of importance, are the cost factors: Price, crowding, and occupancy – which is perceived as being in close proximity to crowding.

The third quadrant (lower left) contains the factors of supervision and regulations, issues on which the policy of the marina should be to maintain the situation.

In the fourth quadrant (upper left) are the factors of location, an area where the marina managers must operate to take advantage of the existing potential.

Contribution of Study

Below, we will present both the academic and the practical contributions of this study.

Academic Contribution

- For the first time, scientific questionnaires have been developed for the marina industry: One questionnaire to investigate the areas of customer satisfaction, and a second to investigate the managerial-strategic behavior of the marina managers.
- For the first time, a unique classification method has been developed for studies on the marina industry, as an infrastructure that enables us to describe the existing knowledge and the knowledge that is still lacking in this growing tourism industry.
- The study offers a method of classifying variables according to which marinas can be characterized. The uniqueness of the classification method is twofold: First, this marks the first time a classification method for the marina industry has been proposed. It enables us to classify marinas according to uniform criteria, making it possible to compare various marinas quantitatively, in addition to qualitatively (Raviv, 2001). Second, these criteria are placed in clusters viewed by the marina managers as being related to one another, adding structure to the process of classification, which is similar to the "conceptual map" that exists in the minds of the marina managers.
- For the first time, an occupancy index has been developed for the marina industry: This study proposes an occupancy index that reflects the occupancy rate as a ratio between the number of anchored boats and the total anchorage capacity at the marina.

Practical Contribution

- A comprehensive description of the world marina industry, according to marina ownership and type of customer to which the marina caters, among other criteria.
- Development of a model that is the first of its kind, adapted to marina management. This model provides tools for strategic planning of an existing marina or planning for building a new marina.
- The conclusions of the study offer a series of recommendations for ongoing management of the marina: Some of the research recommendations have already been applied in marinas in Israel (the marina in Haifa) and worldwide.

As previously stated, this study is a pioneering work in the field of marina management. As such, it asks initial questions and proposes new ways of thinking.

The next chapter will describe the limitations of the study and recommendations for further studies.

Limitations of Study and Follow-up Research

All research is limited in its ability and is given to inherent deviation. This is also the case for research based on questionnaires (Ruth Beyth-Marom *et al.*, 1986).

The current study is pioneering empirical research in the formulation of a strategic business model for marinas. The study provided empirical grounding for several claims and methodological tools for continued development of research in the field. It also presented additional/new questions that require additional research.

The methodology of this study found a certain amount of empirical evidence to show that occupancy can be used as an index for marina profitability. The model, as a whole, cannot be verified, evidently for methodological reasons (lack of reliability of some of the parameters that are factors in the model). This raises methodological questions about performance of studies with global samples.

As noted, the high correlation (Cronbach's α = .77) found (in reliability analysis) between profitability (subjective estimate by the marina manager) and occupancy, provides empirical validation of the hypothesis that occupancy can be used as a proxy indeed for marina profitability. However, it is desirable, and not only in a small sample, to validate the relationship between occupancy and profitability, looking at real profit data. It may be possible to receive this data from public or state-owned marinas and based on the findings make assumptions regarding the accuracy with which the occupancy index reflects profitability.

The fact that this study established factors proven to have an impact on marina occupancy and profitability (associated services, environmental protection, and to some degree, local community) is critical. Two of the factors are exogenous: The local community and environmental protection, factors mangers tend to relate to less as compared to the internal factors at the marina (such as the associated services). It is important to research these exogenous factors (and others) in depth.

In this pioneering study (that dealt with customer perceptions), the "safety and professionalism" analysis of the factors provided the highest percentage of explained differences and returned the highest eigenvalue. Even in this study, security/safety was positioned at the center of the cognitive map for marina managers, as a factor that is most highly related to all other factors. It is important to conduct research that will attempt to shed light on this issue, which is perceived as being central by both customers and managers.

It could be argued that the boating industry was ahead of globalization in establishing two sports cultures: A worldwide culture and a local/national culture. The global culture is supported by international competitions, by the fact that the manufacture of equipment and materials for this support are done in a limited number of places and serves the entire world, and the fact that this is a support that assumes mobility among countries.

The current study relates to the global culture of the boating industry and does not relate to the various local differences that may appear if the data among countries is compared. This issue of a cultural comparison among different countries and the link between local and global culture in the industry, is waiting for follow-up research.

The current study is a pioneering effort in marina management, and it raises questions which have not been addressed in the past and opens new ways of thinking. The answers to the questions will need to be found in complex research, and it would be fitting for other researchers to look for a way to anchor marinas to a stable business shore.

In short, the purpose of this study was to develop a model for strategic management of marinas. The development of new models to analyze industries enables researchers, planners, and managers to create additional tools to understand and cope with existing situations. These tools may form the foundation for evaluating current strategies and developing new strategies for both existing marinas and those being planned.

The researcher studied the business components of the marina industry around the world from the customer perspective and, particularly, from the managers' perspective. The study is the first in the world to cover five continents, and for the first time proposes a taxonomy which allows the world of marinas and its business philosophy to be classified. This study found that despite the fact that marinas are found on different continents, they are similar in the customers' service expectations.

This study provides an initial roadmap for efficient and profitable marina management, while studying a strategic model developed especially for this unique industry.

BIBLIOGRAPHY

Amidon, D. M. 1997. *Innovation Strategy for the Knowledge Economy.* Boston, MA: Butterworth-Heinemann.

Anderson, E. W., Fornell, E., & Lehman, D. R. 1994. Customer Satisfaction, Market Share and Profitability. *Journal of Marketing, 58,* 53-66.

Anderson, J. C., & Gerbing, D. W. 1988. Structural Equation Modeling in Practice. *Psychological Bulletin, 103*(3), 411-23.

Anderson, L. K., Taylor, J. R., & Holloway, R. J. 1996. The Consumer and His Alternatives - An Experimental Approach. *Journal of Marketing Research,* Nov.

Adamson C. 1994. How to Waste Money Measuring Customer Satisfaction. *Managing Service Quality,* 4(5), 9-12.

Athiyaman, A. 1995. The Interface of Tourism and Strategy Research: an Analysis. *Tourism Management* 16(6), 453-47. 113

Bagozzi, R. P., & Phillips, L. W. 1982. Representing and Testing Organizational

Theories: A Holistic Construal. *Administrative Science Quarterly, 27*(3), 459-89.

Bakkal, 1991. Characteristics of West German Demand for International Tourism in the Northern Mediterranean Region. *Applied Economics, 23*(2), 295-304.

Barney, J. B. 1991. Firm Resources and Sustained Competitive Advantage. *Journal of Management, 17*(1), 99-120.

Bennington, L., & Cummane, J. 1998. Measuring Service Quality: A Hybrid Methodology. *Total Quality Management, 9*(6), 395-405.

Bentler, P. M., & Bonett, D. G. 1980. Significance Tests and Goodness of Fit in the Analysis of Covariance Structures. *Psychological Bulletin, 88,* 588-606.

Bentler, P. M. 1989. *EQS: Structural Equations Program Manual.* Los Angeles, CA: BMDP.

Berry, L. L., & Parasuraman, A. 1997. *Marketing Services: Competing Through Quality.* New York, NY: Free Press.

Bitner, M. J., & Booms, B. H. 1990. The Service Encounter: Diagnosing Favorable and Unfavorable Incidents. *Journal of Marketing.* 54(1), 71-84.

Bitner, M. J., & Booms, B. H. 1994. Marketing Strategies and Organizational Structures for Service Firms. In J. Donnelly & W. R. George (Eds.), *Marketing of Services* (47-51). Chicago, IL: American Marketing Association.

Bollen, K. A., & Liang, J. 1988. Some Properties of Hoelter's CN. *Sociological Methods & Research*, 16(4), 492-503. 114

Boston Consulting Group . Strategic Matrix . Explained. At www.valuebasedmanagement.net/methods. Last accessed 03-08-06.

Broetzman, S., Kemp, J., Rossano M., & Marwaha, J. 1995. Customer Satisfaction - Lip Service or Management Tool? *Managing Service Quality*, 5(2), 13-18.

Chan, K. W., & Mauborgne, R. 2000. Knowing a Winning Business Idea When You See One, *Harvard Business Review*, Sep-Oct, 129-38.

Chang, W. H. 2000. *National Recreation Visitors Spending Profiles for 16 Corps of Engineers Lakes.* Michigan State University. Retrieved from http://www.msu.edu/user/changwe4/spend/16main.htm

Comerford, R. A. 1998 *Marina and Boatyard Industry Financial Performance.* Wickford, RI: International Marina Institute.

Cudeck, R., & Henly, S. J. 1991. Model Selection in Covariance Structures Analysis and the "Problem" of Sample Size. *Psychological Bulletin,* 109(3), 512-19.

Dale, F. 1994. Measuring Tourism Motivation. *Annals of Tourism Research*, 21(3), 555-81

Danaher, P. J. 1997. Using Conjoint Analysis to Determine the Relative Importance of Service Attributes Measured in Customer Satisfaction Surveys. *Journal of Retailing*, 73(2), 235-260.

Danaher, P. J., & Haddrell, V. 1996. A Comparison of Question Scales Used for Measuring Customer Satisfaction. *International Journal of Service Industry Management,* 7(4), 4-6.

Denison, D. R., Hooijberg, R., & Quinn, R. 1995. Paradox and Performance: Toward a Theory of Behavioral Complexity in Managerial Leadership. *Organization Science,* 6(5), 524-40. 115

Day, G., & Reibstein, D. 1997. *Wharton Dynamic Competitive Strategy.* New York, NY: Wiley. 233-395.

De Ruyter, K., Bloemer, J., & Peeters, P. 1997. Merging Service Quality and Service Satisfaction. *Journal of Economic Psychology,* 18, 287-406.

Dion, P. A., Javalgi, R., & Dilorenzo, J. 1998. An Empirical Assessment of the Zeithaml, Berry and Parasuraman Service Expectation Model. *The Service Industrial Journal,* 18(4), October, 66-86.

Dunn Ross, E. L., & Iso-Ahola, S. E. 1991. Sightseeing Tourists' Motivation and Satisfaction. *Annals of tourism Research* 10(2): 226-37.

Echtner, C. M. 1995. Entrepreneurial Training in Development Countries. *Annals of Tourism Research*, 22(2), 119-33.

Eisenhardt, K. M., & Sull, D. 2001. Strategy as Simple Rules. *Harvard Business Review*, January, 107-16.

Engel, J. F., Kollat, D. T., & Blackwell, R. D. 1968. *Consumer Behavior.* New York, NY: Holt, Rinehart and Winston.

Evans, P., Pucik, V., & Barsoux JL. 2002. *The Global Challenge.* Boston, MA: McGraw-Hill.

Fleischer, A., & Felsenstein, D. 2000. Support for Rural Tourism: Does it make a difference? *Annals of Tourism Research, 27*(4), 1007-24.

Fitzsimmons, J.A. & Fitzsimmons, M.J., 2000. *Service Management: Operations, Strategy, and Information Technology* (3rd ed.). New York, NY: Irwin/McGraw-Hill. 116

Fred, D. 1986. *Strategic Management and Business Policy*. Prentice-Hall

Gadiesh, O. and Gilbert, J. L. 2001. Transforming Corner-Office Strategy into Frontline Action. *Harvard Business Review,* May.

Grabrun, N. H. 1983. The Anthropology of Tourism. *Annals of Tourism Research, 10*(1), 9-33.

Gronroos, C. 1990. Relationship Approach to Marketing in Service Contexts: The Marketing and Organizational Behavior Interface, *Journal of Business Research, 20*(1), 3-11.

Gronroos, C. 1984. A Service Quality Model and its Marketing Implications, *European Journal of Marketing, 18*(4), 36-44.

Goodman, J., & Ward, D. 1993. The Importance of Customer Satisfaction. *Direct Marketing,* December, 23-26.

Grant, R. M. 2001. *Contemporary Strategy Analysis*. Malden, MA: Blackwell. 29-47 223-25.

Gunn, C.A., 1994. *Tourism Planning*. New York, NY: Taylor and Fracis.

Hall, D.R. 1991. *Tourism and Economic Development in Eastern Europe and the Soviet Union*, London: John Wiley & Sons.

Hall, C. M. 1996. *Tourism and Politics - Policy Power and Place*, London: Wiley.

Hamel, G. 1991. Competition for Competence and Inter-Partner Learning within International Strategic Alliances. *Strategic Management Journal, 12*, 93-103.

Hamel, G., & Prahalad, C. 1989. Strategic Intent. *Harvard Business Review,* May-June, 63-76. 117

Hoelter, J. W. 1983. The Analysis of Covariance Structures: Goodness-of-Fit Indices. *Sociological Methods & Research, 11*(3), 325-44.

Hu, L., Bentler, & Kano, Y. 1992. Can Test Statistics in Covariance Structure Analysis Be Trusted? *Psychological Bulletin, 112*(2), 351-62.

Huba, G. J., & Harlow, L. L. 1986. Robust Structural Equation Models. *Child Development, 58*, 147-166.

Huba, G. J., & Harlow, L. L. 1987. Robust Estimation for Causal Models. In D. L.

Featherman, P. B. Baltes, & R. M. Lerner (Eds.), *Life-span Development and Behavior* (22-38). New Jersey, NJ: Lawrence Erlbaum and Associates.

International Marina Institute. 1995. *Financial & Operational Benchmark Study For Marina Operators*. Washington, DC: International Marina Institute Publication.

Jackson, R., Stynes, D., Propst, D., & Siverts, L. E. 1992. *Economic Impact Analysis as a Tool in Recreation Program Evaluation* (Instruction Report R-92-1).

Vicksburg, MI: US Army Engineer Waterways Experiment Station.

Jackson, R. S., & Stynes, D. J. 1996. *A Summary of the National and State Economic Effects of the 1994 Recreation Program* (Technical Report R-96-1). Vicksburg, MI. US Army Engineer Waterways Experiment Station.

Jacoby, J., Hoyer, W., & Brief, A. 1992. Consumer Psychology. In D. Dunnette & L.

M. Hough (Eds.), *Handbook of Industrial Organizational Psychology* (2nd ed.). Palo-Alto, CA: Consulting Psychologist Press.

Jones, T., Sasser, E., &. 1995. Why Satisfied Customers Defect. *Harvard Business Review,* Nov-Dec, 88-9. 118

Kaplan, R. S., & Norton, D. P. 2001. *The Strategy Focused Organization.* Boston, MA: Harvard Business School Press.

Kemp, P. 1979. *The Oxford Companion to Ships and the Sea.* London: Granada.

Kildow, J. T. 1981. *Boston Harbor Management Study* (MITSG 81-15, NTIS: PB 82-178-864). Cambridge, MA: Massachusetts Institute of Technology.

Kotler, P. & Armstrong, G. 2004. *Marketing Management Analysis Implementation and Control Planning.* Englewood Cliffs, NJ: Prentice-Hall.

Kraemer, H. C., Thiemann. 1987. *How Many Subjects?* Newbury Park, CA: Sage.

Kruskal, J. B., & Wish, M. 1978. *Multidimensional Scaling.* Newbury Park, CA: Sage.

Kurowsky, J. 1999. Consolidation Depends on the Sector. *Boating Industry, 62*(9), 29-33.

Lerner, M. & Haber, S. 2001. Performance Factors of Small Tourism Ventures: the Interface of Tourism, Entrepreneurship and Environment. *Journal of Business Venturing, 16,* 77-100.

Levit, H. J. 1954. A Note on Some Experimental Finding about the Meaning of Price. *Journal of Business, 27,* July, 205-10.

Levy, D. 1994. Chaos Theory and Strategy: Theory, Application, and Managerial Implication. *Strategic Management Journal, 15,* 167-78.

Ley, D.A. & Madison, J. 1996. Romanian Tourism . Status, Limitations and Prospects.

In E. Kaynak, D. Lascu & K. Becker (Eds.), *Restructuring for Global Production, Service Needs and Markets: Business Strategy and Policy Development for a Global Economy and Projection for the Twenty First* 119 *Century.* Proceedings of the Fifth World Business Congress. International Management Development Association, Bermuda.

Lickorish, L., Jefferson, A., Boudlender, J., & Jenkins, C. L. 1994. *Developing Tourism Destination: Policies and Perspectives*, Essex: Longman.

Lundberg, D.E., Krishnamoorthy, M. & Stavenga, M. H. 1995. *Tourism Economics.* New York, NY: Wiley.

Mahoney, J. T., & Pandian, J. 1992. The Resource-Based View Within the Conversation of Strategic

Management. *Strategic Management Journal, 13*, 363-80.

Mangoione, T., Hingcon R., & Barrett, J. 1982. Collecting Sensitive Data: A Comparison of Three Survey Strategies. *Sociological Methods and Research, 10*, 337-46.

Mannell, R., & Iso-Ahola, S. 1987. Psychological Nature of the Leisure and Tourism Experience. *Annals of Tourism Research, 14*(3), 314-33.

Marina Survey, 1998. *The American Marina Statistical Profile*. Brussels: ICOMIA. *Marketing Definitions*. Retrieved from the American Marketing Association Web site: http://www.marketingpower.com/content4620.php

Martin, F. 1994. *Elements of the Competitive Analysis of Marinas and Other Yacht Harbors*. Alicante, Spain: Club Nautico de Campello.

Martin, J. 1998. As Customers Go, So Goes the Dow. *Fortune*, Feb. 16, 88.

Martin, J. A. 1987. Structural Equations Modeling. *Child Development, 58*, 33-7. 120

Menipaz, E. 1999. Global Management Strategies: A Key for Sustainable Growth. *Economie des Region Mediteranéennes et Developpement Durable*, 733-36.

Menipaz, E., Weber, J., Raviv, A., & Hartman, A. 1999, May. *A Taxonomy of Strategic Business Models for Leisure Industry Organizations*. Paper presented at the International Conference on Forging Regional Cooperation in the Mediterranean Basin, Arles, France.

Meyer, M. W. 1999. Permanent Failure and the Failure of Organizational Performance.

In H. K. Anheier (Ed.), *When Things Go Wrong* (197-212). Thousand Oaks, CA: Sage Publications.

Miller, D. C. 1991. *Handbook of Research Design and Social Measurement* (5th ed.). Thousand Oaks, CA: Sage Publications.

Mintzberg, H. 1994. The Fall and Rise of Strategic Planning. *Harvard Business Review*, Jan-Feb, 107-11.

Norton, R. S. & Kaplan, D. P. *The Strategy Focused Organization*. Boston, MA: Harvard Business School Press. 69-133.

Oliver, R. 1981. Measuring and Evaluation of Satisfaction in Retail Settings. *Journal of Retailing, 57*, 25-48.

Parasuraman, A. 1988. .SERVQUAL: A Multiple Item Scale for Measuring Consumer Perceptions of Service Quality.. *Journal of Retailing, 64*(1), 12-40.

Parasuraman, A. 1991. *Marketing Research* (2nd ed.). Reading, MA: Addison-Wesley.

Parasuraman, A., Zeithaml, V., & Berry, L. 1985. A Conceptual Model of Service Quality and its Implications for Further Research. *Journal of Marketing, 49*(4), 41-50. 121

Patterson, P. G., Johnson, L. W., & Spreng, R. A. 1997. Modeling the Determinants of Customer Satisfaction for Business to Business Professional Services. *Journal of the Academy of Marketing Science, 25*(1), 4-17.

Paz-Tal, G. 1998. *Tourism and Leisure Business Management.* Tel Aviv: Lahman - The Israel Association for Tourism and Leisure Culture.

Pendleton, L., Martin, N., & Webster, D. G. 2001. Public Perception of Environmental Quality: A Survey Study of Beach Use and Perceptions in Los Angeles County. *Marine Pollution Bulletin*, 42, 1155-60.

Perales, M. K. 1998. *Profiling Private Dock and Marina Slip Holders at Corps of Engineers Projects* (Technical Report R-92-1 & Natural Resources Technical Note ECN-02). Vicksburg, MI: US Army Engineer Waterways Experiment Station.

Peters, E. E. 1994. *Fractal Market Analysis*, New York, NY: Wiley.

Porter, M. 1991. Towards a Dynamic Theory of Strategy. *Strategic Management Journal*, 12, 95-118.

Porter, M. 1980. *Competitive Strategy.* New York: Free Press.

Porter, M. 2001. Strategy and the Internet. *Harvard Business Review*, 75(3), 63-78

Prahalad, C., & Hamel, G. 1990. The Core Competence of the Organization. *Harvard Business Review*, May-June, 79-91.

Propst, D., Stynes, D., & Jackson, R. 1992. *A Summary of Spending Profiles for Recreation Visitors to Corps of Engineers Projects* (Technical Report R-92-4).

Vicksburg, VA: US Army Engineer Waterways Experiment Station. 122

Propst, D., Stynes, D., Lee, J., & Jackson, R. 1992. Development of Spending Profiles for Recreation Visitors to Corps of Engineers Projects (Technical Report R-92-

4). Vicksburg, VA: US Army Engineer Waterways Experiment Station.

Quinn, J. B., Baruch, J. J. & Zien, K. A. 1997. *Innovation Explosion.* New York, NY: Free Press. Random House College Dictionary. 1975. New-York, NY: Random House.

Rasmussen, D. R. & Mosekilde, M. 1998. Bifurcation and Chaos in a Generic Management Model. *European Journal of Operational Research*, 35, 80-8.

Rathmell J.M. 1966. What is Meant by Services?, *Journal of Marketing*, 30, 32-6.

Raviv, A. 1996, March. *Marina Marketing as a Worthwhile Investment.* Paper presented at the ICOMIA Second International Marina Conference, Genoa, Italy.

Raviv, A. 1999, February. *The World Of Marinas.* Paper presented at the ICOMIA 3rd International Marina Conference, Fort Lauderdale, FL.

Raviv, A. 1999, May. *A Taxonomy of Strategic Business Models for Leisure Industry Organizations.* Paper presented at the International Conference on Forging Regional Cooperation in the Mediterranean Basin, Arles, France.

Raviv, A. 2001, April. *The Regional and Global Marina Industry: A Strategic Business Approach.* Paper presented at The School of Management, Department of Hotel and Tourism Management, Beer Sheba, Israel.

Raviv, A. 2002, March. *Marina Strategic Business Models: Taxonomy and a New Model Proposal*. Paper presented at the ICOMIA Fourth International Marina Conference, Sydney, Australia. 123

Richards, D. 1990. Is Strategic Decision-Making Chaotic? *Behavioral Science, 35,* 219-32.

Reichheld, F., & Sasser, E. J. 1982. Zero Defection: Quality Comes to Service. *Harvard Business Review,* Sep-Oct, 41-7.

Rogers-Harrington, J. 1999. Marina Survey 1999. *Boating Industry, 62*(11), 49-56.

Schneider, B. 1990. The Climate for Service: An Application of the Climate Construct. In B. Schneider (Ed.), *Organizational Climate and Culture.* San Francisco, CA: Jossey-Bass.

Schneider, B. & Bowen, D. 1995. *Winning the Service Game.* Boston, MA: Harvard Business School Press.

Scolari. 2000. The Methodologist's Tool Chest. Version 3.0. Ex-sample Module. Sage Publication Software.

Smith, S. L. J. 1983. *Recreation Geography.* New York, NY: Longman.

Smith, S. L. J. 1989. *Tourism Analysis.* New York, NY: Longman.

Smith, S. L. J. 1994. The Tourism Product. *Annals of Tourism Research, 21*(3), 582-95.

Smith, V. L., & Eadington, W. R. 1992. Introduction: The Emergence of Alternative Form of Tourism. In V. L. Smith & W. R. Eadington, (Eds.), *Tourism Alternatives: Potential and Problems in Development of Tourism.* Philadelphia: University of Pennsylvania Press.

Stynes, D. 1999. *Guidelines for Gathering Recreation/Tourism Spending Data for Use in and Economic Impact Estimation.* Michigan State University. Retrieved from http://www.msu.edu/user/stynes/mirec/howtosp.htm

Swarbrooke, J. 1995. *The Development and Management of Visitor Attraction.* London: Heinemann.

Talheim, D. R. 1993. *The Community Options Model.* Presented at the National Training Conference of the American Society for Public Administration. San Francisco, CA.

Talheim, D. R., Mahoney, E. M., Bishop, G., Lee, H. C., & Tsung, C. W. 1998. *Report on Michigan Marina Census and Needs Assessment* (Research Report 548). East Lansing, MI: Agricultural Experiment Station, Michigan State University.

Tanaka, J. S., Panter, A. T., Winborne, W. C., & Huba, G. J. 1990. Theory testing in personality and Social Psychology with structural equation models. *Review of Personality and Social Psychology, 11,* 217-42.

Taylor, C. 1995. The Case for Customer Satisfaction. *Managing Service Quality, 5*(1), 11-14.

Texas Department of Commerce, Texas Agriculture Extension Service and Texas A&M University. 1992. *Developing Tourism in your Community.* Texas: Texas A&M University.

Thietart, R. A. & Forgues, B. 1995. Chaos Theory and Organization. *Organization Science, 6*(1), 19.

Tsui, A. 1997. A Multiple-Constituency Model of Effectiveness: An Empirical Examination at the Human Resource Subunit Level. *Administrative Science Quarterly, 35,* 458-83.

Van Der Heijden, K. 1996. *Scenarios: The Art of Strategic Conversation.* New York, NY: Wiley.

van Geenhuizen, M., & Nijkamp, P. 1998. .Improving the Knowledge Capability of Cities: The Case of MainPort Rotterdam.. *International Journal of Technology Management, 15*(6-7), 691-709.

Voss, G. B., Parasuraman, A., & Grewal, D. 1998. The Roles of Price, Performance and Expectations in Determining Satisfaction in Service Exchanges. *Journal of Marketing, 62,* 46-61.

Weiermair, K., & Fuchs, M. 1999. Measuring Tourist Judgment on Service Quality. *Annals of Tourism Research, 26*(4), 1001-21.

Wilkie, W. L. 1994. *Consumer Behavior* (3rd ed.). New York, NY: Wiley.

Williams, C. E. and Tse, E. C. Y. 1995. The Relation between Strategy and Entrepreneurship: The U.S. Restaurant Sector. *International Journal of Contemporary Hospitality Management, 7*(1), 22-6.

Wilson, E. O. 1998. *Consilience: The Unity of Knowledge.* New York, NY: Knopf.

Wong, S. and Perry, C. (1991) .Customer Service Strategies in Financial Retailing., *International Journal of Bank Marketing,* 9 (3), 11-16.

Zeithamel, V. A. 1988. Consumer Perception of Price, Quality, and Value: A Means-End Model and Synthesis of Evidence. *Journal of Marketing, 52,* July, 2-22.

Zeithamel, V. A. 1996. *Service Marketing.* New York, NY: McGraw-Hill.

Zeithaml, V., Parasuraman, A., & Berry, L. 1985. *Quality Counts in Services Too.* Englewood Cliffs, NJ: Prentice-Hall.

www.ingramcontent.com/pod-product-compliance
Lightning Source LLC
Chambersburg PA
CBHW080455220526
45465CB00006B/2279